SAY GOOD-BYE TO

ALLERGY-RELATED

AUTISM

BY
DEVI S. NAMBUDRIPAD
D.C., L.Ac., R.N., Ph. D.

The Author of

" Say Good-bye to ..." Series

"The doctor of the future will give no medicine,
But will interest his patients
In the care of the human frame, in diet,
And in the cause and prevention of disease"
Thomas Edison

Published
By
Delta Publishing Company
6714 Beach Blvd.
Buena Park, CA 90621
(888) 890-0670, (714) 523-8900
Fax: (714) 523-3068
Web site: www.naet.com
e-mail: naet@earthlink.net

DEDICATION

This book is dedicated to
all Autistic Children of the world

First Edition: December, 1999

Library of Congress: 98-93777
ISBN: 0-9658242-5-X

Printed in U.S.A.

CONTENTS

A Few Words From NAET Practitioners

NAET is truly awesome. You will want to pass this book on to others and spread the word about this amazing technique. Anyone who has wrestled with a rotation diet or tried to eliminate wheat, sugar and dairy from a small child's diet knows what a struggle that can be. But with the NAET process all of this becomes unnecessary. An allergen can be *eliminated* within 25 hours of treatment! No more having to avoid the food. By finding a NAET practitioner in your area, and following through with the treatments, you and your child can get a new lease on life and tackle new horizons.

Sandra C. Denton, MD.
Anchorage, AK
(907) 563-6200

Dr. Devi Nambudripad has pioneered the greatest leap in the field of energy medicine technology on the doorstep to the 21st Century, at a time when there is greater suffering from allergies than ever before in people all over, especially in children who are suffering from Allergy-Related Autism and Attention-deficit and Hyperactive Disorders. This book offers a glimpse into the miracles that NAET can bring to the lives of frustrated parents and their helpless children!

Rahmie Valentine, L.Ac., O.M.D.
Los Angeles, CA
(323) 936-3162

I was frustrated with diets, therapies and allergy shots and I couldn't find a way out for my son who was diagnosed with a severe type of autism for the past four years. I met an old friend at a professional seminar and she told me about the allergy elimination treatment called NAET. It sounded too good to be true. I enrolled right away. After learning the technique, I immediately began treating my son. Before he even finished the basic ten treatments, I was amazed at his miraculous leap to wellness from his so called "incurable" severe autism.

S. Racette, R.D.
Quincy, MA

As a recently retired psychiatrist, I have witnessed the great devastation and feelings of helplessness, which many families have experienced by having an autistic child in the home. Now, with NAET, we finally have a treatment approach which is providing real improvement in these difficult cases. I applaud Dr. Devi for her great accomplishments in helping to relieve the suffering of her fellow humans.

Robert Prince, MD.
Charlotte, NC
(704) 537-0201

NAET has changed my practice. NAET is a profound and fascinating technique of correcting children's allergies, which is an underlying cause of most pediatric problems.

Sue Anderson, D.C.
Ann Arbor, MI
(734) 662-9140

From my experience with several autistic children with whom I have recently worked, I have found that NAET provides a powerful tool to unravel the mystery of autism and restores a higher level of functioning. It gives hope where there was none before!

Susan LeFavour, LMSW, Ph.D
Atlanta, GA
(770) 643-6784

At the age of three my son was classified as having PDD/Autism. After the shock wore off I decided to stop fighting with the pediatrician, and started listening to my family and friends to go the alternative way. When I learned about NAET I cried I was so happy. Needless to say I did what I had to, to get trained so I could treat my children. My children now 7 and 5 are no longer labeled autistic and attend regular schools. NAET is the answer to so many parents' prayers. Your child doesn't have to live a casein, gluten, food and chemical free life! I can't thank Dr. Devi Nambudripad and NAET enough for giving us our children back. Now I have started treating my autistic patients with NAET. I am so amazed in a short period of time how NAET has transformed many children's lives in my practice!

Maribeth Mydlowski, D.C.
Hamilton Township, NJ

My first autistic patient was a 29-year-old autistic adult. When he began treatment with me, he was unable to communicate with anyone about his needs. He was incontinent and was on diapers. He behaved like a two-year-old. When he finished the first five NAET basic treatments, he was able to communicate with his parents asking for his favorite food - ice cream. When he finished the mineral mix treatment, he stopped his bladder incontinence. By the time he completed his basic fifteen treatments, he was on his way to recovery. Step by step, little by little, I watched how NAET transformed a violent, frustrated, autistic adult into a passive, focused, manageable state. Ever since I have seen many autistic patients go through similar processes. When children get the NAET treatments at a young age the result is phenomenal. The younger the patients, the faster the results. NAET is a simple technique but it is so powerful beyond imagination!

Mala Moosad, R.N., L.Ac.
Buena Park, CA
(714) 523-8900

I have seen NAET create amazing changes in Autistic children that can allow communication breakthroughs that seemed impossible prior to treatment. We have received letters from teachers asking parents what changes have recently been made because their child now suddenly is able to acknowledge and respond to questions that in the past resulted in little more than a blank stare.

Glenn Nozek, D.C.
Tom River, NJ
(732) 255-0600

Sam R. was a 13-year-old who was doing very poorly in school in spite of the massive doses of Ritalin he received and his parents tutoring him four hours every day. Due to the medication he walked like a zombie with no expression on his face or personality. He was underweight for his age. We found him to be severely allergic to milk and cheese, and was consuming dairy products virtually at every meal. After NAET treatments he was able to get off Ritalin, gained 40 pounds and grew 6 inches in height within the next six months. The following year he won an award for the top math student in his grade in the entire school district, and is making straight A's. As the result of Ralph's "Miracle," over 60 patients have come from his geographical area to be treated at our clinic, an eight hour round trip drive! Without NAET we never would have been able to resurrect Ralph nor the many other patients we have helped with behavior problems, attention deficit disorders, hyperactivity, and emotional problems. Thank you Dr. Devi from all of us.

Dr. James H. Winer, D.C.
1320 E. Carson St.
Pittsburgh, PA 15203
412) 431-1724

Dr. Devi's breakthrough approach of treating autism is the perfect example of how alternative medicine can offer the right solution for this disorder. NAET helps you to identify the causes and allows you to not only eliminate them but also lead a productive life.

Alan Bain, D.O.
Chicago, IL
(312) 236-7010

We can look at autism as a dysfunction in the brain's chemistry or electromagnetic frequency, be it a deficiency caused by allergies to certain groups of amino acids or neurotransmitters. Having practiced NAET successfully for a number of years, I have no doubt of its applicability in treating autism in a most remarkable, safe and cost effective way.

George Caldwell, OMD, L.Ac.
Minneappolis, MN
(612) 470-6206

I have been practicing NAET for 9 years. It has changed my practice greatly and has effected many lives positively including many autistic children I have treated over the years. Thank you Dr. Devi for helping me to make a difference in their lives!

Farangis Tavily, L.Ac.
20 Sunnyside ave, A397
Mill Valley, CA 94941
(415) 302-7907

I highly commend Dr. Devi Nambudripad and recommend her book on the subject of Allergy-related Autism in children. This book reveals availability of help to a prevailing and difficult medical problem.

Bess Liganor, MD.
Internal and Pediatrics Medicine, Fresno, CA
thanaw@pesc.com

ACKNOWLEDGMENTS

I am deeply grateful to my husband, Dr. Kris K. Nambudripad, for his inspiration, encouragement and assistance in my schooling and later, in the formulation of this project. Without his cooperation in researching reference work, revision of manuscripts, word processing and proofreading, it is doubtful whether this book would ever have been completed. My sincere thanks also go to the many clients who have entrusted their care to me, for without them I would have had no case studies, no technique and certainly no extensive source of personal research upon which to base this book.

I am also deeply grateful to the parents of Dominic, Steve, John, Steven, James, Matt, Brown, Mark, Ralph, Ann, Bob, Patrick, Eric, Paul, Young, John, Sean, Maureen, Yasue, and hideo and all other children whose names I haven't mention here due to lack of space, for believing in me from the very beginning of my research, supporting my theory and helping me conduct the on-going *detective* work. I like to express my special gratitude to Patrick's mother, Mary Nunan for showing such enthusiasm in not only taking care of her son's problem, but in sharing and spreading information about NAET to all other autistic community within her reach and constantly taking responsibility in educating other parents with similar problem. With the support of mothers (parents) like Mary, we will defeat and destroy autism very soon.

I also like to thank Prasad, Sara, Nathan, Karthik, Peyton and their parents for allowing me to take pictures to share with others for educating them about NAET. I like to express my heartfelt thanks to my friends who are excellent NAET practitioners who supported me by providing case studies, patients' testimonials, and constant encouragements to bring this book out. Without their ardent help, the writing of this book would have been a dream only.

Additionally, I wish to thank Mala, and Mohan for allowing me to work on the book by relieving me from the clinic duties, and helping me in the formulation of this book I do not have enough words to express my thanks to Art Hunter, Janice Barone, and many of my friends who wish to remain anonymous for proofreading the work, and Mr. Sridharan at Delta Publishing for his printing expertise. I am deeply grateful for my professional training and the knowledge and skills acquired in classes and seminars on chiropractic and applied kinesiology at the Los Angeles College of Chiropractic in Whittier, California; the California Acupuncture College in Los Angeles; SAMRA University of Oriental Medicine, Los Angeles; and the clinical experience obtained at the clinics attached to these colleges.

My special thanks also go to the late Dr. Richard F. Farquhar at Farquhar Chiropractic Clinic in Bellflower, California. Under Dr. R. F. Farquhar, I accumulated many hours of special instruction and hands-on practice in kinesiology that led me to find NAET.

I extend my sincere thanks to these great teachers. They have helped me to grow immensely at all levels. My mentors are also indirectly responsible for the improvement of my personal health as well as that of my family, patients and other NAET practitioners among whom are countless doctors of western and oriental medicine, chiropractic, osteopathy, as well as their patients.

Many of the nutritionists instrumental in this process, were professors at the institutions I have mentioned. Their willingness to give of themselves to teach, as well as their commitment of personal time to give the interviews necessary to complete this work, places them beyond my mere expressions of gratitude. They are servants to the greatest ideals of the medical profession.

Dr. Devi S. Nambudripad
Los Angeles, CA

PREFACE

PREFACE

For years, autism was considered a type mild brain disorder with no known cure. Even now, not too many people know that autism is reversible. So many intricate messages and signals are necessary for us to receive, process and retrieve information that one miscue or blockage to the brain might hinder us from communicating normally with another person.

Autism is a biological, neurological disorder, and developmental disorder which severely impairs a child's communication and social interactions. Unable to learn from the natural environment as most children do, the child with autism shows little interest in the world or people around him/her. While some or most children with autism develop some normal and even advanced skills, they exhibit a wide range of behavioral deficiencies and excesses. Some behavioral symptoms of autism are as follows:

■ Disturbances in the rate of appearance of physical, social and language skills.

- Abnormal responses to sensations, such as: sight, hearing, touch, balance, smell, taste, reaction to pain, and the way a child holds his/her body.
- Speech and language are absent or delayed, while specific thinking capabilities may be present.
- Abnormal ways of relating to people, objects, and events.
- Left untreated, autism inhibits a child's developmental growth to such a degree that most will require lifelong support.

The brain and the network of the nervous system do not function normally in autistic people. It seems that the cranial nerves become swollen causing inability to see, smell, hear, think or talk normally. Their vision becomes foggy and images get scrambled causing unclear pictures to float in front of them because of blockages in the nerves supplying the vision center. That's the reason autistic children do not look at you or look into your eyes when you talk to them. They cannot smell because the cranial nerve that is responsible for smell is not getting an adequate nerve energy supply. They cannot hear normally due to poor nerve energy supply to the acoustic nerves. Their thinking, creativity, and imagination is minimal or muddled because the nerves and brain tissue that are responsible for its functioning are not able to do its job due to the poor energy supply. Autistic people cannot speak because their speech center is not receiving messages from other areas to initiate speech or voice. Their sense of fine touch is also impaired. Something in their body causes swelling of the tissue, especially in the brain and cranial nerves, disturbing the energy supply to different parts of the brain that are responsible for such functions in the five senses. From my experience in treating autistic children and adults, I have found that the cranial nerves are highly affected, making the midbrain area most affected in autistic people.

For years, any abnormality of the brain was considered a type of madness. Autism was included in that category by lay people. People were frightened of persons with any brain disorders even if it happened to their close family members. Most of the people with brain disorders ended in mental illness (madness) those days. The mentally sick people were treated badly by their family and friends or were committed to mental institutions. In those days, mental illness was thought to be a hereditary disorder. Some people also believed mental illness was due to a person being possessed by devils or evil spirits. From such assumptions and fears developed various exotic treatments like exorcism, (trying to remove the possessed entities by inflicting pain in the sufferer, burning body parts of the sufferer, etc.), warding off evil spirits by chanting positive affirmation, or reciting certain religious words, etc. Some people were afraid to be associated with a family who had a mentally ill person in it. Other families in town avoided them and would not get involved in relationships with them, like marrying. People were afraid that they might become "crazy" by fraternizing with them, creating fear in family members of the victim. So the family of the "crazy" person did not want anyone else to find out the truth about their sick family member. In order to do that they would kill or hide the person. Since the killing was not a viable solution, they chose to hide the person from everyone. They locked him/her up in a secluded room, perhaps in a dungeon, basement, or in a soundproof room in the house, hidden from the rest of the world.

As I was growing up in a rural village in India, I knew a few innocent people who became victims of such ignorance and spent their lives in total seclusion until they died. The causes of their mental illness were never found out. No one other than some immediate family members or immediate neighbors knew their existence. One such case was an autistic adult. At that time I did not know she was autistic. Now after learning more about autism, examining and treating more patients who suffer from different stages of autism, I know she was just autistic, but labelled as mentally sick. If it was seen in a small village where population was not more than 500 people, I am sure it was probably prevalent in every village and town all over the world This clearly demonstrates that autism is not just a new age health disorder. It was prevalent all over the world years ago. Nobody talked about it or tried to cure the person. They were kept isolated, labeled as mentally unstable or mentally retarded and no one tried to help them overcome their illnesses, probably no one knew how to help these people.

Some of the families I knew in my childhood were sad to have two of their offsprings born mentally retarded. They used to bring doctors from different fields to help their children. One type of treatment given to them interested me so I watched the procedure many times. These teenage patients were made to lie flat on their back (if they did not cooperate, they were restrained), heads were kept soaked in herbal concoction and cold pressed sesame oil for a few hours daily for 41 days at a time, in order to cool their "hot" brain and nervous system. Because those herbal doctors thought their mental instability was due to excess heat in the brain.

Chinese medicine also holds similar principles regarding mental instabilities. It teaches that liver fire can rise to the brain and cause heat in the brain thus mental derangement. The dampness from gall bladder, phlegm from the spleen and cold mist from the heart (due to blockages in respective meridians) reach the brain and cause poor or no mental clarity and severe mental instability.

Today we know many mental disorders are due to various nutritional deficiencies, or chemical imbalances of the brain brought on by nutritional deficiencies. These deficiencies may not be due to lack of intake of nutritious food in most cases, but may be due to allergies to nutritional elements in food causing poor absorption and assimilation of the essential nutrients. Essential nutrients are the precursors to various brain enzymes. In the absence of essential nutrients, incomplete brain enzymes and neurotransmitters are produced. However, taking enzyme supplements without removing the allergy to them is not the answer. If the person is not allergic to the enzymes, appropriate enzyme supplementation will help the person. But if the person is allergic to the enzyme supplements, he/she can get worse. These incomplete brain enzymes can cause malfunctions of various parts of the brain and nervous system leading to abnormal behaviors, including autism, attention deficit hyperactive disorders, schizophrenia, bipolar disorders, manic depressive disorders, anxiety disorders, various kinds of depression, etc.

Many parents prefer to keep most brain-related health disorders of their children as secretive as possible. Unfortunately, autism is one of them. Over the years, I have treated a few cases of autistic children and adults suffering from varying degrees of autism with good success. When the children get well, the parents become reluctant to share their improvement or journey from autism to normalcy with others. They are happy that their children got well but they were not willing to be reminded of their past nightmare. They don't want their children to know their troubled past either. They don't want anyone to know that their child had autism. One of my patient's mothers, a native of another country said that no one in her family (except her husband) knew that her daughter had autism. She brought her to the U.S and to Europe for treatments. If her relatives knew that her child was autistic, it would damage the child's future since autism in her country is still looked upon as insanity. She would have difficulty putting her in a regular school, and later finding a husband for her. Even though she gave her testimonials, I had to promise her that I would never ever reveal her real name under any circumstances. This is not only happening to foreign born parents, this is happening in the U.S also. I have a few autistic children as patients, whose parents are well known doctors, lawyers, investors and actors who refuse to give their identity or give permission to have their names associated with autism. The fear of their future image is the concern here.

Fortunately, I have a few unselfish, compassionate, caring parents who are excited with the possibilities that not only their children but all other autistic children of the world could have a chance to start over and have a new hopeful life with NAET. They are willing to go all the way to educate other parents of autistic children, provide support, pass on the information about NAET, etc. With the help of these committed and caring parents, we are certain to achieve our dream soon... to reach all the autistic communities of the world and make NAET available to all in need. We applaud and extend our heartfelt thanks to these self-

less, caring, humanitarian parents who are eager to see the autism brought under control in the world.

NAET treatments on autism are more effective when the patients are very young. The older they get, the longer it takes to treat successfully. I have treated a few autistic patients who were in their late twenties or early thirties. One of the boys I treated a few years ago was a 29-year-old, no one suspected any allergy in him as a cause of his autism. This boy was very well built physically and had a mind of a three-year-old. After each successful treatment, this autistic boy who weighed 170 lbs and had a height of 5'11" embraced his lean, thin, stressed out father (probably had a height of 5'5', and weighed about 100 pounds) very tight. The father in fact crunched in pain from his rough embrace. Other times, the boy jumped around in the hallway like a three-year-old. Whenever he lost a treatment he grew very agitated, angry, physically violent towards his parents and caretakers, bit his own hand until it hurt him, and some other times he banged his head against the concrete floor or the brick wall. His behaviors were so violent, my other patients and staff were afraid to be near him. I had to schedule him during our days off and had to suggest to his father to medicate him to calm him down during the NAET treatment. If the symptoms are kept under control, NAET works better. When children are small, someone could hold them and control them from physical violence to themselves or others; but when autistic children grow up without treatments, it may not be easy to manage them in a regular clinic. If they have violent and aggressive behaviors, they should be treated with NAET in special clinics or in a hospital where more help is available. Calming medication or herbs should be given after checking and clearing the allergy for the drug or the herb. It is okay to give a non-allergic drug or herb and keep them calm than letting them become violent and agitated during the NAET treatment and during 25 hours waiting period. Physical strength of unmanaged autistic adults are usually very high and you may need more people to help with the treatment. It may be exhausting for the patient, doctor and the assistants. The treatments may not proceed smoothly if their nerves remain agitated. If the autistic children are allowed to remain without treatment, they are unable to attend regular school, unable to find jobs, unable to live by themselves, and they become dependent on others for the rest of their lives. On the contrary, if they get treated for their allergies, get proper schooling, they may be able to function in a normal fashion. They may be able to find jobs and live on their own with minimal help from others. Mild cases of autism and PD can have complete reversal provided they receive appropriate treatment from an early age or as soon as it is discovered. So it is for everyone's benefit to begin NAET treatments as early as possible.

There are many special schools and special clinics in U.S today where the autistic children are taught various behavior modifications. Specially trained people are available there to help bring your child to the wide world as a normal human being. If NAET is provided along with behavior modification, your child will grow to be a healthy, happy normal adult.

We have a lot of work ahead for us if we want people to accept autism as a treatable deficiency disease rather than an incurable mental disorder. If we want autism to be accepted as one of the health disorders caused by allergies, we need to educate the public, parents and the children about autism. We need to do clinical trials and double blind studies to get hard data on records so that skeptics and nonbelievers will provide their support to bring the unfortunate children out of their shells. We know now that an autistic child has deficiency in seeing, hearing and perceiving things as a normal child would. We need to know if these functional deficiencies are in fact due to allergies. We need to know if all types of autism are caused from some form of allergy (food, environmental agents, chemicals, internal toxins, external toxins, defective DNA, defective brain parts, genetically oriented, etc.). Are there causes other than allergies? If so, what are they and how do we find them and solve them?

We study, read and see many health disorders around us every day. How did we recognize or diagnose them? From their history, presenting symptoms and the laboratory tests supporting the symptoms. We prescribe, give and take various herbs, prescription and non-prescription medications to get the symptoms under control. When the pain and/or discomfort gets better we are happy and we don't bother to look into the cause that initiated the symptoms. Then the next episode occurs. The same routine is repeated. When the symptoms are gone no one really has time or interest to look into the cause. Here is an example:

"I was sick yesterday and I couldn't go to work," Jane said.

Maria asked, "What was your problem?"

"I had a migraine headache," Jane replied.

Jane's migraine headache becomes the cause and the sickness. So the symptom becomes the cause to most people. People all over the world are looking at symptoms and treating symptoms. No one looks for a cause or treat the cause.

It is different In NAET. Whatever the symptoms may be, we look for the cause. If we can trace the cause, NAET works faster. If a patient comes to my office with a migraine headache, I will ask, "What caused your migraine headache?" If she doesn't know, NAET has a way to find the cause of the presenting symptoms. All certified NAET practitioners know how to find the cause. May be the pear you ate at lunch; or the make up you put on your face during your lunch break, or the perfume you smelled from one of your customers, or the candybar you ate from the vending machine while returning from lunch, could have triggered this migraine headache. An NAET practitioner will probe until he/she finds out the culprit. When you treat the allergy towards the offending substance the pain and discomfort will clear swiftly never to return again in most cases.

I can relate to the plight of parents searching for a cure for their child's illness, running from western medical doctors to alternative forms of medicine hoping for some reassurance that their child will be able to lead a productive life. After exhausting their energy and finances most parents face a grim future without getting much help. If your child's autism is allergy related, unless you eliminate the allergies, your child may not be able to function normally even if you feed them any amount of expensive good nutrition. You need to find your child's allergies. Now there is an easy way to do that. You have to learn the testing techniques if you want to see your child function normally. I would like to see all parents learn and master this simple technique. Please read Chapter Six and practice to perfection. Then you will know how to help your child.

If you carefully evaluate any health disorders, you may find an allergic factor involved in almost everything, including physical, physiological, psychological, emotional and genetic disorders and autism is not any different.

Let us look at some examples:

A fourteen-year-old boy hurt his knees, sprained his ankles many times within a year while playing soccer. He was found to be allergic to his shin splints, cotton socks and shoes. After he was successfully treated for the above items with NAET, he was able to play soccer and take part in normal sports activities without a problem for the rest of his school years.

A 36-year-old man hurt his lower back while playing tennis. He had to be carried into the doctors office in excruciating pain. He was found to be allergic to the fish meal he had before playing tennis. After he was treated for the abalone fish, he was able to walk out of the office in 30 minutes and play tennis the next day.

A 37-year-old female suffered from high blood pressure (190/120 mm of hg.) for six months. She was found to be allergic to the new mattress she had bought six months ago. When she was successfully treated for the mattress, her blood pressure became normal.

A 28 year old man suffered from a (left) sided migraine headache for nine months. He was found to be allergic to the left lens of the eye glasses that he acquired nine months ago.

A 43-year-old female, who was diagnosed as having schizophrenic disorders, was found to be allergic to many food groups in her daily diet. She was also allergic to household cleaning chemicals, soaps, detergents and pets. She was successfully treated for all of the above and became a normal productive individual again. She returned to school, completed her education, found a job that pays her a large sum, went off the permanent disability on her own and leads a normal productive life now.

A 28-year-old man suffered from extreme depression in the early morning hours. He lived by the ocean in Southern California. He was allergic to the morning cold air and fog. When he was treated for cold air mixed with cold mist, his years-long depression disappeared.

A 14-year-old boy with severe backache, joint pains and bone and muscle aches was found to be allergic to every food group he ate and everything he drank including water. His paternal grandfather suffered a crippling kind of arthritis from a very young age. His father also suffered from severe joint pains and muscle aches that did not respond to analgesics. He was told by previous medical practitioners who examined him that his health problems were genetic in origin. Nothing could be done except to learn to live with the pain. When he was treated for all his food allergies, he became free from his incurable pain.

A 65-year-old male suffered from frequent memory lapses and seizures that resembled some form of epilepsy, Alzheimers disease or perhaps a mild stroke. He would often wander off in total confusion or complete amnesia, sometimes losing track of significant blocks of time. Neurological examination and a CAT scan showed his brain wave pattern to be completely normal. After considerable detective work, the cause in this case turned out to be the airborne spores of a fern tree he had recently planted in his backyard. He became absolutely normal after he was treated successfully for the same fern tree.

When I look back into my childhood days, I recall the multitude of health problems I suffered. Probably each and every one of them may have followed an allergy to whatever I ate, touched or inhaled. I literally lived on prescription medicines and herbs to control my symptoms. No one knew how to find the cause of my heath problems. No one knew how to test the allergy using muscle response testing in those days. In fact The word "allergy" was non-existent in the part of the world where I grew up. People got sick there but no one had any allergies. As an infant, I had severe infantile eczema, which lasted until I was seven or eight-years-old. I was given western medicine and Ayurvedic herbal medicine without a break. When I was eight-years-old, one of the herbal doctors told my parents to feed me white rice cooked with a special herb formula. This special diet helped me a great deal. The herbalist seemed to know what he was doing. But it didn't cure my problem. It only gave temporary relief until I discovered NAET.

In 1976, I relocated to Los Angeles. I became more health-conscious and tried to eat healthy by adding more whole grain products and complex carbohydrates into my daily bland diet. All of a sudden, I became very ill. I suffered from repeated bronchitis, pneumonia and my arthritis returned. My symptoms multiplied. I suffered from insomnia, clinical depression, constant sinusitis and frequent migraine headaches. I felt extremely tired all the time, but I remained wide-awake when I went to bed. I tried many different antibiotics and medicines, changed doctors and consulted nutritionists. All the medications, vitamins and herbs made me sicker, and the consumption of good nutrition made me worse. I was nauseated all the time. Every inch of my body ached. I lived on aspirin, taking almost 30 aspirin a day to keep me going.

I searched everywhere for an answer to my agony. Through my illness and devastation, I continued my search. Whenever I signed up for a class in some health subject, or joined a new school to explore more on health, my husband used to make a statement "You are a glutton for punishment" and I would reply, "This glutton is going to be off the punishment soon." I longed to be free of pain at least for few days but I didn't know how.

While I was a student of oriental medicine and attending one of the courses in electromagnetic energy and its interference with the human body and other surrounding objects, I arrived at a discovery, which resulted in the foundation of my own good health and my family. The integration of the relevant techniques from the various fields I studied, combined with my own discoveries, has since become the focus of my life to help my family, myself and my patients. We were an allergic family —father-mother-son! We were allergic to everything around us. There was no known successful method of treatment for food allergies then (actually even now as I am writing this), using western medicine except avoidance, which means deprivation and frustration. Each of the disciplines I studied provided bits of knowledge, which I used to develop this new allergy elimination treatment called Nambudripad's Allergy Elimination Techniques or NAET for short, that I practice now.

Thousands of sick patients with a variety of health problems have been treated with NAET and have achieved marvellous results. From my own health improvements and watching the thousands who achieved similar or better results, I am convinced now that most of the ailments we see around us stem from some kind of allergies, including almost all genetic disorders. Autism is not any different.

The more extensively I studied the subject of allergies, the more I found it to be a truly fascinating, yet highly complex field.

Although food allergies as causes for multiple physiological problems have been gaining acceptance as a separate area of medical study in the last few years, it certainly has not been given the recognition it deserves. In fact, knowledge of the field is still quite limited not only among the general public, but also among those who treat allergies because of the limited volume of research conducted.

After learning about the prevalence of allergies in children with autism and gathering a great deal of clinical hands-on experience with my young patients from my 15 years of practice as an allergist, I felt motivated to write this book on allergy-based Autism and how to conquer it with NAET.

When I realized that most autistic disorders I treated were allergy-based, my urge to inform and educate people grew. In the meantime, many of my patients and my friends insisted that I put this valuable information in a book form. The best form of education is through published materials. Consequently, "Say Goodbye to Allergy-related Autism," came into shape.

In this book, I do use some specialized terminology, which may give some lay readers a harder time and diminish their reading pleasure and understanding. But rest assured, technical terms are kept to a minimum. Caution has also been exercised in determining the depth of the subject matter. For instance, the way allergies and the nervous system are inextricably interrelated is just now being understood. But since the human nervous system is one of the most complex areas of human anatomy and remains largely uncharted, I decided to deal with it in a sweeping fashion, drawing the reader's attention only to the close link between the nervous system and allergic reactions.

I would feel gratified, indeed, if the up-to-date material compiled in this book were to contribute to the well-being of a great number of Autistic children and give their worried, and frustrated parents a little peace of mind, then my dream would be fulfilled. If this book could provide help to the tired, frustrated mothers of Autistic children in managing their symptoms efficiently, if NAET could reach the misdiagnosed and wrongly treated Autistic children in their autistic community and bring help to those children who are not Autistic in reality, making them calm, responsible, productive individuals, my job is done.

To enhance your understanding of the subject matter, you should check out some of the other relevant books and articles quoted as a part of this book. You will find them under the section marked "BIBLIOGRAPHY," at the conclusion of this book. Since the main focus of this presentation is acupuncture, an understanding of that medical system and an introduction to the basis of Traditional Chinese Medicine (TCM) is mandatory. You should keep in mind, however, that an in-depth introduction to oriental medicine was neither intended nor considered appropriate within the scope of this publication.

Therefore I urge you to refer to appropriate books for more information on this topic. Some of the references are listed in the bibliography.

Dr. Devi S. Nambudripad,
D.C., L.Ac., R.N., Ph.D. (Acu)
Los Angeles, California
December, 1999

Say Good-bye to Allergy-related Autism

FOREWORD

FOREWORD

Say Good-bye to Allergy-Related Autism

**By
David I. Minkoff, M.D.**

It is with great pleasure that I introduce this fourth book of Dr. Devi Nambudripad. I consider her one of my best teacher's and mentors.

Every now and then in the history of medicine there comes along a rare physician who produces a quantum leap in the understanding of disease. Through insight and perception he/she discovers a basic truth about human physiology and is able to utilize that knowledge for the betterment of all mankind.

One such physician is Dr. Devi Nambudripad. She is a pioneer. I first had the pleasure of being her student just nine months ago. Learning the technology of NAET has transformed my practice of medicine, which has progressed from Pediatrics and Infectious Disease to Emergency Medicine, and now to Complementary Medicine.

In that practice I do NAET among a whole variety of other complementary disciplines. Of all of them, NAET is the most important and the most effective. It has completely changed my concept of what allergy is and what dramatic effects it has on the human body.

Using NAET, children's common allergies and recurrent infections are eliminated. Children with mood disorders change their behavior and children with Down's syndrome brighten up. There is no area that I have applied NAET that it has not dramatically changed the condition of the patient for the better. In fact, all of our patients, no matter what they come in for are treated with NAET. We get more successes from our NAET treatments than with any other modality that we use.

I have seen a three year wheel chair bound patient "MS patient," with no feeling in her legs and virtually no muscle movement, **regain** sensation and start walking within two weeks after desensitization to calcium! Another person with a disease called Sarcoid, that was proven by a lung biopsy, who was short of breath and lost sensation in the left side of his body regained feeling and normal breathing after NAET treatments. I know it sounds too good to be true. If I was not seeing it daily in my own practice with my own eyes, I would not believe it either.

This book is about Autism. It is a scourge for anyone connected with it, family, friends, physicians, and the patients themselves. Unfortunately Autism is on the rise by high percentages. The modern concept is that these children suffer from a toxic brain that may be due to a number of insults, including nutritional deficiency, poorly tolerated immunizations, overuse of antibiotics, intestinal yeast overgrowth, in-adequate liver detoxification, heavy metal intoxication, and perhaps secretin deficiency.

Underlying *all of these may be allergy*. Using NAET to treat the allergy, many children can be helped to regain normal function. It occurs rather quickly and painlessly too. I've seen a child with sugar allergy and severe autism regain his awareness of the environment after one treatment!

In this book you will read the miracle stories. They are real. If you like happy endings to things you will enjoy them. For the joy of living includes feeling well and alive, in communication and out of pain.

For Dr. Devi, who discovered this technique I can't express enough gratitude for this gift to the world. Millions of patients can daily attest to that. Nobel prizes for medicine are given to people who make outstanding contributions in the field of medicine, who better have bettered many lives. Such a profile fits Dr. Devi, and were it up to me, she would be bestowed with that honor.

Thank you Dr. Devi.

David I. Minkoff M.D.
Medical Director,
Lifeworks Wellness Center
Clearwater, Florida
(727) 466-6789

INTRODUCTION

INTRODUCTION

Say Good-bye To Allergy-related Autism

It is your child's HUMAN RIGHT to eat whatever he/she wants, live in whatever environment he/she wants to live, wear whatever clothes he/she wants to wear, attend regular school, and grow up normally like other children. If your child is unable to do any of these, you need to pay attention to the matter immediately. You are with your child most of the time. No one understand your child as you do. If any abnormalities are noted you should have your child checked immediately. If there is any problem detected, you should immediately get professional help. The sooner you look into the problem, the better the prognosis. This book "Say Good-bye to Allergy-Related Autism," will help you to search for any possible abnormalities in your child, and assist you in finding the right help for your child.

This book reveals the secrets of a remarkable breakthrough in medical history. It brings a breath of fresh air to the medical field and approaches health care from a new intelligent view point.

This book is filled with so much common sense that it simply cannot be ignored by the medical community. The brain and central nervous system reacts to foods (egg white, milk casein, milk albumin, wheat products, gluten, candida, refined starches, fatty acids, minerals, amino acids, turkey and serotonin, chocolate), heavy metals, chemicals, vaccines, immunizations or other substances as if they were poison when they are really neutral or in some cases beneficial. You can now reprogram your brain to perfect health by eliminating and/or neutralizing the adverse effects and side effects of all these allergens and improve or restore the brain function.

Kinesiology, chiropractic and acupuncture techniques have already been proven and accepted in the medical world. It is important to note that these procedures along with Dr. Nambudripad's discovery of NAET will be beneficial to children suffering from Autism, ADHD, and other learning disabilities.

WHAT IS NAET?

NAET is an acronym for Nambudripad's Allergy Elimination Techniques. Various effective parts of healing techniques from different disciplines of medicine (allopathy, acupuncture, chiropractic, kinesiology and nutrition) have been compiled together to create NAET, to permanently eliminate allergies of all kinds (food and environmental allergies and reactions in varying degrees from mild to severe to anaphylaxis) from the body. NAET is a completely natural, non-invasive and drug-free holistic treatment. Over thirty-five hundred licensed medical practitioners have been trained in NAET procedures and are practicing all over the world. Please look up the NAET websit, **"www.naet.com"** for more information on NAET and a NAET practitioner near you.

WHAT IS AN ALLERGY?

A condition of unusual sensitivity of one individual to one or more substances (may be inhaled, swallowed or contacted vy the skin), which may be harmless or even beneficial to the majority of other individuals. In sensitive individuals, contact with these substances (allergens) can produce a variety of symptoms in varying degrees ranging from slight ADHD to Autism, mild itching to swelling of the tissues and organs, mild runny nose to severe asthmatic attacks, general tiredness or fatigue to severe anaphylaxis. The ingested, inhaled, injected or contacted allergen is capable of alerting the immune system of the body. The frightened and confused immune system then commands the white blood cells to produce immunoglobulin type E (IgE) to stimulate the release of neuro-chemical defense forces like histamines from the mast cells. These chemical mediators are released as part of the body's immune response.

WHAT CAUSES ALLERGIES?

■ Heredity (inherited from parents, grandparents, uncles, aunts, etc.).

■ Toxins (produced in the body from: food interactions, unsuitable proteins, bacterial or viral infections; molds, yeast, fungus or parasitic infestation; vaccinations and immunizations; drug reactions; constant contacts with certain irritants like mercury, lead, copper, chemicals, etc.).

■ Low immune system function (due to surgeries, chronic illnesses, injury, long term starvation, etc.).

■ Radiation (excessive exposure to television, Sun, radioactive materials, etc.).

■ Emotional factors.

WHAT ARE SOME COMMON ALLERGENS

- ■ Inhalants: pollens, flowers, perfume, dust, paint, formaldehyde, etc.

- ■ Ingestants: food, drinks, vitamins, drugs, food additives, etc.

- ■ Contactants: fabrics, chemicals, cosmetics, furniture, utensils, etc.

- ■ Injectants: insect bites, stings, injectable drugs, vaccines, immunization, etc.

- ■ Infectants: viruses, bacteria, contact with infected persons, etc.

- ■ Physical Agents: heat, cold, humidity, dampness, fog, wind, dryness, sunlight, sound, etc.

- ■ Genetic Factors: inherited illnesses or tendency from parents, grandparents, etc.

- ■ Molds and Fungi: molds, yeast, candida, parasites, etc.

- ■ Emotional Factors: painful memories of various incidents from past and present.

HOW DO I KNOW IF MY CHILD HAS ALLERGIES?

If you notice any unusual or strange behavior for the age of your child, that may give you the first clue. If he/she experiences any allergic symptoms or unusual physical, physiological or emotional symptoms in the presence of any of the above listed allergens, you can suspect an allergy contributing towards such changes.

WHO SHOULD USE THIS BOOK?

All parents, teachers, medical professionals, anyone involved with a child with learning disorders should read this book to learn about NAET and to include NAET with your current mode of treatment to enhance the results of your current treatment. This drug-free, non-invasive technique is ideal to treat infants, children, and grown-ups alike to remove the adverse reactions.

HOW IS THIS BOOK ORGANIZED?

The front cover of the book symbolizes " The NAET result." When autism is reversed the real angel hiding within your child will get a chance to come out of his/her cage. The cover is designed by one of our children who was once treated for ADHD, and who is a smart teenager now.

The broken chain at the beginning of each chapter represents the ability of the body to break its existing allergic pattern, and re-program the brain to an allergy-free life, through NAET.

■ Chapter 1 explains the definition of allergy in various disciplines of medicine and also in laymen's terms and how it affects an autistic child. There are numerous autism case studies throughout the book, some are from the author's observation, some are from other NAET practitioners' case notes, and some are from the parents of children who have benefitted from NAET.

■ Chapter 2 describes the various categories of allergens and how they affect an autistic child.

■ Chapter 3 explains Nambudripad's Testing Techniques and gives you information about various allergy testing techniques to detect allergies in your autistic child.

■ Chapter 4 is a step-by-step method of evaluating your child's allergic history.

■ Chapter 5 describes the normal function of the human nervous system and how it creates allergies by receiving wrong stimuli.

■ Chapter 6 discusses kinesiology, acupuncture and how energy blockages can cause allergies and diseases in the human body. It also explains Muscle Response Testing (MRT) to detect allergies, the main testing technique used in NTT.

■ Chapter 7 explains the major acupuncture meridians, and their normal and pathological functions.

■ Chapter 8 describes and illustrates self-balancing techniques and the use of acupressure techniques to give the reader more control over his/her child's reactions.

■ Chapter 9 describes various self-help modalities to balance your child's brain and nervous system with illustrations of the procedure for better understanding.

■ Chapter 10 explains the basic NAET allergens, the most effective treatment approach and the order of treatments.

■ Chapter 11 presents various case studies are presented here in detail including the procedure, the immediate reactions, the immediate response and reactions, and responses after leaving the office during 25 hours after treatment.

■ Actual parent's testimonials are also included where appropriate to help the reader understand the severity of the symptoms and the process involved in undergoing treatment to eliminate those allergic reactions in order to reverse autism. This is done for two purposes:

1. To provide guidance to an inexperienced NAET practitioner in treating autism successfully.

2. To provide an understanding of NAET to the parents and the type of reactions and responses they could expect for their child after each treatment.

■ Chapter 12 emphasizes the importance of essential nutritional elements in your child's diet.

■ Chapter 13 discusses the author's dream to defeat and eradicate autism permanently from the world. Is it possible? Yes, absolutely, if we all work hard at it.

■ The glossary of terms will help you to understand the appropriate meanings of the medical terminology used in certain parts of the book.

■ The resource guide is provided to assist you in finding products and consultants to support you in dealing with your allergies.

■ The Bibliography covers most of the sources of information on autism. A detailed index is included to help you locate your area of interest quickly and easily.

CHAPTER 1

PARENTS, DO YOU KNOW THAT AUTISM IS TREATABLE ?

1

PARENTS, DO YOU KNOW THAT AUTISM IS TREATABLE ?

It was 3 A.M. and my 2 year old son, Dominic was humming along to the song "A Whole New World." It had been another rough night for him as he had awakened at 1 a.m. screaming and banging his head. He had finally settled down after an hour and had requested the Aladdin video as usual. As he drifted off to sleep I sat there watching him. He seemed so peaceful now. It was hard to believe, whenever he had settled down, that he was the same little boy.

I began to wonder, as I had so many times before, what made it so hard for my little one to live in our world. What happened to the little baby who used to smile at me? Where had he gone? What "new world" had he entered? I said a prayer for him. Then I prayed for strength and for an answer that would bring our son back to us.

Dominic had cried since the day he was born. The doctors had told me it was colic and sent me on my way. By 15-months-old, he became more belligerent with his screaming episodes. He would often bang his head and throw himself on the ground in a rage. There was no consoling him as he resisted all comforting, although he did allow only me to try. The doctors did not have an explanation for me and so my husband and I just sat there night after night trying to help our son as he would cling to us then push us away. At a point, I called 911 because I thought he was having seizure. He also had other physical problems such as diarrhea, rashes, hives, stuffy nose, runny nose, fluids in the ears, and ear-aches. Dominic's sleep was often interrupted by these attacks. At 18 months he began to appear withdrawn from the world around him. When he would visit relatives he would hide in a corner or under my chair. The pediatrician thought it was the "terrible two's" that was responsible for his tantrums and strange behaviors. Yet, in my heart, I knew differently. My husband and I were exhausted, and I felt so alone.

Then one day, a special friend of mine handed me Dr. Devi's book, "Say Goodbye to Illness." Until then, I had not heard of alternative therapies, like acupuncture, acupressure, or chiropractic. I was completely dependent on western medicine and western medical doctors. I did not have much time and never thought of going to bookstores to look for health alternatives because I thought, only western medicine exists to cure us from our health problems. I was simply not educated by anyone about any alternative medical therapies. I wish there had been and would be more exposure and discussion about alternative medical therapies and their benefits and importance in our daily lives. There may be millions of desperate mothers all over the world thinking that they have to use just western medical therapies to get well. Many of them may be suffering due to mere ignorance.

Well, I had tried western medicine all along and I had failed to see any results. So I decided to take him to Dr. Devi. Dominic was 100% allergic to 156 items. We began treatments and Dominic began to get some relief. During the initial treatment days, when he would have an attack, we would massage his acupressure points that Dr. Devi taught us to use and he would relax into my arms. My husband would have to hold him down as I massaged his points, because he was very strong during his attacks. At this point, Dominic hardly spoke a word. He would speak in jargon and no one could understand him. He would easily become overwhelmed and was resistant to any change in his routines. Dominic would run in circles and flap his arms. He would hold food in his mouth for an hour at a time and would nervously chew holes in his shirt. He was tested by a regional center and was found to be a year and a half behind in his language and fine motor skills.

He was then referred to a specialist, who told me that he was autistic and needed to be tested for fragile syndrome which causes mental retardation. We were devastated at this news. We could not control our tears as we prayed to God to have mercy on our son. My husband and I cried together many times during those five weeks before we got the results from the doctor's test. Dr. Devi reassured us that it was his allergies contributing to his behaviors. She was kind, confident, and understanding of our pain. She treated me for my emotions. I was an emotional wreck during that time. When Dr. Devi began eliminating Dominic's food allergy one by one (first one was protein, then milk and calcium, then vitamin C, B complex), we began seeing some results. When she treated him for sugar his crying decreased and his head banging ceased. It took two times for him to pass the sugar allergy. He began speaking a few words that made sense to us. He began gesturing for the things he wanted. We continued the treatments and after passing minerals (8th treatment) he began to speak more. At this time his doctor (specialist) did most of his tests once again. This time we received God's Grace and were told that Dominic's genetic test came back normal. He then started special education classes to help with his speech and fine motor skills. It was then I knew that Dr. Devi's treatments would help bring our son back to us. I was amazed at the progress Dominic had made. Now he is just a happy healthy little boy! Our older son also has a learning disability and is currently being treated. He also suffered from asthma and sinusitis from childhood. After five basic NAET treatments, she treated him for grasses, pollens, dust, animal epithelial and dander. He can now play in the grass, and cuddle a cat without an asthma attack. He is also showing progress in his learning. We are very thankful to our friend who shared Dr. Devi's book with me. Otherwise I would have had no way of finding about this unique treatment. We thank Dr. Devi for her kindness to our family during this time. Thanks to her treatments, our son now lives in "our world." Seeing Dominic's changes, a few parents have started NAET treatments on their children and they are also very happy with the results. So many of our children are suffering. I just pray that other doctors who are specializing in treating autistic children, other schools for special education, and parents who have autistic children or who have learning disabilities will find Dr. Devi. I hope they will be encouraged to try the NAET treatments that changed our lives. Thank you Dr. Devi.

Debbie Lopez, Registered Nurse
Fullerton, CA

WHAT IS AUTISM?

A syndrome of early childhood, autism is a biological brain disorder that causes the child to see, feel, smell and hear differently from other people. It is a complex developmental disability that typically appears during the first three years of life. It is characterized by abnormal social relationships, language disorders with impaired understanding, pronominal reversal (saying you for I or me for you, etc.), rituals (wiping the face repeatedly, rubbing the nose, pulling hair, chewing long hair constantly, etc.), compulsive phenomena and uneven intellectual development with mental retardation in most cases if the right treatment is not provided adequately.

Autistic children are born more frequently in this century than ever before. According to the statistics released by the Center for Disease Control and Prevention in 1997, autism and its associated behaviors have been estimated to occur in as many as 1 in 500 individuals, or in other words, in 20 of every 10,000 births and is four times more common in males than females. Autism can occur by itself or in association with other developmental disorders such as learning disabilities, mental retardation, Tourett's syndrome, epilepsy, etc. The exact cause of autism is still unknown. Some research suggests that a physical problem affecting those parts of the brain that process language and information coming in from the senses is the cause. It may be due to an imbalance in the brain chemicals especially those produced in the hypothalamic region, which affects the way the brain uses information from the five senses. Genetic factors may be involved, as well as an imbalance of certain chemicals either in excess or deficiency in the brain. Another possibility may involve some of the messenger neurons turning dormant due to the effect of toxins from various sources and fail to conduct messages appropriately through the energy pathways. Sometimes autism can be the result of a combination of these factors. There are no geographical, social or racial boundaries to autism. It occurs throughout the world in all races, nationalities, and social classes. The most common problems in autism are that the individuals have extreme difficulty learning language and social skills and in relating to people. People with autism also exhibit extreme hyperactivity or unusual passivity in their relations with family members and other people. Behavior problems may exist, which range from mild to severe, aggressive to self-injurious.

Autism prevents individuals from properly understanding what they see and hear. Individuals with autism have extreme difficulty in learning language and social skills and in relating to people. It is considered a brain disorder. Autism affects the way the brain uses information. The imbalance of the brain may be due to various factors: accumulation of certain chemicals in the brain, nuclear radiation, toxins from bacterial and viral infections, toxic exposure from heavy metal, mercury, and silicone; chemically introduced toxins as in vaccination, immunization, etc., genetic factors, food and environmental allergies, sudden emotional shocks, witnessing frightful events in childhood, or a physical problem affecting those parts of the brain that process language and information. A combination of factors is likely to be responsible. Autism is treatable—early diagnosis and intervention are vital to the prognosis of autism.

It is best to consider it as a disability on a scale from mild to severe. The extreme form of the syndrome may include self-injurious, repetitive, highly unusual and aggressive behavior. Individuals with autism show uneven skill development, with deficits in certain areas (usually in the ability to communicate and relating to others) and distinct skills in other areas. It is important to distinguish autism from mental retardation, in which relatively even skill development is shown. People with autism are not physically disabled and "look" just like anybody without a disability. Because of the invisible nature of autism, it can be much harder to create awareness and understanding of the condition.

HISTORY OF AUTISM

Leo Kanner and Hans Asperger were the first to publish any accounts of childhood autism. Working independently, Kanner in Baltimore (1943), and Asperger in Vienna (1944), detailed case studies and attempted to describe the disorder. Before Leo Kanner wrote his paper identifying autistic children, these children were classified as emotionally disturbed or mentally retarded. Kanner observed that the children were not merely slow learners and they didn't fall in the category of emotionally disturbed. He presented 11 children in his study whose behavior was so different from anything he had noticed previously that he felt they needed a new category, which he called "Early Infantile Autism." He noted the features of "autistic aloneness," "desire for sameness," and "islets of ability," which are discernible in all true cases of autism. "Autistic aloneness," refers to the child disregarding or ignoring anything from the outside environment; "desire for sameness," includes the repetitive motions and noises; the ability to recollect poems, complex patterns and sequences are " islets of ability" that represent good intelligence.

Asperger gave detailed descriptions of autistic children. He found that they all had common fundamental disturbances in their social integration. However, he also felt that they had an originality of thought and experience, which might lead them to exceptional achievement as they grow older. He also noted that autistic children's language was unnatural, they followed their own impulses and had many stereotypical movements along with narrow area of intellectual ability. The patients Asperger identified all had speech, so the term Asperger's Syndrome is used to label autistic people with speech, at the higher functioning end of the autism spectrum, while Kanner's Syndrome is used for the classical form of autism.

Before Kanner and Asperger used the word "autism," it already had a meaning. Eugen Bleuler introduced it in 1911. He was a psychiatrist, who originally used the word to refer to a basic disturbance in schizophrenia (also coined by Bleuler) the narrowing of relationships to people and to the outside world. The narrowing became so extreme it excluded everything except the person's own self. The word comes from the Greek word "autos" meaning "self."

CHARACTERISTICS OF AUTISM

The characteristics of autism vary with each individual and may include the following:

Severe delays in language development: language is slow to develop or it may not develop at all. Individuals who do use language usually have peculiar speech patterns or use words without attaching the normal meaning to them. A monotonal voice is often noted when speech is involved.

SEVERE DELAYS IN SOCIAL INTERACTIONS

Autistic individuals often avoid eye contact and appear to "tune out the world." There is an impaired ability to develop friendships, understand someone else's feelings or interact and play with peers.

UNEVEN PATTERNS OF INTELLECTUAL FUNCTIONING

People with autism may have certain skills that they can excel in, such as music, art, math computation (the movie "Rain Man" acted by Dustin Hoffman and Tom Cruise is an example), and memorization of facts. Other autistic people may have varying degrees of mental retardation. This combination of intellectual variation makes autism very perplexing to diagnose and treat.

RESTRICTION OF ACTIVITY

Repetitive body movements, such as twisting, spinning, rocking are common in people with autism. Individuals may repeatedly follow the same route, the same order of dressing, or the same schedule everyday. It becomes extremely stressful for autistic individuals if there are changes in their routine.

INCONSISTENT PATTERNS OF SENSORY RESPONSES

Sometimes people identified as autistic may appear deaf and fail to respond to words or other sounds. At other times they may be distressed by an everyday noise, like a dog barking. There also may be a tendency to be insensitive to pain, unresponsive to heat or cold or they may overreact to any of these.

An allergic reaction may be manifested in varying degrees in an autistic child as mild to severe irritability of the brain and nervous system, inappropriate activity, itching, rashes, hives, ear infections, edema, asthma, joint pains, muscle aches, headaches, restlessness, insomnia, addictions, craving, indigestion, vomiting, anger, depression, disturbed vision, incontinence, repeated infections, panic attacks, brain fatigue, and brain fog.

When you look at an allergy from a holistic point of view, you can say that an allergy is an energy imbalance caused by

WITH JUST SIX NAET TREATMENTS, WE CAN SEE THE DIFFERENCE!

Maureen is 16 years of age. She was born microcephalic. Later she was diagnosed as autistic, attention deficit and hyperactive. She also has a compulsive behavioral problem. A few weeks ago Maureen started NAET treatments with Dr. Nambudripad. She had six basic treatments so far. Her behavioral problems and temper tantrums have reduced greatly. The tantrum has been reduced from 3 or 4 times a week to about 2 times or less. Her speech is clearer and she is more focused. My wife and I are very excited about Maureen's progress. Maureen is going to continue with the NAET treatments and we are positive she is going to be functional very soon.

Stephen Tee
West Hills, CA

the clashing of two or more incompatible charges. This is similar to like-magnetic charges repelling one another with a slight difference. The repulsion of the incompatible energies causes an allergic reaction, an altered action in the body.

An allergy is a hereditary condition: an allergic predisposition or tendency is inherited, but the allergy itself may not manifest until some later date. Researchers have found that when both parents were or are allergy-sensitive, 75 to 100 percent of their offspring react to those same allergens.

When neither of the parents is (nor was) sensitive to allergens, the probability of producing allergic offspring drops dramatically to less than 10 percent. Most of us suffer from allergic manifestation in varying degrees because of our different levels of parental inheritance.

Studies have shown that, in some cases, even when parents had no allergies, their offspring still suffered from many allergies since birth. In these cases, various possibilities exist:

■ The parents may have suffered from a serious disease or condition. For example, the parents had rheumatic fever before the child was born, which caused an alteration in the genetic codes.

■ The pregnant mother may have been exposed to harmful substances such as radiation (X-rays); chemicals (an expectant mother taking too much caffeine, alcohol, chemical exposures, carbon monoxide poisoning, etc.); circulating internal toxins as the result of a disease (streptococcal infection as in strep-throat, measles, chickenpox, candidiasis, parasitic infestation, diabetes, etc.); drug-induced toxins as a result of allergic reactions to vaccinations, immunizations, antibiotics, other drugs, emotional trauma (sudden loss of loved ones, various kinds of abuses like mental torture, rapes, fearful events like a major fire in the living quarters, falls, etc.).

■ The parents may have suffered severe malnutrition (not getting enough food or not assimilating due to poor absorption or allergies) possibly causing the growing embryo to undergo cell mutation during its development in the womb. The altered cells do not carry over the original genetic codes or do not go through normal development. The organs and tissues that are supposed to develop from the affected cells have impaired function.

■ In our modern day life, many parents leave their infants in front of a color television permitting the infant to bathe in a continuous flow of radiation for hours. Excess assimilation of television radiation can cause energy blockages and cell mutation in the growing infant.

We cannot ignore the fact that we are moving toward the twenty-first century where technology will be even more predominant than today. There is nothing wrong with the technology, but the allergic patient must find ways to overcome adverse reactions to chemicals and other allergens, in order to live a better life.

The symptoms, diagnosis and treatment of sensitivities, hypersensitivities and intolerance, (non-IgE mediated reactions), and allergies (IgE mediated reactions) often overlap. Both intolerances and allergies, in varying degrees, can be tested by Muscle Response Testing (MRT) either by producing a weak MRT (weakness of the indicator muscle in the case of an allergy), or a strong MRT (strong resistance by the indicator muscle in the case of no allergy). All of these allergic reactions are capable of producing autism, but can successfully be treated by NAET. MRT and NAET are explained in detail in Chapter Six.

WHAT IS NAET?

A thorough treatise on biochemistry is not appropriate for the purpose of an introduction to this new method of treatment for people suffering from allergies. Instead, this discussion will concentrate on the basic constructs of this treatment method and give some insight into the lives of people that it has helped. This is not a new technology. It is actually a combination of knowledge and techniques that uses much of what is already known from allopathic (western medical knowledge), chiropractic, kinesiology, acupuncture (oriental medical knowledge) and nutrition. Each of the disciplines I studied provided bits of knowledge, which I used to develop this new allergy elimination treatment. There is no known successful method of treatment for food allergies using western medicine except avoidance, which means deprivation and frustration.

I developed this new technique to eliminate allergies and allergy-related symptoms, employing the knowledge from these above mentioned fields of medicine, to identify and treat the reactions to many substances, including food, chemicals, and environmental allergens.

Through many long years of research, and after many trials and errors, I devised this combination of "hands-on techniques" to eliminate energy blockages (allergies) permanently and to restore the body to a healthy state. These energy blockage elimination techniques together are called Nambudripad's Allergy Elimination Techniques or NAET for short.

ALLOPATHY AND WESTERN SCIENCE

Knowledge of the brain, cranial nerves, spinal nerves and autonomic nervous system from western medicine enlightens us about the body's efficient multilevel communication network. Through this network of nerves, vital energy circulates in the body carrying negative and positive messages from each and every cell to the brain and then back to the cells. A cell or tissue sends one message to brain. The brain sends out the reply in a matter of nanoseconds to the rest of the body. Knowledge about the nervous system, its origin, travel route, organs and tissues that benefit from its nerve energy supply (target organs and tissues), helps us to understand the energy distribution of the spinal nerves emerging from the 31 pairs of spinal nerve roots. If the energy supply reaches all the respective organs and tissues, through their miles-long nerve fibers, they all remain healthy and happy. If the energy distribution is reduced or stopped in one or more of the spinal nerves, the respective organs and tissues will have diminished function or partial or complete shut down. By evaluating the condition of its target organs and tissues, changes in energy distribution via any spinal nerve can be detected (Gray's Anatomy, 36th edition).

KINESIOLOGY

Kinesiology is the art and science of movement of the human body. Kinesiology is used in NAET to compare the strength and weakness of any muscle of the body in the presence or absence of any substance. This is also called Muscle Response Testing (MRT) to detect allergies. It is hypothesized that this measurable weakness of a particular muscle is produced by the generation of an energy obstruction in the particular spinal nerve route that corresponds to the weakened muscle when the specific item is in its energy field. Any item that is capable of producing energy obstruction in any spinal nerve route is called an allergen. Through this simple kinesiological testing method, allergens can be detected, obstructed spinal nerves and their routes can be identified, and the affected organs, tissues, and other body parts can be uncovered.

CHIROPRACTIC

Chiropractic technique helps us to detect the nerve energy blockage in a specific nerve energy pathway by detecting and isolating the exact nerve root that is being pinched. The exact vertebral level in relation to the pinched spinal nerve root helps us to trace the travel route, the destination and the target organs of that particular energy pathway. D.D. Palmer, who is considered the "Father of Chiropractic" said, "too much or too little energy is disease." According to chiropractic theory, a pinched nerve can cause disturbance in the energy flow. The presence of an allergen in its energy field can cause a pinched nerve or obstruction of the nerve energy flow. Chiropractic medicine postulates that a pinched nerve or any such disturbance in the energy flow can cause disease in the target organ and tissues, revealing the importance of maintaining an uninterrupted flow of nerve energy. A pinched nerve or an obstruction in the energy flow can result from an allergy. Spinal manipulation at the specific vertebral level of the pinched nerve can relieve the obstruction of the energy flow and help the body come to a state of homeostasis (i.e. a state of perfect balance between all energies and functions).

ACUPUNCTURE/ORIENTAL MEDICINE

Yin-Yang theory from oriental medical principles also teaches the importance of maintaining homeostasis in the body. According to oriental medical principles, "when the Yin and Yang are balanced in the body (a state of perfect balance between all energies and functions), no disease is possible." Any disturbance in the homeostasis can cause disease. Any allergen that is capable of producing a weakening effect of the muscles in the body can cause disturbance in the homeostasis. By isolating and eliminating the cause of the disturbance (in this case an allergen), and by maintaining an absolute homeostasis, diseases can be prevented and cured. According to acupuncture theory, acupuncture and/or acupressure at certain acupuncture points is capable of bringing the body into a state of homeostasis, by removing the energy blockages from the twelve (meridian) energy pathways.When the blockages are removed, energy can flow freely through the energy meridians bringing the body into perfect balance.

NUTRITION

You are what you eat! The secret to good health is achieved through correct nutrition. What is correct nutrition? How do you get it? When you can eat nutritious foods without discomfort and assimilate the nutrients from the food, that food is the right food for you. When you get indigestion, bloating, other digestive troubles, constipation, diarrhea, depression, hyperactivity, mood swings, anger, insomnia, sleepiness, fatigue, poor concentration, diminished clarity of thinking, brain fog, pain in the joints and muscles, nervousness, heart palpitation, itching anywhere in the body upon or after eating a particular food, that food is not helping you to function normally. However natural, expensive or packed with high quality nutrition, if a food item causes one or more of these symptoms upon ingestion, it is not the right nutrition for you. This is due to an allergy to that food. Different people react differently to the same food. So, it is very important to clear the allergy to the nutrients, which are in the food. Allergic people can tolerate food that is low in nutrition better than nutritious food. After clearing the allergy, you should try to eat more wholesome, nutritious foods. Above all, you should avoid refined, bleached foods devoid of nutrients.

Many people who feel poorly due to undiagnosed food allergies may take vitamins or other supplements to increase their vitality. This can actually make them feel worse if they happen to be allergic to these nutrients as well. Only after clearing those allergies can their bodies assimilate them properly .

To comprehend NAET, some understanding of the brain and its functions is necessary. Many books on the subject of the brain are available in bookstores and libraries. A brief introduction to the brain function related to NAET is given here. For more information, please consult the references in the bibliography.

THE BRAIN

The brain is the master control center of the body and constantly receives information from the senses about conditions both inside and outside the body. It rapidly analyzes this information and then sends out messages that control body functions and actions. It also stores all information from past experiences, which makes learning and remembering possible. In addition, the brain is the source of thoughts, moods and emotions.

The brain works somewhat like a computer and a chemical factory. Brain cells produce electrical signals and send them from cell to cell along pathways called "circuits." As in a computer, these electrical circuits receive, process, store, and retrieve information. Unlike a computer but more like a battery, the brain creates its electrical signals by chemical means. The proper functioning of the brain depends on many complicated chemical substances produced by the brain cells.

Hard working scientists in the fields of neuroscience, neurobiology and neuro-physiology are constantly looking for more ways to understand the complete functions of the brain. According to these researchers, approximately 10% of the functions of the human brain can be explained. The rest remain to be discovered.

The Brain Has Three Main Divisions

1. The cerebrum
2. The cerebellum
3. The brain stem

Each division contains nerve cells or neurons and supporting cells or glia. The cerebral cortex is the thin outermost layer which has three parts:

Step 1.   The sensory cortex receives messages from the sensory organs as well as messages of touch and temperature from the body.

Step 2.   The motor cortex sends out nerve impulses that control the movements of all the skeletal muscles.

Step 3.   The association cortex analyzes, processes and stores information, making possible all our higher mental abilities, such as thinking, speaking, storing, retrieving, correcting and restoring information that is shared by the peripheral nerves.

The cerebrum is divided into right and left hemispheres. Most of the cerebrum beneath the cortex consists of nerve cell fibers. Some of these fibers connect parts of the cortex. Others link the cortex with the cerebellum, brain stem and spinal cord (autonomic or sympathetic and para-sympathetic nervous system), and through these nerves, they are able to link each and every nerve cell of the peripheral areas of the body.

The cerebellum is responsible for balance, posture and coordination of movement. The cerebellum is located below the back part of the cerebrum. It has a right hemisphere and left hemisphere, which are joined by vermis. Nerve pathways connect the right half of the cerebellum with the left cerebral hemisphere and the right side of the body; pathways of the left half of the cerebellum connect with the right cerebral hemisphere and left side of the body.

The brain stem connects the cerebrum with the spinal cord. The bottom part of the brain stem is called the medulla. This contains nerve centers that control breathing, heartbeat and many other vital body processes. The major sensory and motor pathways between the body and the cerebrum cross over as they pass through the medulla. Each cerebral hemisphere thus controls the opposite side of the body.

Just above the medulla is the pons, which connects the hemispheres of the cerebellum. The pons also contains nerve fibers that link the cerebellum and the cerebrum. Above the pons lies the midbrain. Nerve centers in the midbrain help control movements of the eyes and the size of the pupils.

At the upper end of the brain stem are the thalamus and the hypothalamus. There are actually two thalami, one on the left side of the brain stem and one on the right side. Each thalamus receives nerve impulses from various parts of the body and directs them to the appropriate areas of the cerebral cortex. The thalami also relay impulses from one part of the brain to another. The hypothalamus regulates body temperature, hunger, sensitivity (hyper or hypo and allergic reactions) and various other internal functions.

The human brain has approximately 10 billion to 100 billion neurons and a great number of glia. The neurons transmit nerve impulses and glia surround and support the neurons. A thin membrane forms the outermost layer of each neuron. A neuron's membrane is highly specialized to carry nerve impulses. Each neuron consists of a cell body and a lot of nerve fibers. Short fibers are called dendrites, and the long fibers of each nerve are called axons.

The axon carries nerve impulses from the cell body to other neurons. The dendrites pick up impulses from the axons of other neurons and transmit them to the cell body. The point where any branch of one neuron transmits a nerve impulse to a branch of another neuron is called a synapse. Each neuron may form synapses with thousands of other nerve cells.

The receiving and interpreting of sensory messages is chiefly the task of the cerebral cortex. The various areas of the cerebrum interpret the nerve impulses from the sense organs as visual images, sounds, tastes and smells. The brain cells and other neurons accomplish the task of transmitting the messages across the miles-long nervous system communication network through efficient chemical messengers called neurotransmitters. Some of the notables ones are acetylcholine, dopamine, nor-epinephrine and serotonin.

The hypothalamus is a small area at the base of the brain. It has a key role in regulating the body's general level of activity. The hypothalamus helps to control the autonomic nervous system, the part of the nervous system that regulates automatic body processes such as breathing, heart rate, lowering or increasing blood pressure, initiating and ending allergic reactions and regulating various hormonal functions by regulating the pituitary gland. It also regulates many functions like thirst, hunger, retrieving genetic memory, helping the rest of the brain, body or any particular part of the body to remember or recall information as needed regarding any past memory, emotions, or emotional associations and links to present events, etc. This is the specialized quality of the hypothalamus and the rest of the brain, along with the ability of the rest of the nervous system (autonomic nervous system), to recognize, transmit messages, regulate, control, adjust, correct and reprogram the functions of the body.

The special selective quality of the hypothalamus also helps to prevent the adverse or harmful chemical agents entering from the circulation into the brain tissue (blood-brain barrier). These all help us to find the energy blockages in the system that are inhibiting its normal function and enable us to make appropriate corrections to our advantage.

We need the complete cooperation of the whole brain and nervous system for NAET to show the best results. NAET involves the whole brain and its network of nerves as it reprograms the brain by erasing the previous harmful memory regarding the allergen, and imprinting a new useful memory in its place.

EMOTIONS

Emotions involve many areas of the brain as well as other body organs. A part of the brain structure called the limbic system plays a central role in the production of emotions. This system consists of parts of the temporal lobe, hypothalamus and thalamus.

An emotion may be provoked by a message from a sense organ or by a thought in the cerebral cortex. In either case, nerve impulses are produced that reach the limbic system. These impulses stimulate different areas of the system depending on the kind of sensory message or thought. For example, the impulses might activate parts of the system that produce pleasant feelings involved in emotions like joy and love. We can easily be inspired and energized by impulses that activate parts of the system that uplift our spirits and bring forth feelings of harmony and well being. These grand moments of reverie are in our power. On the other hand, the impulses that stimulate unpleasant feelings associated with anger and fear can produce negative results.

Scientists have only an elementary understanding of the extraordinarily complicated processes of thinking and remembering. Explanations for much of this area of thinking are still beyond our grasp.

INCOMPATIBILITIES / IMBALANCES

The energy blockages in the human body are caused by incompatible electro-magnetic charges around the body. When there is an incompatible charge around the body, there is an altered reaction in the body. Energy incompatibilities that are capable of producing various ailments are used synonymously with "allergy" in this book.

When we talk about health conditions, there is hardly a human disease or condition that may not involve an allergic factor; autism spectrum disorders are not any different. Any portion of the body, organ, or group of organs may be involved, though the allergic responses may vary greatly from one item to another and from one person to another.

In 1983, I originated NAET to eliminate the food and environmental allergic reactions, to balance the unbalanced energies, to remove the adverse reaction of foreign energies and make them compatible with the body, successfully restoring normal body functions, applying simple chiropractic and acupuncture principles, manipulating the 31 pairs of spinal nerve roots and associated sympathetic and parasympathetic nerve fibers.

Major illnesses, severe reactions to foods, drinks, drugs, bacterial toxins, chemicals, radiation, emotional stresses, etc., are capable of causing damage to the central and autonomic nerve fibers and inhibiting their conductivity. This poor conductivity causes allergy and allergy-related illnesses. So these allergic reactions and allergy-related illnesses can be eliminated or reduced in their intensity by treating with NAET.

The brain, through 31 pairs of spinal nerves, operates the best network of communication ever known. Energy blockages take place in a person's body due to contact with adverse energy of other substances. When two adverse energies come close, repulsion takes place. When two compatible energies get together, attraction takes place.

NAET can unblock the blockages in the energy pathways and restart normal energy circulation through the once blocked energy channels. This enhances the supply of right nutrients to the brain. When the brain receives right nutrients it can function normally and coordinate with the rest of the body to operate the body functions appropriately. When the brain is not coordinating with the vital organs, physiological functions are impaired. When the circulation of the energy is restored in the energy pathways, the vital organs resume their routine work and function properly. The brain and body together will remove any toxic build-up through the body's natural excretory mechanisms.

When the energy channels are filled with vibrant energy, and the energy circulates through the channels freely, the body is said to be in perfect balance or in homeostasis. When the body is in homeostasis, it can function normally, and allergies and diseases do not affect the body. In this state, the body can absorb all the necessary nutrients from the foods consumed.

The energy channels need energy to function normally. This energy is produced from the nutrients consumed, such as vitamins, minerals, and sugars, etc. The attraction or repulsion of the electromagnetic energy field is created in the body by the interaction of the various charged nutrients inside the body. Each cell is an electricity-generating unit loaded with positively charged potassium and some sodium ions. Most of the sodium is outside the cell. The sodium and potassium keep circulating in and out of the cell in the presence of water with the help of other nutrients like proteins and sugars. The charged molecules of the central nervous system and the autonomic nervous system (sympathetic and parasympathetic nervous system) thus can share, transfer and transmit the charges with other nerve cells in the body. These charged molecules inside the body make the whole body an electrical unit with an electrical field around it. This electrical field allows the body to interact with other electrical fields (of other people and substances) positively or negatively whenever it comes in contact with other people or objects.

When the central, sympathetic and parasympathetic nerves are not coordinating well, the energy does not circulate properly and certain parts of the body gets diminished energy and nutrient supply. When this happens, the highly blocked area or the weakest part of the body fails first. If the weakest part of the body happens to be the brain or any part of the brain, if the energy supply to the brain is blocked, abnormalities or poor functions of the brain is seen. Then a person can demonstrate autistic disorders, manic depressive disorders, schizophrenic, and other neurological disorders, etc. all due to lack of energy and nutrient supply to the brain. This can be tested and demonstrated by various equipment. E.E.G (electro-encephalogram), EDS (electro-dermal screening, HRV (Heart Rate Variability) machines and brain and autonomic balance recording machines can be used to monitor and record the range of activity of the brain and nervous system.

EFFECT OF NAET
ON A GROUP OF AUTISTIC CHILDREN

A clinical study was done on a non-verbalizing group of 14 children with autism spectrum disorder. The details of the study are given below.

Total number of participants selected-----------20
Total number of participants in the study-------14
Number of children that did not show up--------6
Status of children:

> Made no eye contact.
> Unable to talk
> Unable to communicate.

Study began = August 15, 1999
Study ended = December 10, 1999
Frequency of the treatments = 2 x week

Number of Basic allergens treated = 25

TESTING MODALITIES BEFORE AND AFTER THE STUDY

History /Symptom Survey
Muscle Response Test
Heart Rate Variability test
EAV test

TREATMENT: NAET Basic-25

Comments: Children showed 40-50% improvements in their overall symptoms. They need to be treated for 50 or more NAET allergen groups since these children are also highly sensitive to more foods other than the essential nutrients treated in this program (NAET Basics), as well as chemicals and environmental substances, antibiotics and medications.

We also need to do a study on a large number of autistic population with 50 or more NAET treatments to understand how much NAET can contribute to their complete recovery.

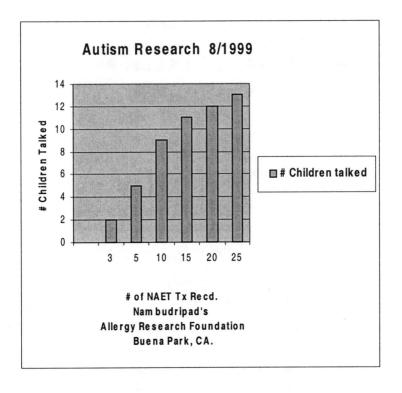

Children Began Talking

Study began: 8/15/99
Study ended: 11/15/99
Number of patients took part: 14

# of NAET Tx Recd: 3   5   10   15   20   25

# of Children Talked: 2   5   9   11   12   13
      after Tx

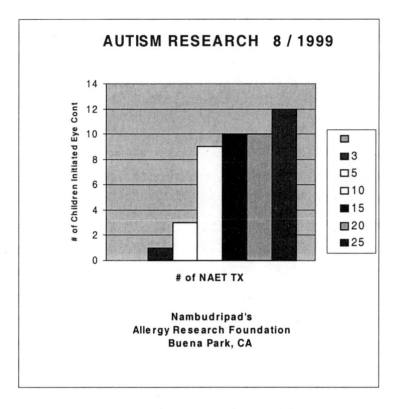

Children Initiated Eye contact

Study began: 8/15/99.
Study ended: 11/15/99
Number of Patients: 14

# of NAET Tx Recd: 3   5   10   15   20   25

# of Children Initiated: 1   3   9   10   10   12
eye contact after Tx:

COMMONLY SEEN AUTISTIC TRAITS

If your child exhibits more than ten of these symptoms from the following list, you should consult a medical specialist to evaluate your child's condition. If any abnormalities are detected, appropriate measures should be taken right away to monitor and treat the condition. The prognosis is better if the treatment is started as soon as the autism is identified. Early detection of autism can give your child the best chance to recover completely.

___ Abnormal appetite.
___ Abnormalities in speech.
___ Accident prone.
___ Aggressive.
___Always climbing on objects.
___Appears deaf and/or dumb.
___ Biting nails.
___ Biting own body parts.
___ Bladder problems.
___ Cannot be pacified.
___ Cannot determine right from wrong.
___ Cannot tie shoes.
___ Clumsiness.
___ Compulsive touching.
___ Constant motion.
___ Destructive.
___ Dizziness.
___ Does not ask for help when needed.
___ Eating dirt.
___ Enuresis (bed wetting).
___ Erratic disruptive behavior.
___ Excessive drooling.

___ Excessive flatulence.
___ Excessive salivation.
___ Excessive sweating.
___ Facial changes.
___ Fat craving.
___ Fatigued, weak, weary, listless.
___ Following routines to precise detail.
___ Frequent and repetitive activity.
___ Frequent burping.
___ Frequent flu and colds.
___ Greater than normal crying as an infant.
___ Growing pains.
___ Hair pulling.
___ Hand flapping.
___ Head banging.
___ High pain threshold.
___ Holds on to people and objects.
___ Impaired ability to role-play.
___ Impaired social play.
___ Impaired ability to initiate speech.
___ Impaired peer relationships.
___ Impulsive.
___ Increased thirst.
___ Irritable.
___ Lacks concentration.
___ Nightmares.
___ Loud talk.
___ Muscle aches.
___ Nervous.
___ Nightmares.
___ No eye contact while communicating.
___ Non-stop talk.
___ Normal or high I.Q. in certain areas.
___ Not aware of other people's feelings.
___ Onset of unusual activity in infancy or childhood

___ Parrot-like talking
___ Picking at skin, hair, nose.
___ Pinches or hurts others.
___ Poor eye-hand coordination.
___ Post nasal drip.
___ Preoccupation with parts of objects.
___ Preoccupations in narrow interests.
___ Presence of unusual body movements.
___ Profuse sweating.
___ Protruding abdomen.
___ Puffy below the eyes.
___ Pushing people away.
___ Red cheeks.
___ Red earlobes.
___ Repetitious.
___ Restless sleep.
___ Restlessness.
___ Ring around anus.
___ Rocking.
___ Salt craving.
___ Screaming inconsolably.
___ Self abusive.
___ Sensitive to cold or heat
___ Sensitive to odors
___ Sensitive to sound or light
___ Spinning.
___ Spurns affection and cuddling.
___ Staring at people without acknowledgment
___ Sugar craving.
___ Tantrums.
___ Totally nonverbal.
___ Twisting
___ Uncontrollable body movements.
___ Uncooperative.
___ Violent behavior at times

AUTISM FOLLOW-UP RECORD SHEET

Name of the Child_____Sex _____

Date of Birth /age_____ Today's date_____

Select 10-20 characteristics from the list of "Commonly Seen Autistic Traits," which describe your child's behavior. List them on this sheet and keep follow-up records on a weekly basis.

Scoring: Score the child's behavior using "0 -10" scale where "10" is maximum discomfort or disturbance (probably pretreatment value) and "0" is normal state of health or normal behavior. Use value between one and ten for status of improvement.

Symptoms   Pretreatment 1wk 2wk 3wk 4wk

1._____

2._____

3._____

4._____

5._____

6._____

7._____

Say Good-bye to Allergy-related Autism

8._____

9._____

10._____

11._____

12._____

13._____

14._____

15._____

16._____

17._____

18._____

19._____

20._____

COMMONLY SEEN ALLERGIC SYMPTOMS

Name of the Child_____Sex _____

Date of Birth /age_____ Today's date_____

    If your child exhibits any of these symptoms from the following list, you should consult an NAET specialist to evaluate your child for possible allergies and try to eliminate them as soon as you can. Untreated allergies can increase the autistic behaviors.

____ Addictions to carbohydrate
____ Addiction to coffee, chocolate, caffeine
____ Addiction to drugs
____ Addiction to food
____ Allergy to chemicals
____ Allergy to cold
____ Allergy to heat
____ Allergy to milk products
____ Allergy to mold
____ Allergy to peanuts
____ Allergy to penicillin
____ Allergy to pets, animals or humans.
____ Allergy to plastics
____ Allergy to prescription drugs & immunizations,
____ Allergy to radiation
____ Allergy to shellfish
____ Allergy to Sun
____ Allergy to clothing
____ Anxiety
____ Anxiety attacks
____ Attention deficit
____ Bad breath
____ Bronchitis

Say Good-bye to Allergy-related Autism

___ Candida/Yeast
___ Chronic fatigue
___ Colitis
___ Depression
___ Diarrhea
___ Distractibility
___ Dyslexia
___ Ear infections
___ Eating disorders
___ Eczema
___ Excessive appetite
___ Fibromyalgia
___ Flatulence
___ Food cravings
___ Frequent colds
___ Frequent infections
___ General itching
___ Headaches
___ Hives
___ Hyperactivity
___ Hypoglycemia
___ Impulsivity
___ Indigestion
___ Insomnia
___ Irritable bowel syndrome
___ Leaky gut syndrome
___ Migraines
___ Mood swings
___ Nervous stomach
___ Night sweats
___ O.C. D.
___ Parasitic infestation
___ Phobias
___ Poor appetite
___ Poor memory

___ Restless leg syndrome
___ Sinusitis
___ Toxicity to mercury
___ Toxicity to Heavy Metal

These nearly 90% effective, redundant NAET treatments are available to the whole world. It is up to the health professionals to learn them and use them on their patients correctly, and it is up to the public to get them from their doctors to receive full benefits of this new, remarkably effective treatment method.

Thousands of doctors of allopathic, chiropractic, osteopathy, dentistry, naturopathy, and acupuncture/oriental medicine from all over the United States, Canada, Europe, Australia, Israel and other countries, have been trained to treat their patients with this new revolutionary technique. Regular training sessions are being conducted several times a year to prepare many more licensed medical professionals to meet the challenge. This book will educate individuals to test themselves and locate the cause of their problem.

Steps of treatments are not given here because that is beyond the scope of this book. The information about the NAET training available for licensed medical practitioners can be received from the following sources:

NAET
6714 Beach Blvd
Buena Park, CA 90621
Tel: I-714-523-0800 / (714) 523 8900
Fax: 1-714-523-3068
E-mail: naet@earthlink.net
Web site: www.naet.com

We Will All Be Smiling Soon!

Dear Dr. Devi,

Three weeks ago, my eight-year old-son was referred to you by his pediatrician Dr. Levine for evaluation and NAET treatment. Patrick was diagnosed as having moderate to severe autism spectrum disorder a few years ago. After your examination, you said, Patrick has severe food and chemical allergies. You began treatment on the same day. You treated him for egg mix on his first visit. Patrick was asked to return once a week for treatments.

On his first visit you noticed that he had no eye contact, was restless, ran aimlessly in and out of the building. He could not speak any legible words; sometimes he mumbled something which no one could understand. You used me as a surrogate to treat him. I was asked to hold on to his wrist while you performed acupressure treatments on my back acupuncture points. It wasn't easy to hold on to him and keep him still for that two minutes-long acupressure treatment.

Now he completed three treatments: Egg mix, Calcium mix and vitamin C mix. After just three treatments, I am feeling very optimistic about Patrick's progress.

He has become more social, with improved eye contact, and is using more legible words spontaneously. Until recently he spoke a few words only when prompted. After the last treatment (Vitamin C), he appears more restful, and tries to sit in one place or next to me for minutes at a time. He is initiating more requests and is generally more cooperative in all respects.

We did notice increased sleep disturbances following the calcium treatment for several nights but they have abated.

I also suffer from a lot of aches and pains. I attributed to exhaustion from work and caring for my disabled son. You evaluated me and said that I had lots of food allergies and Patrick could have inherited the allergic tendency from me. So I decided to take a few NAET treatments myself. After just one treatment (egg mix), I have much more energy and improved concentration. If this is indicative of how Patrick is feeling, we will all be smiling soon.

Mary Nunan
Orange, CA
November, 1999

Say Good-bye to Allergy-related Autism

CHAPTER 2

AUTISM
OR
BRAIN ALLERGY?

2

AUTISM
OR
BRAIN ALLERGY?

Statistics indicate that approximately one in 500 children may be affected by autism or associated neurological behaviors in this country. Autism is four times more prevalent in boys than girls. Left untreated, autism inhibits a child's developmental growth to such a degree that most patients will require life-long support. Over one million people in the U.S. today have autism or some form of pervasive developmental disorder.

We are discussing allergy-related autism in this book. There are hardly any human diseases or conditions in which allergic factors are not involved directly or indirectly. Autism is not any different. Any substance under the sun, including sunlight itself, can cause an allergic reaction in any individual.

In other words, potentially, you can be allergic to anything you come in contact with. If you begin to check people around you—not only people with autism, even so called healthy people—you will find them reacting to many things around them.

But every one reacts differently to allergens. There is no single type of reaction that can be established to every allergic person with a particular allergen. You can be allergic to: foods, drinks, drugs, childhood immunizations, herbs, vitamins, water, clothing, jewelry, cold, heat, wind, food colors, additives, preservatives, chemicals, and formaldehyde, etc. Undiagnosed allergies can produce symptoms of various health disorders including autism.

By learning the simple Nambudripad's Testing Technique (NTT), anyone, professional or layman, can easily learn to recognize various allergens and the symptoms they cause. This will help the sufferer begin to seek the appropriate diagnostic studies and pursue proper health care as needed. When the patient's diagnosis is correct, results are less frightening than an uncertain diagnosis from a doctor.

Science and technology have altered the lifestyle of mankind enormously. The reactions and diseases arising from responses to these changes are also very different. Our quality of life has improved from these scientific achievements. Yet, these same scientific accomplishments have become everlasting nightmares for people suffering from autism.

Technology is becoming more pervasive over time. Let's face it, technology will always be with us. But people with autism and other related neurological disorders must find ways to overcome adverse reactions to new chemicals and other allergens they are exposed to and created by the new technology. NAET will fit right in with the 21st century life style of the modern world. Even though it requires a series of detailed treatments, NTT and Nambudripad's Allergy Elimination Treatments (NAET) offer the prospect of relief to people who suffer from constant irritations from allergies.

COMMONLY SEEN SYMPTOMS OF AUTISM

- Communication difficulties: non-verbal, repeats what is said, no response to "stop" command, runs or moves away, covers ears, and looks away constantly.
- May appear argumentative, stubborn, belligerent, may incessantly ask "Why?" or answers "No" to all questions.
- Will have difficulty interpreting body language, and facial expressions, jokes, and teasing.
- May be poor listeners, may not seem to care what others have to say, may lack eye contact.
- May have passive monotonal voices with incorrect and/ or unusual pronunciations, often sounds like a computer generated robot.
- Difficulty in judging personal space: may stand too close or too far away, may stare at people.
- May persevere on topics that interest them, may repeatedly ask the same questions about their area of interest. They may not see another person's point of view
- They are very honest, perhaps too honest, and not tactful.
- May not recognize danger. May not differentiate be-

tween minor or major problems. May not know how and where to get help. May not be able to give answers to questions.

■ May have candida, yeast problems, parasite infestation, chronic fatigue, immune disorders, hormonal imbalances, ear infections, and pediatric problems.

■ May have digestive disorders, anxiety disorders, various other mental disorders, depression, and various emotional imbalances, etc.

■ Symptoms include circulatory disorders, sleep irregularity, chemical sensitivity, nutritional disorders, restless leg syndrome, skin ailments, and genito-urinary disorders.

This clearly points out that there are no typical responses to allergens in the real world. If we are depending on allergies to produce a uniform set of responses for all people, we may misdiagnose and provide the wrong treatment. We cannot duplicate and package a standard medication as an antidote for any specific allergy - each individual case is different. We must not oversimplify our treatment of patients. Not everyone exhibits typical allergic symptoms (whatever we perceive typical to be). Should we do so, we risk missing a myriad of potential reactions that may be produced in some people in response to their contact with substances - that are for them - allergens.

CATEGORIES OF ALLERGENS

Common allergens are generally classified into nine basic categories; based primarily on the method in which they are contacted, rather than the symptoms they produce.

1. Inhalants
2. Ingestants
3. Contactants
4. Injectants
5. Infectants
6. Physical Agents
7. Genetic Factors
8. Molds and Fungi
9. Emotional Factors

INHALANTS

Inhalants are those allergens that are contacted through the nose, throat and bronchial tubes. Examples of inhalants are microscopic spores of certain grasses, flowers, pollens, powders, smoke, cosmetics, perfumes, different aromas from spices, coffee, popcorn, food-cooking smells, different herbs and oils and chemical fumes such as paint, varnish, pesticides, insecticides, fertilizers, and flour from grains, etc.

It is typical for a person with autism to react to most of these environmental allergens. The symptoms of a person with autism arising from the interactions with the above allergens, varies greatly from a typical response of an environmentally sensitive person. In a child with autism the first organ in the body that is affected is the brain and the typical symptoms of brain allergy are exhibited.

INGESTANTS

Ingestants are allergens, which are contacted through the mouth and find their way into the gastrointestinal tract. These include foods, condiments, drugs, beverages, chewing gum, and vitamin supplements, etc. We must not ignore the potential reactions to things that are touched, then inadvertently transmitted into the mouth through our hands.

The area of ingested allergens is one of the most difficult to diagnose because the allergic responses are often delayed from several minutes to several days. This makes the direct association between cause and effect very difficult. Some people can react violently in seconds after they consume an allergen. In extreme cases, just touching or coming near the allergen is enough to forewarn the central nervous system that it is about to be poisoned resulting in a premature allergic reaction. Usually more violent reactions are observed in ingested allergens than in any other forms.

Such was the case of 4-year-old Austin, who doubled over or rolled over on the ground and cried every time he ate any food. He became very irritable at times. He just rocked back and forth in his chair, or ran in circles non-stop until he got tired. He was becoming antisocial, refusing to meet other children and/or go out and play with them.

Say Good-bye to Allergy-related Autism

He was referred to us by one of their family friends. Austin was examined by NTT, and found to be allergic to all the basic 30 groups of foods from the NAET list and many from the environmental groups. His treatments progressed slowly. He was highly allergic to egg white, vitamin C, milk casein, tyramine, lactic acid, wheat, gluten, gliadin, mineral mix, salt mix, food colorings, tomato, pesticides, formaldehyde, and MMR (immunization). His strange behavior and stomach ache was under control when he passed the treatment for gliadin one of the natural substances seen in wheat. He appeared cheerful, became focused, attentive, and friendly by the time he was ready for school.

We live in a highly technological age. New substances are being introduced into our diets to preserve color, flavor, and extend the shelf life of our foods. There are some additives used in foods as preservatives that have caused severe health problems. Some artificial sweeteners cause mysterious problems in particular people. They may mimic symptoms of serious disorders (autism, ADHD and other brain disorders, etc.). Clinical depression, anti-social behaviors, itching and hives, confusion, insomnia, vertigo, are also reactions from an allergy to food coloring and preservatives. The majority of these additives are harmless to most people but can be disabling and life-threatening to those who react to these substances.

Great care must be taken to know exactly what is contained in anything a person with allergies puts into his/her mouth. If everyone could become proficient in MRT, simple testing before eating foods could prevent most hazardous reactions from food allergies.

CONTACTANTS

Contactants produce their effect by direct contact with the skin. They include environmental allergens, fabrics, cats, dogs, rabbits, cosmetics, soaps, skin creams, detergents, rubbing alcohol, latex gloves, hair dyes, various types of plant oils, and chemicals such as gasoline, dyes, acrylic nails, nail polish, fabrics, formaldehyde, etc.

Allergic reactions to contactants can be different in each person, and sensitive children may exhibit symptoms of autism.

Various natural or synthetic fabrics can affect autistic children and adults. Many children react to cotton. Cotton is used in numerous items. It is not easy to find a fabric that is made from only one type of material anymore. Many products seen in shops are a blend of many things. Cotton fibers are used in carpets, elastics, bed sheet, fleece material, cosmetic applicators, toilet paper, paper towels, etc. Wool may also cause brain imbalances in sensitive persons. Some people who are sensitive to wool also react to creams with a lanolin base since lanolin is derived from sheep wool. Some people can be allergic to cotton socks, nylon socks or woolen socks, causing them to have abnormal behaviors. Children can also be allergic to carpets, drapes and ceramic tiles or marbles, and these items can cause similar reactions in sensitive children.

A lot of children are allergic to crude oils, plant oils and their derivatives, which include plastic and synthetic rubber products as well as latex products. Many children react to their favorite toys or teddy huggers. Can you imagine the difficulty of living in this modern society, attempting to be completely free from products made of crude oil? A person would literally be immobilized. The phones we use, the milk containers we drink from, the polyester fabrics we wear, most of the face and body creams we use... all are made from a common product – crude oil!

Food items normally classified as ingestants—may also act as contactants on persons who handle them constantly over time. They can cause migraines, headaches, brain irritability, anger, temper tantrums, fatigue, brain fog, confusion, crying spells, mood swings, insomnia, and depression, etc.

Other career-produced allergies have been diagnosed in cooks, waiters, grocery store-keepers, clerks, gardeners, school teachers, teaching assistants, etc. Virtually no trade or skill is exempt from contacting allergens and producing allergic symptoms.

One could be allergic to cooking smells, cleaning agents, paper napkins, paper products, paper bags, books, ink, pens, pencils, plants, fertilizers, coloring books, pencils, crayons, etc. One can also be allergic to toilet paper, and currency bills. Care must be taken to isolate the allergen efficiently so that treatment can be provided precisely.

INJECTANTS

Allergens are injected into the skin, muscles, joints and blood vessels in the form of various serums, antitoxins, vaccines, childhood immunizations, and drugs. Injectants also include substances entering the body through insect bites. As with any other allergic reaction, the injection of a sensitive drug into the system creates the risk of producing dangerous allergic reactions. To the sensitive person, the drug actively becomes a poison with the same effect as an injection of arsenic. The seemingly harmless substance can become more allergenic for certain people over time without the person being aware of the potential risk. For example, take the increasing number of incidents of allergies to the drug penicillin. The reactions vary from hives to diarrhea to anaphylactic shock and death.

Various vaccinations and immunizations may also produce such allergic reactions. History of the most autistic children I have seen revealed that they were normal in their growth and developments before they reached 18 months or so. Then they began showing different health and behavioral disorders. Some parents could trace their children's behavioral changes beginning from reactions to antibiotics and booster doses of immunizations. While receiving their usual immunizations, many children become extremely ill physically, physiologically, and emotionally. Some children do not exhibit any immediate reactions. If a child is allergic to the injected vaccine, if he/she did not exhibit any immediate symptoms, he/she could have a delayed reaction. How does the delayed reaction take place? The child is allergic to the substances. It is causing energy blockages in certain meridians only. Because of the Yin-Yang relationships of the meridians, eventually, the blockage will spread through other meridians and begin to develop reactions in deeper levels. Various neurological disorders, hyperactive disorders, attention deficit disorders, mental retardation, manic disorders, Crohn's disease, chronic irritable bowel syndrome, tumors, and cysts, etc., could manifest as a delayed reaction of a childhood immunization.

Such was the case of a 5-year-old boy Daniel, who became very sick after a regular MMR booster dose. He had a continuous fever (102 degrees Fahrenheit) that lasted for six weeks. Finally, when the fever came down to a normal level, he became irritable, aggressive, short tempered, anti-social. He couldn't play with other children without kicking, hitting, biting or spitting on them. He talked constantly and craved sweets all the time. He ran around the house playing hide and seek in the middle of the night instead of sleeping. His worried parents brought him to see me. His problem was traced to the MMR immunization after testing with NTT. He was treated for all the basics and MMR vaccine with NAET after which he became well again.

INFECTANTS

Infectants are allergens that produce their effect by causing sensitivity to an infectious agent, such as bacteria. For example, an allergic reaction may result when tuberculin bacterium is introduced as part of a diagnostic test to determine a patient's sensitivity or reaction to it. A typical reaction to the tuberculin test may be seen as an infectious eruption under the skin. This type of reaction may occur with a skin patch or scratch tests preformed in the normal course of allergy testing in traditional medical approach.

Infectants differ from injectants because of the nature of the allergic substance; that is a substance, which is a known injectant and is limited in the amount administered to the patient. A slight prick of the skin introduces the toxin through the epidermis and a pox, or similar harmless skin lesion will erupt if the patient is allergic to that substance. For most people, the pox soon dries up and forms a scab that eventually heals, without much discomfort. However, in some cases the site of the injectant becomes infected and the usual inflammatory process can be seen (redness, swelling, pain, drainage of pus from the site for many days). Some sensitive individuals may experience fainting, nausea, fever, swelling (not only at the scratch site but also over the whole body), and respiratory distress, etc., if left untreated.

In other words, the introduction of an allergen into a reactive person's system creates the potential risk of causing a severe response regardless of the amount of the toxic substance used. Great care must be taken in the administration of traditional allergy testing procedures in highly sensitive individuals. However, if NAET is administered correctly and immediately, it can stop such adverse reactions.

It should be noted that bacteria and virus are contacted in numerous ways. Our casual contact with objects and people expose us daily to dangerous contaminants and possible illnesses. When our autoimmune systems are functioning properly, we pass off the illness without notice. It is when our systems are not working at maximum performance levels that we experience infections, fevers, and other discomforts. Children with autism should not be allowed to come in contact with other people who suffer from infections like upper respiratory infections, flu virus, and bacterial infections, etc.

From a strictly allergenic standpoint, however, contact with an injectant does not always produce the expected reaction. The intensity and type of reactions vary from individual to individual depending on their immune system, age and the length of exposure.

PHYSICAL AGENTS

Heat, humid air, cold, cold mist, sun radiation, dampness, drafts, changes in barometric pressure, high altitude, air conditioning; other types of radiation like computer, microwave, X-ray, geopathic radiation, electrical and electro-magnetic radiation, fluorescent lights, radiation from cellular and cordless telephones, and radiation from power lines are irritants. Vibrations from a washer and dryer, hair dryer, electric shaver, massager, motion vibrations from a moving automobile, motion sickness (car sickness, sea sickness), sickness while playing sports, roller coaster rides and/or horseback riding are mechanical irritants. Airplane sounds, traffic noises, loud music and voices in a particular pitch may also cause allergic reactions. All the above are known as physical allergens. Burns may also be included in this category. When the patient suffers from more than one allergy, physical agents can affect the patient greatly. If the patient has already eaten an allergic food item, then walks in cold air, he might develop upper respiratory problems, a sore throat, asthma or joint pains, etc., depending on his/her tendency toward particular health problems.

It is not uncommon for children with autism to suffer from repeated canker sores. They suffer from sluggish digestion due to many food allergies, and food remains longer in the small bowel. According to oriental medical principles, when food remains in the small bowel too long, the undigested food produces a large amount of heat. The heat escapes through the mouth causing the delicate mucous membrane of the mouth to blister and form canker sores.

One of the young patients, Alan who came to our office had a history of canker sores whenever he ate pizza for dinner. He turned out to be highly allergic to tomato sauce (spices and tomato). After the basics, he was treated for tomato mix and pepper mix. He has never been bothered by canker sores again.

Many symptoms of autism spectrum patients become exaggerated on cold, cloudy or rainy days. The patients could suffer from a severe allergy to carbon dioxide (their own breath), electrolytes, cold or a combination of all. Some people, especially people who suffer from mental imbalances, also react to moonlight or moon radiation.

Some autism spectrum patients experience fear, and anxiety attacks when taking a hot shower. They are also allergic to humidity and can be successfully treated with NAET. A glass jar with a lid is filled half way with hot water. An NAET practitioner administers the NAET treatment while the patient or surrogate holds the jar. In certain cases, salt is added to the hot water sample, creating salty and humid vapor (in order to treat someone who reacts to the atmosphere in coastal climates). Samples of very hot water used in treatment of mild to moderate types of burns have shown excellent results. Cold, high altitude, low altitude, wind, dampness, dryness, rain water, and other physical agents can be treated in a similar way.

Some patients react to heat or cold violently, suffering from extreme chills and shaking uncontrollably. They need to bundle up with three-four layers of clothing during a cold day or experience icy cold hands and feet even if they are clad in mittens and warm socks. These patients are simply allergic to cold and combinations with other substances. An allergy to cold makes the blood sticky and the circulation will be poor. The body will not be able to get rid of its toxins. Allergy to anti-oxidants like vitamin C, A, etc. makes the elimination of the toxins difficult.

If patients are allergic to iron, hormones, heat, etc., their reactions are just the opposite in hot weather. They feel very uneasy in the heat. They may need treatments for vitamin C, iron, cold, hormones, and their own blood, alone or in combination. When they finish the treatment program, they are less prone to feeling cold or getting sick with changes in temperature.

GENETIC FACTORS

Discovery of possible tendencies toward allergies carried over from parents and grandparents open a large door to achieving optimum health. Most people inherit the allergic tendency from their parents or grandparents. Allergies can also skip generations or manifest differently in parents than in their children.

Bea, 38-years-old, had suffered from various allergies since she was an infant. When she was three-weeks-old, she broke out in a rash, which transformed into big heat boils. Her parents tried various medications in attempts to cure her including allopathy, homeopathy, and herbal medicines. Finally, herbal medicine brought the problem somewhat under control. Even with the herbal treatment, she still occasionally suffered from outbreaks of skin lesions. When she was ten-years-old, she developed a type of severe migraine headaches, severe insomnia, and mood swings.

After evaluation, she was found to be reacting to parasites. We learned that both her parents were in the Peace Corps before she was born. They were somehow infected with parasites and were seriously ill for months, but had no idea that their health problems were caused by the parasites until later. After she was treated successfully with NAET for parasites, her health took a quantum leap.

MOLDS AND FUNGI

Many autistic children suffer from yeast, candida, mold, and fungus overgrowth in the body. Molds and fungi are in a category by themselves because of the numerous avenues through which they can come into contact with people in everyday life. They can be ingested, inhaled, touched, or even (as in the case of penicillin) injected. They can also come in the form of airborne spores making up a large part of the dust we breathe or pick up in our vacuum cleaners, in fluids such as our drinking water, the dark fungal growth in the corners of damp rooms. They can appear on the body as athlete's foot and in particularly fetid vaginal conditions commonly called "yeast infections." Molds and fungi also grow on trees and in the damp soil, are a source of food (truffles and mushrooms), disease (ringworm and the aforementioned yeast infections), and even of medicine (penicillin).

People with autism suffer from severe allergy to sugar, starches, and carbohydrates. Consumption and poor digestion of sugar products create yeast, candida, etc. in the gut of the person. Overgrowth of these will cause them to travel to other parts of the body. Molds and fungi, belong to the same family and share the same energy fields. Reactions to these substances make people irritable, depressed, and they can suffer from a variety of mental imbalances, which can be easily mistaken for autism. When they get appropriate treatment to eliminate their yeast, candida, mold and fungi, they become symptom-free.

Allergies to toilet papers, toilet seat covers, etc., also cause yeast-like infections in some people. One of the patients reacted to everything she ate from her freezer. More investigation proved that she was allergic to the molds found in the freezer.

CHAPTER 3

NAMBUDRIPAD'S TESTING TECHNIQUES

3

NAMBUDRIPAD'S
TESTING TECHNIQUES

S ymptoms of allergy vary from person to person depend
ing upon the status of the immune system, degree of in -
volvement of the organs and systems, age, and degree of
inheritance. An allergy is a hereditary condition. An allergic predisposition is inherited, but may be manifested differently in family
members.

There are many types of conventional allergy tests available
to detect allergies; however, if it is done properly, the most reliable and convenient method of allergy testing is NTT testing. This
is a modified form of kinesiological muscle testing. Allergies can
be tested by NTT and treated very effectively with NAET. Please
read Chapter 7 for more information on NTT and MRT.

NAMBUDRIPAD'S TESTING TECHNIQUES

1. History

A complete history of the patient is taken from a parent. A symptom survey form is given to the parent to record the level and type of discomfort the child is suffering. Parents or caretakers usually observe this daily and have accurate information.

2. Physical examination

Observation of the mental status, face, skin, eyes, color, posture, movements, gait, tongue, scars, wounds, marks, body secretions, etc.

3. Vital signs

Evaluation of blood pressure, pulse, skin temperature and palpable energy blockages as pain or discomfort in the course of meridians, etc.

4. SRT

Skin Resistance Test for the presence or absence of a suspected allergen is done through a computerized electro-dermal testing device; differences in the meter reading are observed (greater the difference, stronger the allergy).

5. MRT

Muscle Response Testing is conducted to compare the strength of a pre-determined muscle in the presence and absence of a suspected allergen.

6. Dynamometer Testing

Hand-held dynamometer is used to measure finger strength (0-100) in the presence and absence of a suspected allergen. The dynamometer is held with the thumb and index finger and squeezed to make the reading needle swing between 0-100 scale. Initial baseline reading is observed first, then during contact with an allergen. The finger strength is compared in the presence of the allergen. If the second reading is more than the initial reading, there is no allergy. If the second reading is less than the initial reading, then there is an allergy. For example - if the initial (baseline) reading is 40 on a scale of 1-100, and if the reading in the presence of an allergen (apple) is 28 - the person is allergic to the apple. If the second reading is 60 - or higher there is no allergy. Another benefit of dynamometer testing is that the degree of the weakness/strength is measured in numbers. This gives us some understanding of the degree of allergy.

7. MRT To Detect Allergies

Muscle Response Testing is the body's communication pathway to the brain. Through MRT, the patient can be tested for various allergens. MRT is a standard test used in applied kinesiology to compare the strength of a predetermined test muscle in the presence and absence of a suspected allergen. If the particular muscle (test muscle) weakens in the presence of an item, it signifies that the item is an allergen. If the muscle remains strong, the substance is not an allergen. More explanation on MRT will be given in Chapter 6.

8. SRT (Electro-Dermal Test-EDT)

After the MRT, the Skin Resistance Test (SRT) is administered. The patient is tested on a computerized instrument that is designed to painlessly measure the body's electrical conductivity at specific, electrically-sensitive points on the skin, particularly on the hands and feet.

The computerized tester also helps determine the various intensities of the allergies based on a 0 - 100 scale. This is probably one of the most accurate tests available today to determine allergies. The machine is designed to test food, environmental and chemical allergies, as well as allergies to molds, fungi, pollens, trees, grasses, proteins, vitamins, drugs, radiation, etc. It can be used to test allergies and their intensities before and after treatment so we are able to compare and show the body's response to the treatment.

The procedure does not involve breaking or puncturing the skin. There is no pain or discomfort. Hundreds of allergies can be tested on the patient in minutes. Since the testing probe only touches the skin for less than a second for each allergy tested, this method can be used for infants and children as well as adults. Another advantage of this machine is that it has a TV/computer monitor where the patient can read his/her own allergies as they are being recorded. A printout is produced and the data is saved for future comparison.

9. ALCAT Test

One of today's most reliable and effective tests to detect allergies and sensitivities to food, chemicals, and food additives is the ALCAT test. This system is designed to measure blood cell reactions to foods, chemicals, drugs, molds, pesticides, bacteria, etc. The methodology of this simple test includes using innovative laboratory reagents allowing accurate cell measurement in their native form. Individually processed test samples, when compared with the "Master Control" graph, will show cellular reactivity (cell count and size) if it has occurred. Scores are generated by relating these effective volumetric changes in white blood cells to the control curve.

10. Scratch Test

Although other available methods of allergy testing are plentiful, traditional methods of testing have never been very reliable. Western medical allergists generally depend on skin testing (scratch test, patch test, etc.), in which a very small amount of a suspected allergic substance is introduced into the person's skin through a scratch or an injection. The site of injection is observed for any reaction. If there is any reaction at that area of injection, the person is considered to be allergic to that substance. Each item has to be tested individually.

This manner of testing is more dangerous, painful and time-consuming than SRT. Some patients can go into anaphylactic shock due to the introduction of extremely allergic items into the body. The painful procedure can cause soreness for several days. The patient must wait for a few days or weeks between tests because only one set of allergens can be tested at a time. This method is not very effective in identifying allergies to foods. Since it is not normal to inject foods under the skin, it is not surprising that there usually isn't a significant reaction.

11. Provocative/Neutralizing Technique

This test evaluates cellular immunity by determining patient response to the intradermal injection or topical application of one or more antigens. A minute amount of allergen (a weak dilution) is injected skin deep. It is strong enough to provoke the allergic symptoms in a person. The dilution and the amount of allergen used are noted. The allergen can produce skin erythema and/or wheal around the injected site. A record is kept of the amount, dilution and time injected. After a period of time, the size and shape of the wheal is observed. If the patient feels any reaction (dizzy spells, nausea, etc.), the tester will inject a smaller dose (weaker dilution) of the allergen that is capable of neutralizing the provocative action. This usually takes away the unpleasant symptoms or allergic reactions the patient felt from the initial injection. This is called the neutralizing dose. The neutralizing dose is used to relieve the allergic symptom and keep the patient under control for days.

12. Intradermal Test

The intradermal test is considered to be more accurate for food allergies than a plain scratch test. The name comes from the fact that a small portion of the extract of the allergen is injected intradermally, between the superficial layers of skin. Many people who show no reaction to the dermal or scratch type of testing show positive results when the same allergens are applied intradermally.

As in scratch tests, some patients can go into anaphylactic shock when extremely allergic items are injected into the body. The painful procedure can cause soreness for several days. The patient must wait a few days or weeks between tests, because only one set of allergens can be tested at a time.

13. Radioallergosorbant Test (RAST)

The radio-allergosorbant test or RAST measures IgE antibodies in serum by radioimmunoassay and identifies specific allergens causing allergic reactions. In this test, a sample of patient's serum is exposed to a panel of allergen particle complexes (APCs) on cellulose disks. Radiolabeled anti-IgE antibody is then added. This binds to the IgE-APC complexes. After centrifugation, the amount of radioactivity in the particular material is directly proportional to the amount of IgE antibodies present. Test results are compared with control values and represent the patient's reactivity to a specific allergen.

14. ELIZA

Another blood serum test for allergies is called the "ELIZA" (enzyme-linked immuno-zorbent assay) test. In this test, blood serum is tested for various immunoglobulin and their concentrations. Previous exposure to the allergen is necessary for this test to be positive in the case of an allergy. Eliza can identify an antibody or antigen, and replaces or supplements radioimmunoassay and immunofluorescence. To measure a specific antibody, an antigen is fixed to a solid phase medium, incubated with a serum sample. Then it is incubated with an anti-immunoglobulin-tagged enzyme. The excess unbound enzyme is washed from the system and a substrate is added. Hydrolysis of the substrate produces a color change, quantified by a spectrophotometer. The amount of antigen or antibody in the serum sample can then be measured. This method is safe, sensitive, and simple to perform and provides reproducible results. For this test to show some positive results the patient must be exposed to particular foods within a certain amount of time. If the patient has never been exposed to certain foods, the test results may be unsatisfactory.

15. EMF Test (Electro Magnetic Field Test)

The electromagnetic component of the human energy field can be detected with simple muscle response testing. The pool of electromagnetic energy around an object or a person allows the energy exchange. Human field absorbs the energy from the nearby object and processes through the network of nerve energy pathways. If the foreign energy field shares suitable charges with the human energy field, the human field absorbs the foreign energy for its advantage and becomes stronger. If the foreign energy field carries unsuitable charges, the human energy field causes repulsion from the foreign energy field. These types of reactions of the human field can be determined by testing an indicator muscle (specific muscle) before and during contact with an allergen. The electro- magnetic field of the humans or the human vibrations can also be measured by using the sophisticated electronic equipment developed by Dr. Valerie Hunt, Malibu, California. This genius researcher, a retired UCLA professor of physics, has proven her theory of the Science of Human Vibrations through 25 years of extensive research and clinical studies. Her book "Infinite Mind" explains it all.

16. Sublingual Test

Another prevalent allergy test, which is used by clinical ecologists and some nutritionists, is called a sublingual test. It involves the instillation of a tiny amount of allergen extract under the tongue. If the test is positive, symptoms may appear very rapidly. The symptoms may include dramatic mental and behavioral reactions in addition to physical reactions. Some kinesiologists also use sublingual testing, but only for food items. A tiny amount of the food substance is placed under the tongue, and the patient is checked by muscle response testing.

17. Cytotoxic Testing

Cytotoxic testing is a form of blood test that was developed a few years ago. Many nutritionally oriented practitioners use this test. In this method, an extract of the allergic substance is mixed with a sample of the person's blood. It is then observed under the microscope for changes in white cells. Since foods and other allergic substances do not normally get into the blood in this manner, cytotoxic testing does not give reliable results.

20. Pulse Testing

Pulse testing is another simple way of determining food allergy. This test was developed by Arthur Coca M.D., in the 1950's. Research has shown that if you are allergic to something and you eat it, your pulse rate speeds up.

Step 1:   Establish your baseline pulse by counting radial pulse at the wrist for a full minute.

Step 2:   Put a small portion of the suspected allergen in the mouth, preferably under the tongue. Taste the substance for two minutes. Do not swallow any portion of it. The taste will send the signal to the brain, which will send a signal through the sympathetic nervous system to the rest of the body.

Step 3:   Re-take the pulse with the allergen still in the mouth. An increase or decrease in pulse rate of 10% or more is considered an allergic reaction. The greater the degree of allergy the greater the difference in the pulse rate.

This test is useful to test food allergies. If you are allergic to very many foods and if you consume a few allergens at the same time, it will be hard to detect the exact allergen causing the reaction just by this test.

21. Blood Pressure Test

This test is similar to the pulse test. Systolic blood pressure reading is checked for changes in reading before and after contact with the allergen.

Step 1:   Establish your baseline by checking the systolic blood pressure.

Step 2:   Put a small amount of the suspected allergen in the mouth, preferably under the tongue. Taste the substance for two minutes. Do not swallow any portion of it. The taste will send the signal to the brain, which will send a signal through the sympathetic nervous system to the rest of the body.

Step 3:   Re-take the systolic blood pressure with the allergen still in the mouth. An increase in systolic blood pressure rate of 10% or more is considered an allergic reaction. The greater the degree of allergy the higher the blood pressure change will be.

22. The Elimination Diet

The elimination diet, which was developed by Dr. Albert H. Rowe of Oakland, California, consists of a very limited diet that must be followed for a period long enough to determine whether or not any of the foods included in it are responsible for the allergic symptoms. If a fruit allergy is suspected, for example, all fruits are eliminated from the diet for a specific period, which may vary from a few days to several weeks, depending on the severity of the symptoms. For patients who have suffered allergic symptoms over a period of several years, it is sometimes necessary to abstain from the offending foods for several weeks before the symptoms subside. Therefore, the importance of adhering strictly to the diet during the diagnostic period is very important. When the patient has been free of symptoms for a specific period, other foods are added, one at a time, until a normal diet is attained.

23. Rotation Diet

Another way to test for food allergy is through a "rotation diet," in which a different group of food is eaten every day for a week. In this method seven groups of food are eaten each week, with something different each day. The rotation starts again the following Monday. This way reactions to any group can be traced and eliminated. All of these diets work better for people who are less reactive. The inherent danger in any of these methods is clear: If you are highly allergic to a certain food item you can become very sick if you eat that particular food during testing even if you have not touched it for years.

24. Like Cures Like

There are other allergy treatment methods in practice. Homeopaths believe that if an allergen is introduced to the patient in minute concentrations at various times, the patient can build up enough antibodies toward that particular antigen. Eventually, the patient's violent reactions to that particular substance may reduce in intensity. In some cases, reactions may subside completely and the patient can use or eat the item without any adverse reaction.

25. Urine Therapy

The theory behind giving the urine shots (injection) and own blood serum shots work similarly. A patient is asked to eat a particular suspected allergen at different intervals in a day. The urine of that person is collected after several hours and injected into the body. When a person eats a certain substance, the body creates antibodies for that substance, that are excreted in the urine. This urine is injected into the person, and his own antibodies are introduced into the body as an injectant. This supposedly builds up more antibodies, and the theory holds that the allergic person eventually will not react violently toward the allergen.

26. Blood Sample Injection

The same idea is applied when injecting one's own blood sample intramuscularly. When you suffer from any autoimmune disorder, you create many antibodies in your body. The body creates special antibodies to fight its problems. A sample of blood is taken (about 2 cubic centimeter) and injected into the person, (his/her own antibodies are re-introduced into the body as an injectant). This supposedly builds up more antibodies, and the theory holds that an allergic person eventually will not react violently toward the allergens.

27. Sit With The Allergen In Your Palm

NAET patients are taught to test the allergen in another easy and safe way. Place a small portion of the suspected allergen in a baby food jar and ask the person to hold it in his/her palm touching with the fingertips of the same hand for 15 minutes to 30 minutes. An allergic person will begin to feel uneasy when holding the allergen in his/her palm for a while giving rise to various unpleasant symptoms: feeling hot, itching, hives, irregularities in heart beats (fast or slow heart beats), nausea, light headedness, etc. Since the allergen is inside the glass bottle, when such uncomfortable sensation is felt, the allergen can be put away immediately and hands washed to remove the energy of the allergen from the fingertips. This should stop the reactions immediately. In this way, the patient can detect the allergens easily.

All of the above methods work on a certain percentage of people. Curiously, people who had undergone all of these treatments were still found to be allergic to their identified allergies when they were tested again by muscle response testing. They still had to be treated by NAET to make them non-reactive.

CHAPTER 4

IS IT REALLY AUTISM?

4

IS IT REALLY AUTISM?

The diagnostic process for autism must begin with a formal medical history. Most people are interested in understanding the differences and/or the similarities of the methods of diagnosis, the effectiveness and length of treatment between traditional western medicine and oriental medicine. Since the purpose of this book is to provide information about the new treatment method of NAET, more attention will be given to oriental medicine and NAET.

The American Psychiatric Association periodically publishes an updated manual of diagnostic criteria for various mental conditions and behavioral abnormalities. The most recent edition, as of this writing is the *Diagnostic and Statistical Manual 1V (DSM 1V)*. It includes guidelines for diagnosis of autism. DSM 1V is for experienced professionals and is not intended for self-diagnosis of autism or any other condition described in the manual.

WHAT ARE THE SIGNS OF AUTISM?

Professionals, who diagnose autism, use the diagnostic criteria set forth by the American Psychiatric Association (1994), in *The Diagnostic and Statistical Manual of Mental Disorders, DSM-1V* released in 1994.

According to DSM-1V the most obvious signs associated with this disorder are inattentiveness (short attention span, failure to listen, failure to follow instructions, inability to finish projects and stay focused); severe language deficits, social isolation, uneven fine and gross motor skills, temper tantrums and insistence on sameness.

In addition to these problems, depending on the child's age and developmental stage, parents and teachers may see temper tantrums, frustration, anger, bossiness, difficulty in following rules, disorganization, social rejection, low-self esteem, poor academic achievement, and inadequate self-application.

There are many books written on the subject of autism and every book you read will give you all the standard criteria or diagnostic guidelines to detect and diagnose autism. So I am not going into details about diagnosing an autistic child or adult through standard criteria in this book. But I am going to spend some time explaining things that you absolutely need to understand to recognize this health disorder, so that you can look for appropriate help.

WISH WE HAD KNOWN ABOUT NAET SOONER!

It has been four weeks today since we started NAET treatments on our son Adam, who has been diagnosed as autistic for the past 3 years. We tried many different treatments on him ever since he was diagnosed as autistic. We wish we had known about NAET earlier!

Our five-year-old son has shown tremendous improvement already. He is more awake, calmer and focused now than ever before. His inaudible speech is much clearer too. I would like to inform all parents and caregivers of autistic children to find NAET for your children. NAET has given us great hope and expectations and is something everybody needs to look into. We have been searching for the past 3 years for some relief of our son's problem. Now after many treatments, NAET has given us hope to move on with our lives.

Thank you Dr. Devi, Mala, Kris, Mohan, Janna and Vickie for giving us your support when we needed the most.

Yours' gratefully
Mr & Mrs. John . T
The Parents of Adam
Orange, CA
November, 1999

THE BEST DIAGNOSTIC TOOL

A detailed clinical history is the best diagnostic tool for any medical condition.

It is extremely important for the patient or his/her parents or guardians to cooperate with the physician in giving all possible information about the child to the doctor in order to obtain the best results. It is my hope that this chapter will help bring about a clearer understanding between NAET specialists and their patients; because, in order to obtain the most satisfactory results, both parties must work together as a team.

The doctor should gather a detailed history of the child before formulating a diagnosis of autism. Your doctor's office may ask you to complete a relevant questionnaire during your first appointment. It is important to cooperate with the office staff and provide as accurate a history as possible.

THE AUTISTIC PATIENT-QUESTIONNAIRE

Prenatal History: (socio-economic factors, exposures to substance abuse, cadmium, lead, mercury, coffee, alcohol, chemical toxins, carbon monoxide poisoning, bacterial toxins, emotional traumas during fetal development), delivery, birth records including birth weight and APGAR scores.

GROWTH AND DEVELOPMENTAL HISTORY

Illnesses During Early Infancy?
- Colic——
- Constipation——
- Diarrhea——

- Feeding problem——
- Excessive vomiting———
- Excessive white coating on the tongue ——
- Excessive crying ——
- Poor sleep ——
- Disturbed sleep ——
- Frequent ear infection ——
- Frequent fever ———
- Immunizations———
- Response to the immunizations ——
- Common childhood diseases like measles, chickenpox, mumps, strep-throat, etc.——
- Any other unusual events (fire in the house, accidents, earthquakes, etc).——

DEVELOPMENTAL MILESTONES

AGE OF THE CHILD
- Walked alone———
- Talked———
- Toilet trained for bladder and bowel——
- Enrolled in school——

MEDICAL HISTORY
- Surgeries—
- Hospitalizations—
- Diseases—
- Allergies—
- Frequent colds—
- Fevers—
- Ear infections—
- Asthma—
- Hives——
- Bronchitis—
- Pneumonia—
- Seizures—
- Sinusitis—

- Headaches—
- Vomiting—
- Diarrhea—
- Current medication—
- Any reaction to medication —
- Antibiotics and drugs taken —
- Parasitic infestation —
- Visited other countries —

Social History:

- **Learning:** Responsiveness to teaching methods, interaction between friends and teachers, interaction between family members, activities at school, ability to speak, ability to learn sign language if unable to speak (many autistic children seem to be dumb and deaf), phobias, problems with discipline, and language delays.
- **Behaviors:** cooperative, uncooperative, disruptive and/or aggressive behaviors; overactive, restless, or very passive, inattentive, uncooperative with his/her peers and adults.
- **Habits:** temper tantrums, excessively active, constantly moving in seat or room, low self esteem, short attention span, unusual fears.
- **Hobbies:** collecting things, painting, coloring, singing, etc.

Family History

The medical history of the immediate relatives, mother, father, and siblings should be noted. The same questions are asked about the patient's relatives: grandparents, aunts, uncles, and cousins. A tendency to get sick or have allergies is not always inherited directly from the parents. It may skip generations or manifest in nieces or nephews rather than in direct descendants.

Other Questions:

ALCOHOLISM, DRUG ABUSE, MENTAL DISORDERS, AND OTHER
HEALTH DISORDERS. THE CAREFUL NAET SPECIALIST WILL ALSO
DETERMINE WHETHER OR NOT DISEASES SUCH AS TUBERCULOSIS,
CANCER, DIABETES, RHEUMATIC OR GLANDULAR DISORDERS EXIST,
OR HAVE EVER OCCURRED IN THE PATIENT'S FAMILY HISTORY. ALL
OF THESE FACTS HELP GIVE THE NAET SPECIALIST A MORE
COMPLETE PICTURE OF THE HEREDITARY CHARACTERISTICS OF THE
PATIENT. A *TENDENCY* IS INHERITED. IT MAY BE MANIFESTED
DIFFERENTLY IN DIFFERENT PEOPLE. UNLIKE THE TENDENCY, AN
ACTUAL MEDICAL CONDITION SUCH AS AUTISM IS NOT ALWAYS
INHERITED. PARENTS MAY HAVE HAD CANCER OR RHEUMATISM,
BUT THE CHILD CAN MANIFEST THAT ALLERGIC INHERITANCE AS
AUTISM.

PRESENT HISTORY

When the family history is complete, the practitioner will need
to look into the history of the patient's chief complaint and its
progression. Some typical preliminary questions include: "When
did your child's first symptom occur?" Did you notice your child's
problem when he/she was an infant or a child, or did you first
notice the symptoms during adolescence, or fully grown? Did it
occur after going through a certain procedure? For example, did
it occur for the first time after a dental procedure like a root canal,
the first antibiotic treatment or after installing a water filter? Did it
occur after acquiring a waterbed, tricycle, or after a booster dose
of immunization or vaccination? One of my patients reported that
her son's autism began a few months after he received a booster
dose of MMR.

Once a careful history is taken, the practitioner often discovers that the patient's first symptoms occurred in early childhood. He or she may have suffered from infantile eczema, or asthma, but never associated it with autism, which may not have appeared until a later age.

Next, the doctor will want to know the circumstances surrounding and immediately preceding the first symptoms. Typical questions will include: "Did you change the child's diet or put him/her on a special diet? Did he/she eat something that he/she hadn't eaten lately, (perhaps for two or three months)? Did you feed him/her one type of food repeatedly, every day for a few days? Did the symptoms follow a childhood illness, (whooping cough, measles, chicken pox, diphtheria, polio) or any immunization for such an illness? Did they follow some other illness such as influenza, pneumonia or a major operation? Did the problem begin after your vacation to an island, to another country, or after an insect bite? When did the first symptom appear?

Any one of these factors can be responsible for triggering a severe allergic manifestation or precipitate the first noticeable symptoms of an allergic condition. Therefore, it is very important to obtain full and accurate answers when taking the patient's medical history.

Other important questions relate to the frequency and occurrence of the attacks. Although foods may be a factor, if the symptoms occur only at specific times of the year, the trouble most likely is due to pollens. Often a patient is sensitive to certain foods but has a natural tolerance that prevents sickness until the pollen sensitivity adds sufficient allergens to throw the body into an imbalance. If symptoms occur only on specific days of the week, they are probably due to something contacted or eaten on that particular day.

The causes of autism in different patients can, at first, appear random. Regular attacks of mental irritability was caused in one patient after eating potato chips. The super heated fat in the potato chips caused a severe reaction in this child. Another child refused to eat anything but deep fried foods. Brain irritability in this patient caused depletion of fatty acids. He was highly allergic to all components of fat: animal, fat, vegetable fat, fatty acids, and deep fried fatty finger foods, etc.). A child of eight suffered severe insomnia on Friday nights. The cause was traced to the Friday night's traditional pizza. A 29-year-old autistic man complained of a severe headache every Saturday morning. The cause was traced to eating a traditional Italian dish every Saturday night with his family. He was allergic to the tomato in the food. Still another patient had an allergic attack of sneezing, runny nose, mental irritability, and headaches on Friday night. I traced the allergy to the chemical compounds in the coloring books.

The time of day when the attacks occur is also of importance in determining the cause of an allergic manifestation. If it always occurs before mealtime hypoglycemia may be a possible cause. If it occurs after meals, an allergy to carbohydrates and starch complexes or something in the meal should be suspected. If it occurred regularly at night, it is quite likely that there is something in the bedroom that is aggravating the condition. It may be that the patient is sensitive to: feathers in the pillow or comforter, wood cabinets, marble floors, carpets, side tables, end tables, bed sheets, pillows, pillow cases, detergents used in washing clothes, indoor plants, shrubs, trees, or grasses outside the patient's window. One of my patients suffered from severe insomnia and irritability at night. After spending a few minutes in bed, he regularly got up agitated and uptight and would spent the rest of the night without sleep. He was found to be allergic to his blue colored silk bed sheet and pillow cases; he was found to be allergic to the color blue, which instead of calming him, made him very quiet and passive.

Many patients react violently to house dust, different types of furniture, polishes, house plants, tap water and purified water. Most of the city water suppliers change the water chemicals only once or twice a year. Although, this is done with good intentions, people with chemical allergies may get sicker if they ingest the same chemicals over and over for months or years. Contrary to traditional western thinking, developing immunity can be the exception rather than the rule.

Occasionally, switching the chemicals around gives allergic patients a change of allergens and a chance for them to recover from the existing reactions. In this way, repeated use of the same chemicals can be avoided.

Across the United States, chlorination is used as the primary disinfectant in water systems. Although chlorination will kill most of the bacteria, viruses are not destroyed by any of these cleansing processes. Tri-halomethanes, which are a by-product of chlorine, are also used to clean the water. Ozone is used as a disinfectant for drinking water. Some of these chemicals are known to cause birth defects, nervous system disorders, damage to body organs and many other irreversible sicknesses.

The doctor should ask the patient to make a daily log of all the foods he/she is eating. The ingredients in the food should be checked for possible allergens. Certain common allergens like corn products, MSG (monosodium glutamate or Accent), citric acid, etc., are used in food preparations.

Allergy to corn is one of today's most common allergies, especially in autistic patients. Unfortunately, cornstarch is found in almost every processed food and some toiletries and drugs too. Chinese food, baking soda, baking powder, and toothpaste contain large amounts of cornstarch. It is the binding product in almost all vitamins and pills, including aspirin and Tylenol. Corn syrup is the natural sweetener in many of the products we ingest, including soft drinks. Corn silk is found in cosmetics and corn oil is used as a vegetable oil. For sensitive people this food adds another nightmare.

Other common ingredients in many preparations that autistic people may react severely to are various gums (acacia gum, xanthine gum, karaya gum, etc.). Numerous gums are used in candy bars, yogurt, cream cheese, soft drinks, soy sauce, barbecue sauce, fast food products, macaroni and cheese, etc.

Carob, a staple in many health food products, is another item that causes brain irritability among allergic people. Many health-conscious people are turning to natural food products in which carob is used as a chocolate and cocoa substitute. It is also used as a natural coloring or stiffening agent in soft drinks, cheeses, sauces, etc. We discovered that some of the causes of "holiday flu" and suicidal attempts are allergies to carob, chocolate, and turkey.

When assessing a child in whom autism is suspected, care must be taken not to misdiagnose him/her. Misdiagnosis of autism can probably hurt the child and his family's peace of mind for a long time.

As I have stated earlier, in my opinion, the majority of people labelled as having autism are not suffering from autism. They may be suffering from simple undiagnosed allergies.

If a child is suffering from any of the symptoms described in the diagnostic criteria for autism, it may not necessarily mean that he/she is absolutely suffering from autism. Many food and environmental allergic symptoms overlap or mimic a variety of diseases including many neurological and brain disorders.

After completing the patient's history, the NAET specialist should examine the patient for the usual vital signs. A physical examination is performed to check for any abnormal growth or condition. If the patient has an area of discomfort in the body, it should be inspected. It is important to note the type and area of discomfort and its relationship to an acupuncture point. Most pain and discomfort in the body usually occurs around some important acupuncture point.

Twelve major meridians combined with their channels and branches cover almost every part of the human body. The NAET specialist should examine all these meridians and branches for possible energy blockages. An acupuncturist is trained to understand the exact location of the pathways of these meridians. For this reason, the exact symptoms are very important. By identifying the symptoms, you can identify the area of the energy blockage. From this location, the experienced acupuncturist/NAET specialist can detect the meridians, organs, muscles and nerve roots associated with the blockage. The NAET specialist will then be able to make an appropriate diagnosis by evaluating the presenting symptoms (read Chapter 7 for possible pathological symptoms), and determine what particular allergen is causing the specific problem. When the source of the problem is identified, treatment becomes easier.

CHAPTER 5

ESSENCE OF NAET

5

ESSENCE OF NAET

The word "kinesiology" refers to the science of movement. It was first proposed in 1964 by Dr. George Goodheart, a Detroit doctor of chiropractic medicine. As a function of his practice, Dr. Goodheart learned a great deal about a patient's condition by using isolated movements of various muscles. Isolation techniques—a chiropractic procedure, made it possible to test the strength of an individual muscle or muscle group without the help of other muscles. Dr. Goodheart, with the help of Dr. Hetrick and others concluded after many experiments, that structural imbalance causes disorganization of the entire body. This disorganization results in specific disorders of the glands, organs and central nervous system. His findings were similar to what pioneer Chinese doctors had observed.

Kinesiology holds that when the body is disorganized, the structural balance or electrical force is not functioning normally. When that happens, the electrical energy–life force doesn't flow freely through the nerve cells and causes energy blockages in the person. According to the Chinese, the free flow of energy is necessary for the normal functioning of the body. When your flow of energy gets blocked, you become ill. The messages both from and to the brain also pass through this energy channel. The energy and the messages travel from cell to cell in nanoseconds.

Many years ago, pioneer Chinese doctors and philosophers had studied these energy pathways and networks of the human body energy system by observing living people and their normal and abnormal body functions. The Chinese had learned to manipulate these energy pathways, or meridians, to the body's advantage. About 4,000 years ago, there was no scientific equipment available to feel or observe the presence of the energy flow and its pathways. Now, it is possible to study and trace the energy flows and pathways by using Kirlian photography and radioactive tracer isotopes. Although the existence of energy pathways in the human body has only been confirmed relatively recently, the Chinese doctors hypothesized and established their existence long ago.

Chinese medical theory points out that free-flow of Chi through the meridians is necessary to keep the body in perfect balance. In the United States during the 19th century, the founder of Chiropractic medicine, Daniel David Palmer, said, "Too much or too little energy is sickness." Even though it is believed that Palmer may have had no knowledge of Chinese medicine, his theory corresponded with the ancient Chinese theory of "free flow of energy."

In late 1800's, American chiropractic medicine developed under Dr. D. D. Palmer. Through him, doctors of chiropractic learned about the importance of stabilizing energy and manipulating the spinal segments and nerve roots to keep them perfectly aligned, bringing the body to a balanced state. In the East, acupuncture developed based on the ancient Chinese theory. Eastern acupuncturists tried to bring balance by manipulating the energy meridians at various acupuncture points, inserting needles to remove blockages and reinstating the "free flow of Chi" along the energy pathways. East and West, unaware of each other's findings, worked in a similar manner toward the same goal: to balance the energy and to free sick people from their pain.

Both groups realized that the overflow or underflow of energy, or in other words, too much or too little energy is the cause of an imbalance. When the flow is reinstated, the balance is restored.

HOW CAN YOU REMOVE THE CAUSE OF BLOCKAGE?

A trained acupuncturist can differentiate between the overflow and underflow of Chi, and its affected meridians and organs. When treatment is administered to strengthen the under flowing or hypo-functioning organ, while draining the overflowing meridians and the organs, balance is achieved faster. This is the practice of acupuncture. NTT and NAET are built on acupuncture theory, but have taken it one step further. Using the ideas from acupuncture theory, without using actual needle insertion, meridians can be unblocked, overflowing meridians can be drained and the excess energy can be rerouted through the empty meridians and associated organs. Thus the entire body reaches homeostasis. NAET is perhaps the missing link that various professionals have been searching for years. NTT and NAET will be discussed in detail in later chapters.

When the body senses a danger or a threat from an allergen, sensory nerves carry the message to the brain and the brain alerts the whole body about the imminent danger. Muscles contract to conserve energy, other defense forces like lymph, blood cells, etc., get ready to face the emergency. Spinal nerves also get tightened due to the contracted muscles. Vertebrae go into misalignment causing impingement at the affected vertebral level. Energy is blocked due to the impingement. So, a good chiropractic adjustment can remove the nerve impingement at the specific vertebral level and this can unblock the blocked energy pathway making the energy circulate again freely.

Herbs can cause similar healing. Electromagnetic forces of special herbs actually have the ability to enter selective energy pathways and push energy blockages out of the body to restore the energy balance. A well-trained herbologist can bring about the same result as an NAET specialist. Chiropractic, kinesiology, acupuncture and herbology are blended together to create NAET.

Brain chemicals are not produced or distributed correctly in autistic patients. If given a chance, appropriate stimulation to the spinal nerves, the brain, and nervous system, can produce substances within the body and distribute them appropriately including adrenaline, thyroxin, pituitropin, serotonin, dopamine, endorphin, dynorphin, enkephalin, interferon, cytokines, interleukin, leukotriene, prostaglandin, and other immune mediators to heal many problems. The brain has the ability to create appropriate remedial secretions that release to the target tissue and organs, when needed to heal infections, allergies, imbalances, and immune deficiency diseases, etc., as long as the brain receives the right directions and commands. This has been demonstrated repeatedly and proven in many cases when treated with NAET.

According to western medical researchers, the actual cause of autism is not known. Scientific evidence suggests that in many cases, the disorder is genetically transmitted, results from a chemical imbalance and/or an allergy, or a deficiency in certain neurotransmitters. These are chemicals that help the brain regulate behavior. A study conducted by the National Institute of Mental Health showed that the rate at which the brain uses glucose, its main energy source, is lower in subjects with autism than in subjects without autism (Zametkin et al." 1990).

When body functions do not take place freely, the body begins to succumb to health problems: fatigue, headaches, sleep disturbances, irritability, forgetfulness, confusion, depression, cravings, eating disorders, difficulty in thinking, poor concentration, phobias, crying spells, suicidal thoughts, feelings of loneliness even in crowds, burning sensations on the skin and on the limbs (hands, feet, palms and soles). Most of these symptoms are experienced by autistic patients.

If you fail to eliminate the blockage immediately, the adverse energy eventually takes over the body and causes problems at deeper levels. For example, the headaches can turn into irritability, hyperactivity, and other brain disorders; neuropsychological complaints such as anger, irritability, confusion, and depression, etc., may turn the sufferer into a psychiatric case, possibly leading to institutionalization.

We treated a 28-year-old computer programmer who began to feel extreme fatigue, irritability, depression, and mood swings, a year after he started working with a well-known computer firm. He had a wife and two children. When he started experiencing incapacitating exhaustion, he began dreading his work. His output also started to slow down. He was diagnosed as having "chronic fatigue syndrome." His energy was drained to the point that he was unable to walk without assistance. Finally, he had to file for disability insurance. His health improved when he was away from work for a while. Once he returned to work, his problems started all over—even though he was given regular physical therapy and supportive treatments.

After four years of illness, he came to our office and it was discovered that he was highly allergic to plastic products and his computer keyboard. He was also allergic to computer radiation. After he was treated by NAET for plastics, keyboard, and radiation, he was able to resume his regular work.

NAET treatment works with the entire body: the physical body (organs, brain, nervous system and tissues), physiological body (circulation of blood, fluids and nerve energy) and emotional body (mind, thoughts and spirituality). It helps to detoxify the system by clearing the adverse energies of the allergens from the entire body. Thus it enables the body to relax, absorb and assimilate appropriate nutrients from the food that once caused allergies and support the proper growth of the entire body.

The human nervous system controls every function of every system in the body. This complicated maze of nerves is still not completely understood. Some basic knowledge about the human nervous system will help you to understand the relationship between the human body and allergies. More importantly, it opens the door of knowledge to the concepts that lead to the treatment of allergies and allergy related diseases. It allows you to make readjustments to the nervous system rather than having to depend on a lifetime of allergy shots, antihistamines, and various extensive, expensive types of allergy treatments.

The nervous system is without a doubt the most complex, widely investigated and least understood system in the body known to man. Its structures and activities are interwoven with every aspect of our lives: physical, cultural and intellectual. Accordingly, investigators of many different disciplines, all holding their own methodologies, motivations, and persuasions, converge in its study. Depending on the context, there are many appropriate ways of embarking upon a study of the nervous system.

For purposes of understanding the relationship between the human body and the nervous system, it is essential to look at some of the structures and functions of the nervous system that are both directly or indirectly involved in the adaptation process. This section will not cover the structural aspects of the human nervous system, such as the location of nerve ganglions, trunks, cells, endings, etc.; rather, you are urged to refer to appropriate sections in Gray's or other anatomy texts for such information. In this section, we will try to enlighten you on the chemical and electrical energy aspects only.

The central nervous system consists of the brain and the spinal cord. The peripheral nervous system consists of all of the nerves that leave the spinal cord and go to muscles and various parts of the body. This includes the motor and sensory nerves that are responsible not only for muscle movements of the body, but also for carrying the sensations of heat, cold and touch from various parts of the body to the spinal cord. The autonomic nervous system consists of the sympathetic and parasympathetic nervous systems, which are composed of the nerves regulating the functions of various vital smooth muscle organs such as the heart, liver, and brain, etc.

One of the primary functions of the human nervous system is gathering and processing of information. As the total human being consciously senses and responds according to the stimuli presented by the environment, millions of minor adjustments are constantly being made automatically without our conscious decision-making. For instance, when you are hot, you consciously move yourself away from the sun, or turn on the air conditioning. But the body is already unconsciously making several hundred minor adjustments that trigger changes in the blood flow and the heart rate, expanding and contracting the blood vessels near the skin surfaces, activating the lymph glands, turning on the sweat glands, and so on. These actions of the autonomic nervous system are reprogrammed into the very cells of the body that respond to conscious activity. The autonomic responses are constantly readjusting to respond appropriately to the changing environment.

It is extremely important to recognize the body's attempts to maintain a homeostatic state (balance within the organism). The total balance takes place in various steps, utilizing assistance from a number of functional units. These functional units are large bodies of tissues composed of many microscopic cells, each having a specialized job in the body. These special tissues provide assistance in creating homeostasis at the lowest levels within the individual's cells themselves.

The process through which this occurs is very complex, requiring considerable understanding of the biochemical and bioelectrical properties of the cells. Simplified, it can be said that all cells are surrounded by a plasma membrane similar to a microscopic plastic bag. The walls of this membrane are thick enough to contain the intracellular materials while maintaining the cell shape and size. It is also strong enough to protect the cells from invasion of the intracellular materials that surround each and every cell.

Conversely, it is thin enough and permeable enough to allow the free flow of nutrients. The ionic or magnetic properties of the atoms that make up the fluids inside the cell differ from the fluids surrounding the cells. Because of the differences in ionic composition, it follows that there are differences in their electrical properties. The disparity in electrical energies can be measured in laboratory experiments on various kinds of tissues. But more importantly, it can assess the individual cell's responses to the electrical charges, which add up to millions of measurements per minute.

As a stimulus is applied on some point on the organism, it sets up a sequence of events that is eventually transmitted to the surfaces of the excitable cells, which in turn redistributes the ions across the surface. This becomes a transient, reversible wave of change which presumably affects the permeability of cell membranes, allowing fluids to penetrate. The transfer of fluids changes the cell shape, size and function until it turns back to its original or homeostatic state.

In some primitive multicellular and all uni-cellullar life forms, individual cells are capable of reacting to stimuli; whereas most complex life forms (that make up the processing nervous system) consist of a system of specific cells to accept and interpret stimuli. Thus, in the human body we have highly specialized receptor cells whose total function is to receive stimuli. These receptor cells work in accord with neurons (nerve cells), for the integration and conduction of information; the effector cells (the contractile and glandular cells) operate the action of the responses.

This is the foundational premise upon which the understanding of allergies is based; the muscle response testing detects allergies and NAET eliminates allergies.

The ends of various dendrites and axons do not connect together to create a wire link; rather, they are interlaced, without touching. The space between the ends of the threadlike axons and dendrites are called synapses. The electrical impulses, or energy impulses, jump these spaces in their journey to the brain and back.

Enzymes, on the surface of the neurons act as mediators (like cholinesterase) and complete the circuit. These enzymes are known as neurotransmitters and are extremely important in making intercommunication possible among the cells, neurons, tissues, organs and different body parts. These neurotransmitters vary among neurons, depending upon the specificity of tissue. Although vastly different in chemical composition, all these enzymes share a common origin. They are produced by the neurons, then released into the synapses as the nerve impulse arrives.

The actions and neurological functions of these enzymes in our bodies are still not completely understood, primarily because of the wide distribution of such enzymes throughout the body. These enzymes include mono-amino acids, known as nor-adrenalin, serotonin, histamines, (all of which have an excitatory affect on the body's nervous system) and dopamine, which has an inhibitory effect.

The ability of the central nervous system to react almost instantaneously to a stimulus (such as the sensation of heat, cold, smell, etc.), even on the most remote part of the extremities, is probably the result of the common origin of the nervous system. The body is made up of trillions of individually well-equipped cells. Each cell has the memory to reproduce any number of chemicals and functions in the body. For some reason, in autistic patients, some of these cells remain dormant or have lost the memory to reproduce the neurochemicals (appropriate neuro-transmitters) temporarily. Due to the inactive chemical messengers, messages do not transfer appropriately to the other neurons. So their nervous system does not work smoothly as a normal person's nervous system.

If the stimulus reaches the brain (providing it is not short-circuited by nerve damage, blockage, or missed chemical response due to some defect in the neurotransmitters), the brain accepts the message. It then formulates and transmits a response to all other receptors in the body. In turn, the receptors receive the message as either harmful or harmless. If the receptors receive the message as harmful, they repel it and confirm their findings to the brain. If more stimuli with negative reactions reach the brain, the brain accepts the rejection message from the majority of receptors. Since the brain's responses are impartial, the receptors corresponding to the area of the stimuli will react accordingly, setting in motion evasive actions. In the worst case scenario, where the body cannot effectively avoid or reject the stimulus, it will set up a reaction in an effort to cleanse the body of the stimulus. In an autistic person, incorrect or incomplete stimulus reaches the brain repeatedly and as a result an inappropriate response is set forth.

Activities of the sympathetic system prepare the body for increased activities. Biochemically, the action of the sympathetic system is characterized by the formation of noradrenaline and adrenaline (along with some other basic enzymes) to prepare the body for reaction.

Chiropractors and acupuncturists are stimulating the sympathetic nerve activity, removing the nerve energy blockages to reinstate the nerve energy circulation in the body. These two groups of medical practitioners from East and West have learned to manipulate the sympathetic nerves to the patient's advantage and promote healing power within the body itself without the introduction of foreign chemicals.

Beyond this point, the nervous system becomes a matter of complicated medical study. It is sufficient to say, however, that even a very minor stimulus sensed by any receptor nerve cell located on the body, will set in motion the manufacturing process of hundreds of different kinds of chemicals. Each assists the nerves in producing appropriate responses to the particular stimulus.

CHAPTER 6

LEARN TO TEST YOUR
CHILD AT HOME

6

MUSCLE RESPONSE TESTING

M uscle response testing is one of the tools used by the NAET specialists to test the imbalances and allergies in the body. The same muscle response testing also be used to detect various allergens that cause imbalances in the body.

When the allergen's incompatible electromagnetic energy comes close to a person's energy field, repulsion takes place. Without recognizing this repulsive action, we frequently go near allergens (whether they are foods, drinks, chemicals, environmental substances, animals or humans) and interact with their energies. This causes energy blockages in the meridians. These blockages cause imbalances in the body. The imbalances cause illnesses, which creates disorganization in body functions. The disorganization of the body and its functions involve the vital organs, their associated muscle groups and nerve roots giving rise to brain disorders.

To prevent the allergen from causing further disarray after producing the initial blockage, the brain sends messages to every cell of the body to reject the presence of the allergen. This rejection will appear as repulsion, and the repulsion will produce different symptoms related to the affected organs.

Your body has an amazing way of telling you when you are in trouble. As a matter of habit, you often have to be hurting severely before you look for help. If you went for help at the earliest hint of need, you would save yourself from unnecessary pain and agony. This applies to allergies, too. If you expose your allergies before you are exposed to them, you won't have to suffer the consequences. If you understand your body, your brain and their clues, you can avoid the causes that contribute to the energy blockages and body imbalances.

When some people are near allergens (adversely charged substances), they receive various clues from the brain, such as: an itchy throat, watery eyes, sneezing attacks, coughing spells, unexplained pain anywhere in the body, yawning, sudden tiredness, etc. You can demonstrate the changes in the weaknesses of the muscles by testing a strong indicator muscle in the absence of an allergen and then in its presence. The muscle will stay strong without any allergen in its electromagnetic field, but will weaken in the presence of an allergen. This response of the muscle can be used to your advantage to demonstrate the presence of an allergen near you.

MUSCLE RESPONSE TESTING

Muscle response testing can be preformed in the following ways (See Illustrations of Muscle Response Testing on the Following Pages).

1. Standard muscle response test can be done in standing, sitting or lying positions. You need two people to do this test: the person who is testing, the "tester," and the person being tested, "the subject."

2. The "Oval Ring Test" can be used in testing yourself, and on a very a strong person with a strong arm. This requires only one person if you are self-testing. You need two people if you are testing another person.

Figure 6-1

Standard Muscle Response Testing

3. Surrogate testing can be used in testing an infant, invalid person, extremely strong or very weak person, or an animal. The surrogate's muscle is tested by the tester, subject maintains skin-to-skin contact with the surrogate while being tested. The surrogate does not get affected by the testing. NAET treatments can also be administered through the surrogate very effectively without causing any interference with the surrogate's energy.

Two people are required to perform standard muscle response testing. The person who performs the test is called the tester, and the person who is being tested is called the subject. The subject can be tested lying down, standing or sitting. The lying-down position is the most convenient for both the tester and the subject; it also achieves more accurate results.

Step 1:   The subject lies on a firm surface with one arm raised (left arm in the picture below), 90 degrees to the body with the palm facing outward and the thumb facing toward the big toe.

Step 2:   The tester stands on the subject's (right) side. The subject's right arm is kept to his/her side with the palm either kept open to the air, or in a loose fist. The fingers should not touch any material, fabric or any part of the table the arm is resting on. This can give wrong test results. The left arm of the subject is raised 90 degrees to the body. The tester's left palm is contacting the subject's left wrist (Figure 6-1).

Step 3:   The tester using the left arm tries to push down on the subject's raised left arm toward the subject's left big toe. The subject resists the push of the tester on the arm (the indicator muscle or pre-determined muscle). The PDM remains strong if the subject is well balanced at the time of testing. It is essential to test a strong PDM to get accurate results. If the muscle or raised arm is weak and gives way under pressure without the presence of an allergen, either the subject is not balanced, or the tester is performing the test improperly; For example, the tester might be trying to overpower the subject. The subject does not need to gather up strength from other muscles in the body to resist the tester with all his/her might. Only five to 10 pounds of pressure needs to be applied on the muscle for three to five seconds.

Figure 6-2

MRT with allergen

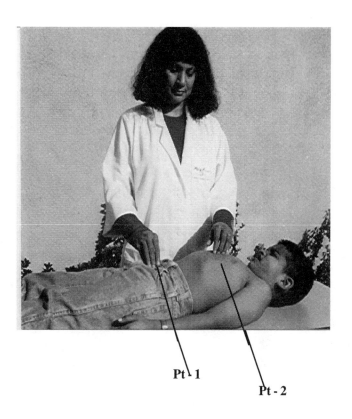

Pt - 1

Pt - 2

Figure 6-3

Balancing The Patient

When the subject's fingertips touch the allergen, the sensory receptors sense the charges of the allergen and relay the message to the brain. If it is an incompatible charge, the strong PDM will go weak. If the charges are compatible to the body, the indicator muscle will remain strong. This way, you can test any number of items to determine the compatible and incompatible charges of the items against the body.

Step 5: This step is used if the patient is found to be out of balance as indicated by the indicator muscle or raised arm presenting weak— without the presence of an allergen. The tester then places his or her fingertips of one hand at 'point 1' on the mid-line of the subject, about one and a half inches below the navel. The other hand is placed on 'point 2', in the center of the chest on the mid-line, level with the nipple line. The tester taps these two points or massages gently clockwise with the fingertips about 20 or 30 seconds, then repeats steps 2 and 3. If the indicator muscle tests strong, continue on to step 4. If the indicator muscle tests weak again, repeat this process.

Point 1:
Name of the point: **Sea Of Energy**
Location: One and a half inches below the navel, on the mid-line.

This is where the energy of the body is stored in abundance. When the body senses any danger around its energy field or when the body experiences energy blockages, the energy supply is cut short and stored here. If you tap or massage clockwise on that energy reservoir point, the energy starts bubbling up and emerges from this point.

Figure 6-4

`O' Ring Test To detect Allergies

If the muscle shows weakness, the tester will be able to judge the difference with only that small amount of pressure. Much practice is needed to test and sense the differences properly. If you cannot test properly or effectively the first few times, there is no need to get discouraged or frustrated. Please remember that practice makes you perfect.

Step 4: If the indicator muscle remains strong when tested- a sign that the subject is found to be balanced - then the tester should put the suspected allergen into the palm of the subject's resting hand. The sensory receptors, on the tip of the fingers, are extremely sensitive in recognizing allergens. The fingertips have specialized sensory receptors that can send messages to and from the brain.

Point 2:
Name of the point: **Energy Controller.**
Location: In the center of the chest on the midline of the body, level with the fourth intercostal space. This is the energy dispenser unit. From this center, energy is distributed to different tissues and organs as needed. This is the point that controls and regulates the energy circulation or Chi, in the body. When the energy rises from the Sea of Energy, it goes straight to the Dominating Energy point. From here, the energy is dispersed to different meridians, organs, tissues and cells as needed to help remove the energy blockages. It does this by forcing energy circulation from inside out. During this forced energy circulation, the blockages are pushed out of the body, balancing the body's state. You sense this through the strength of the indicator muscle. Continue this procedure several times. It is very unlikely that any person will remain weak after repeating this procedure two to three times.

The "Oval Ring Test" or "O Ring Test" can be used in self-testing, since this requires one person to perform the test. This can also be used to test a subject, if the subject is physically very strong with a strong arm and the tester is a physically weak person.

Step 1: The tester makes an "O" shape by opposing the little finger and thumb on the same hand. Then, with the index finger of the other hand he/she tries to separate the "O" ring against pressure. If the ring separates easily, you need to use the balancing techniques as described in step 5 of the muscle response test.

Step 2: If the "O" ring remains inseparable and strong, hold the allergen in the other hand, by the fingertips, and perform step 1 again. If the "O" ring separates easily, the person is allergic to the substance he/she is touching. If the "O" ring remains strong, the substance is not an allergen. Muscle response testing is one of the most reliable methods of allergy tests, and it is fairly easy to learn and practice in every day life. This method cuts out expensive laboratory work.

After considerable practice, some people are able to test themselves very efficiently using these methods. It is very important for allergic people to learn some form of self-testing technique to screen out contact with possible allergens to prevent allergic reactions in order to have freedom to live in this chemically polluted world. After receiving the basic 30-40 treatments from a NAET practitioner, you will be free to live wherever you like if you know how to test and avoid unexpected allergens from your surroundings. Hundreds of new allergens are thrown into the world daily by non-allergic people who do not understand the predicament of allergic people. If you want to live in this world looking and feeling normal among normal people, side by side with the allergens, you need to learn how to test on your own. It is not practical for people to treat thousands of allergens from their surroundings or go to an NAET practitioner every day for the rest of their lives. You will not be free from allergies until you learn to test accurately. It takes many hours of practice. But do not get discouraged. I have given enough information on testing methods here. You have to spend time and practice until you reach perfection.

A TIP TO MASTER SELF-TESTING

Find two items, one that you are allergic to and another that you are not, for example an apple and a banana.

You are allergic to the apple and not allergic to the banana. Hold the apple in the right hand and do the "Oval Ring Test" using your left hand. The ring easily breaks. The first few times if it didn't break, make it happen intentionally. Now hold the banana and do the same test. This time the ring doesn't break. Put the banana down, rub your hands together for 30 seconds. Take the apple and repeat the testing. Practice this every day until you can sense the difference. When you can feel the difference with these two items you can test anything around you.

SURROGATE TESTING

This method can be very useful to test and determine the allergies of an infant, a child, a hyperactive child, an autistic

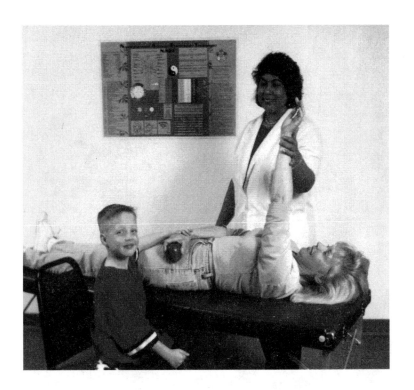

**Figure 6-5
Surrogate Testing**

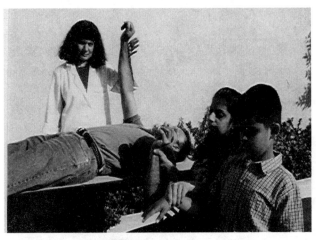

Figure 6-6
Extended Surrogate Testing

child, disabled person, an unconscious person, an extremely strong, and a very weak person, because they do not have enough muscle strength to perform an allergy test. You can also use this method to test an animal, plant, and a tree.

An extended surrogate testing is used when the patient (a hyperactive, an autistic, frightened), is uncooperative. Three people are needed for this test as shown in Figure 6-6. NAET treatments can also be administered through the extended surrogate very effectively without causing any interference to the surrogates' energy.

The surrogate's muscle is tested by the tester. It is very important to remember to maintain skin-to-skin contact between the surrogate and the subject during the procedure. If

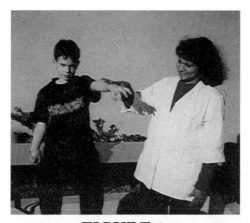

FIGURE 6-7

MRT In Sitting Or Standing Position

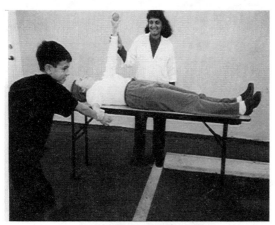

FIGURE 6-8

Testing A Hyperactive Child

Figure 6-9

**Testing To See If The Son
Is Allergic To The Father.**

FIGURE 6-10

**Testing To See If The Father
Is Allergic To The Son.**

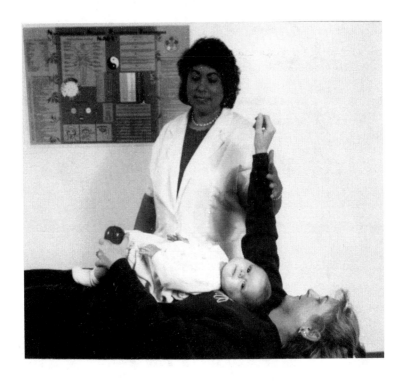

Figure 6-11
Testing An Infant Through a Surrogate

you do not, then the surrogate will receive the results of testing and treatment.

NAET treatments can also be administered through the surrogate very effectively without causing any interference to the surrogate's energy. The testing or treatment does not affect surrogate as long as the subject maintains uninterrupted skin-to-skin contact with the surrogate.

As mentioned earlier, muscle response testing is one of the tools used by kinesiologists. Practiced in this country since 1964, it was originated by Dr. George Goodheart and his associates. Dr. John F. Thie advocates this method through the "Touch For Health" Foundation in Malibu, California. For more information and books available on the subject; interested readers can write to "Touch For Health" Foundation.

Muscle response testing can be used to test any substance for allergies. Even human beings can be tested for each other in this manner. When you are allergic to another human (father, mother, son, daughter, grandfather, grandmother, caretaker, baby sitter, etc.) you or your child could experience similar symptoms as you would with foods, chemicals or materials, whenever you or your child spends some time with the allergic person.

The subject lies down and touches the other person he or she wants tested (Figure 6-9, 6-10). The tester pushes the arm of the subject as in steps 2 and 3. If the subject is allergic to the second person, the indicator muscle goes weak. If the subject is not allergic, the indicator muscle remains strong.

If people are allergic to each other, (between husband and wife, mother and child, father and son, patient and doctor, etc.) the allergy can affect a person in various ways. The father and/or mother allergic to the child, or child allergic to a parent or parents, child can get sick or remain sick indefinitely. The same things can happen to the parents too. If the husband is allergic to the wife or wife towards the husband, they can be fighting all the time and/or their health can be affected. The same things can happen among other family members too. It is important to test the family members and other immediate associates with your child for possible allergy and if found, they should be treated for each other to obtain good health and happiness.

Muscle response testing for allergies should be taught in every school and in every establishment. Everyone should learn to test to detect their allergies even if the treatment is not available. If you know your allergies, you can easily avoid them and that will help you somewhat.

Let's look at the history of 6-year-old Dominic who suffered from severe autism for 4 years. His mother Debbie brought Dominic to the office regularly for treatments. Before the treatment, he was spitting up every meal whether it was water or milk. He suffered from severe constipation, insomnia, irritability, colic pains and severe crying spells. He could not talk or communicate in words about his discomfort. Debbie spent extra time in the office to learn about autism and the NAET connection. She also took a special interest in the series of patient education seminars given in our office to the new patients once a week. Through the patient education seminars she learned ways to detect Dominic's untreated allergens before he was exposed to them. This made their lives easier.

She and her husband tested every food before they bought it from the store. Whenever they found an allergen, they avoided it until they brought the child to treat it with NAET. This helped Dominic immensely. He stopped having skin rashes and hives. He did not have too many temper tantrums any more. He slept well without nightmares and crying spells. Soon after Dominic received about 15-20 treatments, his disposition changed. He started talking, became friendlier, and his behavior changed. He was admitted to regular school. His mother became a teacher's assistant in his class so that she could keep a close watch on him. His parents continued to test him for everything before they introduced anything new to him. His parents took special care to feed him allergy-tested, or non-allergic food items only so that he could continue normal activities without interruption. Because of his mother's special attention, Dominic responded well to the treatment faster than any other autistic child I have ever treated before and he was able to have a normal school life. He is a healthy, intelligent ten-year-old now.

Just by knowing MRT and the testing procedure, Dominic's mother could prevent unwanted visits to the doctor's office. If we can teach these simple testing skills to all the parents of autistic children, the special education teachers, and the caretakers, and encourage them to use non-allergic products in the house, schools, and work-place, most allergy related autism could be controlled easily and these children could have a future like all other normal children.

Medical professionals as well as the public should be educated to listen and look for various types of allergies causing problem in various ways to all. Parents should form support groups to encourage other parents to learn MRT testing. Your normal children should be educated in testing. Schools should begin teaching muscle testing procedures to the children as a normal learning curriculum. Community centers, adult schools, hospitals involved in patient education sessions should take interest to teach MRT to all their attendees. Allergies and allergy-related problems are on the rise due to our scientific advancements. If we learn to manage our adverse reactions towards the scientific advancements, we can enjoy the benefit of the modern inventions too. Unless you are educated to know about the MRT testing, you do not know what to look for. As you have seen, the theory of energy blockages and diseases comes from oriental medicine. Oriental medicine also teaches that, if given a chance, with a little support, the body will heal itself.

CHAPTER 7

BRAIN-BODY

CONNECTIONS

7

BRAIN-BODY CONNECTIONS

The human body is made up of bones, flesh, nerves and blood vessels, which can only function in the presence of vital energy. Without this energy, the body is like an advanced efficient computer without an electrical power supply. Vital energy is not visible to the human eye, neither is electricity. No one knows how or why the vital energy gets into the body or how, when or where it goes when it leaves. However, it is true that without vital energy none of the body functions can take place. When the human body is alive vital energy flows freely through the energy pathways, the blood will be circulating through the blood vessels and distributing appropriate nutrients to various parts of the body.

The blood helps to exchange oxygen and carbon dioxide cleaning up the impurities of the body. When blood receives proper nutrients, the body and bones grow, and the flesh and nerves, in turn, can protect the body; all body parts will work as a unit, like an efficient factory with all functions working as designed. When vital energy stops flowing through the energy pathways, the human machine ceases to function and the person is pronounced dead.

The human body is the most efficient, well-organized, functional unit known. Many branches of channels and energy pathways connect each and every cell of the body (the basic building block) with every other cell. In turn, every body part is connected and interlinked by a meshing networks of channels and branches, creating a perfect communication system within the body. The brain is the commander of this system. When the vital energy activates this system, the brain takes over the responsibilities. Under the brain's command, all parts of the body are activated; there is open communication between the brain, cells from different parts of tissue and other body parts. This communication takes place in a matter of nanoseconds; thus the brain maintains complete control of the body functions.

If for some reason a blockage takes place in the energy pathways, normal physiology is disrupted. This energy disruption will lead to certain visible effects in the human body and pathological symptoms will begin to appear. In the beginning, these pathological symptoms are seen around the blockage(s). Then they spread along the channels and branches to related tissues and organs. If the blockages affect the nerves that supply the different parts of the brain, diminished function of the brain is the result.

Traditional Chinese medicine describes the meridians as well as the symptoms of each of the primary channels. This chapter will explain the 12 primary channels and how blockages in these channels present physical and emotional symptoms, which cause illness, disease, and mental disorders. Many of the symptoms relating to blockages in the meridians will be familiar to the parents of children with autism. Only a brief overview is given in this chapter to aquaint you with energy meridians. You are encouraged to read or refer to any of the respective acupuncture textbooks named in the bibliography. Please read "Say Good-bye To Illness," by the author, for more extensive information about these meridians.

LUNG MERIDIAN

The inability of the lung meridian to accept fresh energy at 3:00 a.m. causes problems in the lung energy meridian. This blockage in the first meridian transmits into all other meridians as a chain reaction, and energy circulation gets disrupted.

Pathological Symptoms

■ Afternoon fever, acute bronchial asthmatic attacks, asthma worse after 3:00 a.m., shortness of breath, burning in the eyes and nostrils, chest congestion, cough, coughing up blood, dry mouth and throat, emaciated look, fever, itching of the nostrils, headaches between eyes, nasal congestion, nose bleed, postnasal drips, runny nose with clear discharge, red or painful eyes, sneezing, throat irritation, swollen throat, and swollen cervical glands.

■ Excessive perspiration in some cases and lack of perspiration in others, husky voice, infection in the respiratory tract, influenza, irritability, low voice, lack of desire to talk, laryngitis, nasal polyps, night sweats, other chest infections, pleurisy, pneumonia, red cheeks, red eyes, pain in the eyes, sinus infections, and sinus headaches.

■ Abdominal bloating, nausea, vomiting, constipation or loose stools, body ache, irritability, and restlessness.

■ Chronic hives, cradle cap, eczema, excessive sweating, skin rashes, skin tags, moles, warts, scaly and rough skin, heat sensation with hot palms, hair loss, thinning of the hair, poor growth of hair and nails, rough ridges on the nails, and brittle nails.

Main Emotion : Grief

■ Related emotions: a tendency toward humiliating others, always apologizing, comparing self with others, contempt, dejection, depression (early morning), despair, emotionally super sensitive, expressions of over-sympathy, false pride, low self-esteem, hopelessness, insulting others, and intolerance.

■ Liking onion, peppers, garlic and cinnamon, pungent and spicy foods, and sometimes craving them.

■ Loneliness, meanness, melancholy, over demanding, prejudice, seeking others' approval, self-pity and weeping frequently without reason.

Essential Nutrition

■ Clear water, proteins, citrus fruits, cinnamon, onions, garlic, green peppers, black peppers, rice, vitamin C, bioflavonoids, and vitamin B-2.

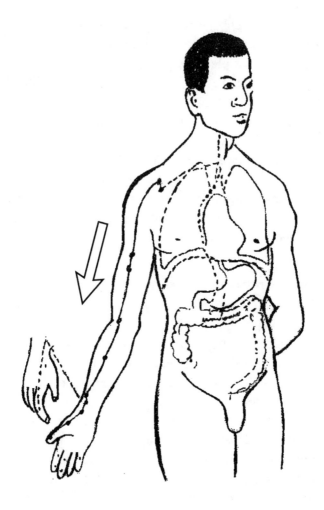

Figure 7-1

Lung Meridian (LU)

LARGE INTESTINE MERIDIAN
PAthological Symptoms

■ Dry mouth, throat, sore throat, nose bleed, toothache on lateral incisors, first lower and second lower bicuspid, red and painful eyes, swelling of the neck and swelling of the lateral part of the knee joint, pain in the shoulders, knees, parts of the thighs, and along the course of the meridan.

■ Lower abdominal cramps, constipation or diarrhea, spastic colon, spasms of the rectum and anal sphincter, itching of the anus, generalized hives, intestinal noise, flatulence, bleeding from the rectum, colitis, and dizziness.

■ Abdominal pain, bloating, bad breath, belching, chest congestion, shortness of breath and sinus headaches on the sides of the nose, between the eyes, and over the eyes.

■ Acne, blister/inflammation of the lower gum, dermatitis, feeling better or tired after a bowel movement, hair loss, hair thinning, hives, and warts.

Main Emotion: Guilt

■ Related Emotions: Grief, sadness, seeking sympathy, weeping, crying spells, and defensiveness.

■ Haunted by past painful memories, bad dreams, nightmares, talking in the sleep, rolling restlessly in sleep, and inability to recall dreams.

Essential Nutrition

Vitamins A, D, E, C, B complex, especially B-1, wheat, bran, oat bran, yogurt, and roughage.

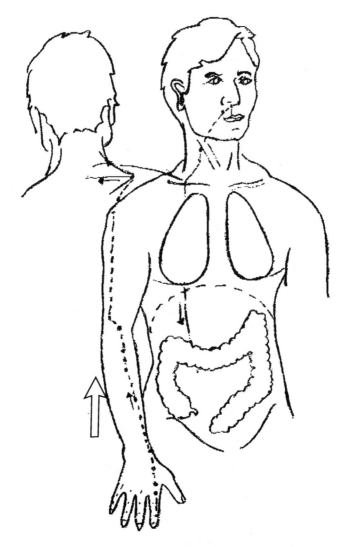

Figure 7-2

Large Intestine Meridian (LI)

STOMACH MERIDIAN
Pathological Symptoms

■ Frequent fever, sore throat, coated tongue, flushed face, fever blisters, herpes, sores on the gums and inside the lips, red painful boils on the face, sweating, cracks on the center of the tongue, bad breath, fatigue, insomnia, seizures, toothache, pain on the upper jaw and upper gum diseases, fibromyalgia and temporo-mandibular joint problems (TMJ).

■ Pain in the eye and chest, pain along the course of the channel in the leg or foot, swelling on the neck, facial paralysis, and coldness in the lower limbs.

■ Acne, heat boils or blemishes, black and blue discoloration along the channel, itching and red rashes along the lateral aspect of the lower leg below the knee.

■ Abdominal bloating, fullness or edema, abdominal cramps, vomiting, nausea, anorexia, bulimia, hiatal hernia, and discomfort when reclining.

■ Insomnia, restlessness, mental confusion, personality changes, double personality, hyperactivity in children or adults, manic-depressive behaviors, learning disorders, schizophrenia, lack of concentration, and aggressive behaviors.

■ Obsession, obsessive compulsive behaviors, panic disorders, headaches on the forehead, and behind the eyes (dull, sharp, pressure or burning pain behind the eyes).

Main Emotion: Disgust
Related emotions: bitterness, disappointment, greed, emptiness, deprivation, restlessness, obsession, ego tism, and despair. Lack of concentration, nostalgia,

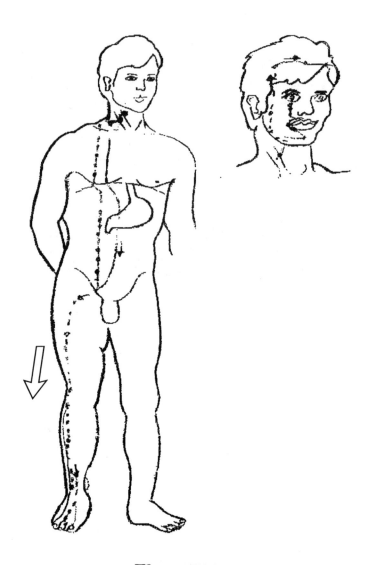

Figure 7-3

Stomach Meridian

mental confusion, mental fog, manic disorders, schizophrenia, hyperactivity, extreme nervousness, butterfly sensation in the stomach, and aggressive behaviors, paranoia, fear of losing control, fear of dying, terror (a sense that something unimaginably horrible is about to occur and one is powerless to prevent it), and perceptual distortions.

Essential Nutrition

B complex especially B-12, B-6, B-3 and folic acid and plenty of water.

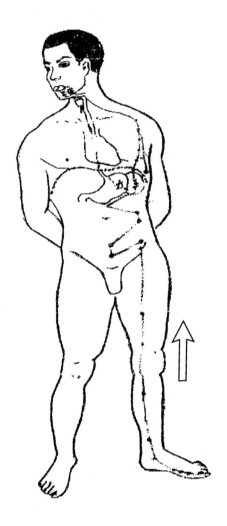

Figure 7-4

Spleen Meridian

SPLEEN MERIDIAN
Pathological Symptoms

■ Heaviness in the head, abdominal pain, fullness or distension, incomplete digestion of food, intestinal noises, nausea, vomiting, lack of taste, stiffness of the tongue, lack of smell, hard lumps in the abdomen, reduced appetite, craving sugar, loose stools, diarrhea constipation, hypoglycemic reaction, general feverishness, and body aches.

■ Low self-esteem, procrastination, depression, and intuitive and prophetic behaviors. Pallor, sleepy in the afternoon, latent insomnia, dreams that makes you tired, light-headedness, jaundice, fatigue, weak limbs, anemia, bleeding disorders, and hemorrhoids.

Main Emotion: Worry
Related Emotions:
■ Over-concern, nervousness, keeps feelings inside, likes loneliness, hyperactivity in children or adults, manic depressive disorder, obsessive compulsive disorder, panic attack, enjoy talking to self, and does not like crowds.
■ Lack of self-confidence, gives more importance to self, hopelessness, irritable, likes to take revenge, likes to be praised, unable to make decisions, shy, timid, restrained, easily hurt, likes to get constant encouragement, otherwise falls apart, likes to live through others, over-sympathetic to others.

Essential Nutrition
Vitamin A, vitamin C, calcium, chromium, and protein.

HEART MERIDIAN

Pathological Symptoms

This is one of the meridians often seen imbalanced in people with autism.

■ Poor circulation and dizziness, general feverishness, headache, and dry throat.

■ Mental disorders, nervousness, hyperactivity in children or adults, bipolar disorder, manic depressive disorder, depression, panic attack, obsessive compulsive disorder, emotional excesses, sometimes abusive, and irritability.

■ Vertigo, nausea, dizziness, or light-headedness.

■ Shortness of breath, excessive perspiration, insomnia, chest distension, palpitation, heaviness in the chest and sharp chest pain, irregular heart beats, and chest distention.

Main Emotion: Joy

■ Over-excitement, emotional excess (excessive laughing or crying), sadness or lack of emotions.

■ Abusive nature, bad manners, anger, easily upset, aggressive personality, insecurity, hostility, guilt, does not make friends, and does not trust anyone.

Essential Nutrition

Calcium, vitamin C, vitamin E, B complex and plenty of water.

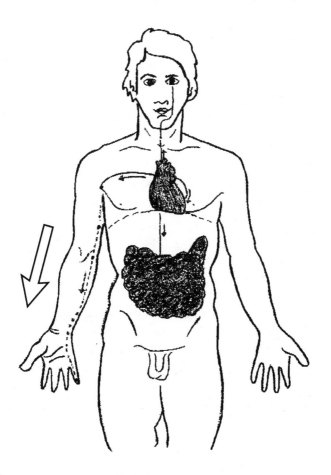

Figure 7-5

Heart Meridian

SMALL INTESTINE MERIDIAN

Pathological Symptoms
- Distension and pain in the lower abdomen, pain radiating around the waist, and to the genitals.
- Abdominal pain with dry stool, constipation, and diarrhea. Knee pain, shoulder pain and frozen shoulder.

Main Emotion: Insecurity
- Related emotion: emotional instability, feeling of abandonment, or desertion.
- Joy, over-excitement, sadness, sorrow, and suppression of deep sorrow.
- Absent-mindedness, poor concentration, daydreaming paranoia, and sighing.
- Irritability, easily annoyed, lacking the confidence to assert oneself, and shy.
- Becoming too involved with details, introverted, and easily hurt.

Essential Nutrition
Vitamin B complex, vitamin D, vitamin E.
Acidophilus, yogurt, fibers, wheat germ, and whole grains.

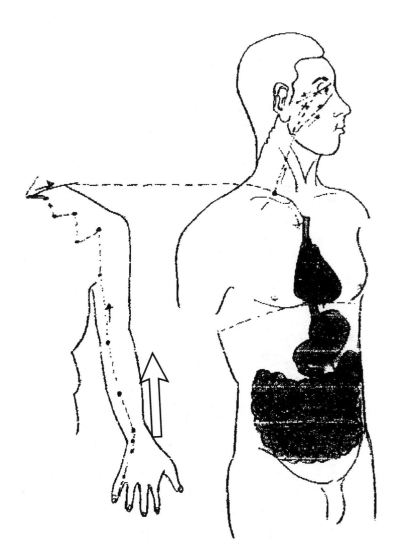

Figure 7-6

Small Intestine Meridian

BLADDER MERIDIAN
Pathological Ssymptoms

- Frequent, painful and burning urination, loss of bladder control and bloody urine.
- Chills, fever, headaches (especially at the back of the neck), stiff neck, nasal congestion, and disease of the eye.
- Pain: in the lower back, along back of the leg and foot, along the meridian, in the lateral part of the ankle, in the lateral part of the sole, in the little toe, and be hind the knee.
- Pain and discomfort in the lower abdomen, sciatic neuralgia, spasm behind the knee, spasms of the calf muscles, weakness in the rectum and rectal muscle.
- Pain in the lower abdomen, enuresis, retention of urine, burning urination, bloody urine, painful urination, frequent bladder infection, fever, and mental disorders.
- Chronic headaches at the back of the neck and pain at the inner canthus of the eyes.

Main Emotion: Fright
Related emotions: holds on to sad, disturbing and im pure thoughts, unable to let go of unwanted past memories, timid, inefficient, annoyed, highly irritable, fearful, unhappy, reluctant, restless, impatient, and frustrated.

Essential Nutrition
Vitamin C, A, E, B complex, B-1, calcium, and trace minerals.

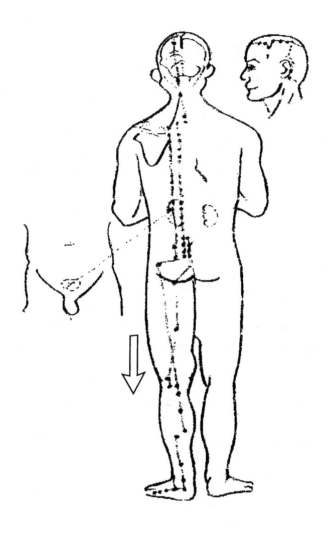

Figure 7-7

Bladder Meridian

KIDNEY MERIDIAN

Pathological Symptoms

- Pain: along the lower vertebrae, in the low back, and in the sole of the foot.
- Puffy eyes, bags under the eyes, and dark circles un der the eyes.
- Motor impairment or muscular atrophy of the foot, dryness of the mouth, sore throat, pain in the sole of the foot, pain in the posterior aspect of the leg or thigh, and lower backache.
- Pain and ringing in the ears, light-headedness, and nausea.
- Frequent burning, scanty and painful urination.

- Fever, fever with chills, irritability, vertigo, facial edema, blurred vision, ringing in the ears, spasms of the ankle and feet, swelling in the legs, and swollen ankles.
- Loose stools, chronic diarrhea, constipation, abdominal distention, vomiting, tiredness, dry mouth, excessive thirst, poor appetite, and poor memory.

Main Emotion: Fear

Related emotions: Indecision, terror, caution, confusion, seeks attention, unable to express feelings, lack of con centration, and poor memory.

Essential Nutrition

Vitamin A, E, B, essential fatty acids, calcium, and iron.

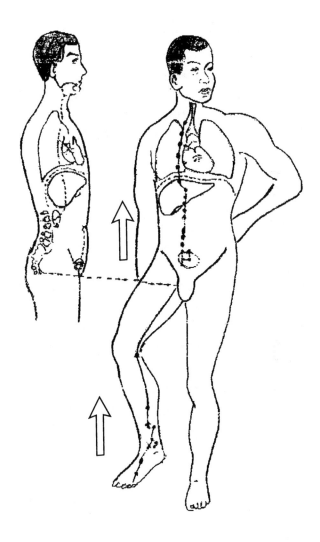

Figure 7-8

Kidney Meridian

PERICARDIUM MERIDIAN

Pathological Symptoms

- Stiff neck, spasms in the arm, in the leg, spasms of the elbow and arm, frozen shoulder, restricting movements hot palms, and pain along the channels.
- Impaired speech, fainting spells, flushed face, irritability, fullness in the chest, heaviness in the chest, slurred speech.
- Sensation of hot or cold, nausea, nervousness, pain in the eyes, and sub-axillary swellings.
- Motor impairment of the tongue, heaviness, palpitation and pain in the chest due to emotional overload.
- Irritability, excessive appetite, fullness in the chest, and sugar imbalance.

Main Emotion: Hurt Or Joy

Related emotions: over-excitement, regret, jealousy, sexual tension, stubbornness, manic disorders, heaviness in the head, light sleep with dreams, fear of heights, various phobias, imbalance in sexual energy like never having enough sex or in some cases no sexual desire.

Essential Nutrition

Vitamin E, vitamin C, chromium, and trace minerals.

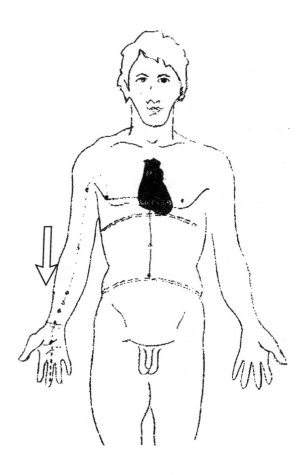

Figure 7-9

Pericardium Channel

TRIPLE WARMER MERIDIAN
Pathological Symptoms

- Swelling and pain in the throat, pain in the cheek and jaw, excessive hunger, redness in the eye, deafness, and pain behind the ear.

- Abdominal pain, distention, hardness and fullness in the lower abdomen, enuresis, frequent urination, and edema.

- Dysuria, excessive thirst, excessive hunger, always feels hungry even after eating, vertigo, indigestion, hypoglycemia, hyperglycemia, and constipation.

- Pain in the medial part of the knee, shoulder pain, and fever in the late evening.

MAIN EMOTION: Hopelessness

Related emotions: depression, despair, grief, excessive emotion, emptiness, deprivation, and phobias.

Essential Nutrition

Iodine, table salt, trace minerals, vitamin C, calcium, fluoride, and water.

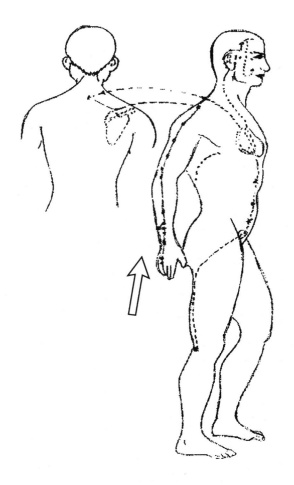

Figure 7-10

Triple Warmer Meridian

GALL BLADDER MERIDIAN

Pathological Symptoms

This meridian is unbalanced in people with autism.

■ Alternating fever and chills, headache, ashen complexion, pain in the eye or jaw, swelling in subaxillary region, scrofula, and deafness.

■ Pain along the channel in the hip region, leg or foot and along the channel, tremors or twitching of the body or parts of the body.

■ Vomiting and bitter taste in the mouth, ashen complexion, swelling in the sub-axillary region and deafness.

■ A heavy sensation in the right upper part of the abdomen, sighing, dizziness, chills, fever, and yellowish complexion.

Main Emotion: Rage

Related Emotions: assertion, aggression, shouting, and talking aloud.

Essential Nutrition

Vitamin A, calcium, linoleic acids, and oleic acids (for example, pine nuts).

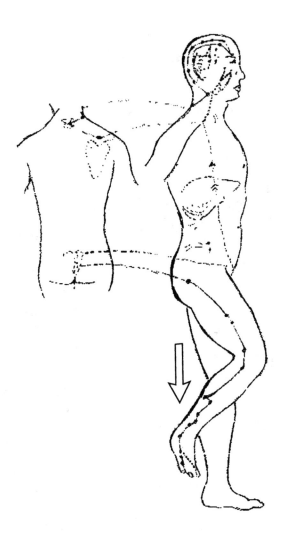

Figure 7-11

Gall Bladder Meridian

LIVER MERIDIAN

Pathological Symptoms
This meridian is unbalanced in people with autism.

- Headache at the top of the head, vertigo, and blurred vision.
- Feeling of some obstruction in the throat, tinnitus, fever, spasms in the extremities, abdominal pain, and hard lumps in the upper abdomen.
- Pain in the intercostal region, hernia, PMS, pain in the breasts, vomiting, jaundice, loose stools, and pain in the lower abdomen.
- Irregular menses, reproductive organ disturbances, and excessive bright colored bleeding during menses.
- Enuresis, retention of urine, dark urine, dizziness, and stroke- like condition.

Main Emotion: Anger
Related emotions: aggression, hyperactivity, frustration, unhappiness, complaining all the time, and finding faults with others.

Essential Nutrition
Beets, green vegetables, vitamin A, trace minerals, and unsaturated fatty acids.

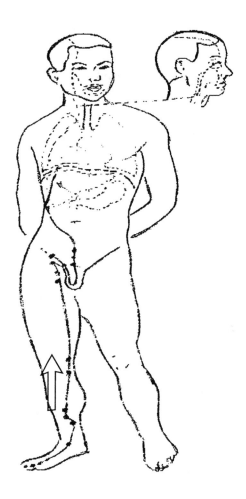

Figure 7-12

Liver Meridian

CHAPTER 8

SUPPLEMENTARY
PROCEDURES

8

SUPPLEMENTARY PROCEDURES

Most of the acupuncture points used in eliminating the energy blockages lie near vital organs. The information about the treatment points and the techniques for needling the specific points to remove allergy are not described in this book. Each of these points is needled with special techniques, which are taught in acupuncture colleges. Teaching these techniques id beyond the scope of this book and has been intentionally excluded. Needling in these areas requires proper education and extensive practice. Improper needling can cause damage to vital organs and even greater damage to health, sometimes leading to fatal accidents.

There are thousands of doctors trained in NAET treatment methods all over the country. Please visit our website "naet.com" to find a practitioner near you.

Information regarding a few important acupuncture points is discussed in this chapter. They can be used to help control autism at any age. It is not a cure. It is going to provide temporary relief from the symptoms.

In Chapter Seven we learned about the twelve acupuncture meridians and their pathological symptoms when the energy circulation is blocked in those meridians (diagrams 7-1 to 7-12). In Chapter 6, "Muscle-Response Testing," we learned to detect the cause of energy blockages by testing via MRT for allergies. We also found that allergies may be the causative agents for energy blockages in particular meridians. We have learned to test and find the causes in general. Practice these testing techniques and make a habit of testing your child for everything before exposing yourself, or your child to food, clothing, household chemicals, drugs, immunizations and environmental agents, etc., which you know or suspect are allergens.

Point Name	Related Meridian	Related Organ
Pt 0	Brain Test Pt	Brain
Pt 1	LU test pt	Lung
Pt 2	PHT(physical heart)	Pericardium
Pt 3	LIV test pt	Liver
Pt 4	GB test pt	Gall bladder
Pt 5	Heart test pt	Heart
Pt 6	ST test pt	Stomach
Pt 7	Kid test pt	Kidney
Pt 8	Sp test pt	Speen
Pt 9	Colon test pt	Colon
Pt 10	TW test pt	Triple warmer
Pt 11	SI test pt	Small Intestine
Pt 12	BI test pt	Bladder

Table 8-1

Points To Balance The Organs

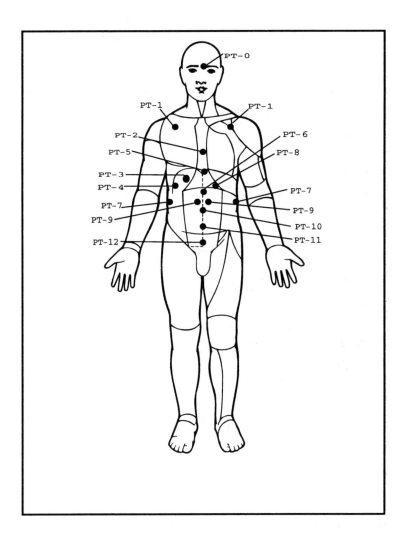

Figure 8-1

Points to Balance the Organs

ISOLATING THE BLOCKAGES

Testing and isolating the particular blockages can be done in many ways. One method, described here, is fairly easy to understand and with some practice, this art can be mastered by anyone.

STEP 1. Balance the patient and find an indicator muscle. Refer to Chapter 7 to learn more about NTT and MRT to test your allergies.

STEP 2. The patient lies down on his back with the allergen (e.g., an apple) in his resting palm. When it is needed, surrogate testing can also be used.

STEP 3. The tester touches the point in diagram 8-1 one at a time, and tests the pre-determined muscle and compares the strength of the PDM in the absence and presence of the allergen. For example, touch point '1' in diagram 8-1 with the finger tips of one hand and with the other hand test the indicator muscle (while the patient is still holding the allergen in one hand). The muscle goes weak, indicating that the meridian or the energy pathways connected to that particular point has an energy blockage.

Point '1' relates to the lung meridian. Obstruction in the energy flow anywhere in the lung meridian can make this point weak. Test the PDM, while touching each point in the lung meridian (for more information regarding point location in the meridians please refer to the appropriate books on acupuncture given in the bibliography). The indicator muscle becomes weakest when the tester touches sites of the blocked area in the meridian. For point-meridian relationships, refer to table 8-1. Using this technique, you can trace all weak meridians and the specific weak sites in your body. Finger pressure therapy can be used temporarily to restore the energy flow in the blocked energy meridians.

STEP 1. The first step for finger pressure therapy is to find the organ or meridian being blocked. Find the related organ point in the table and then in the diagram 8-1.

STEP 2. Apply slight finger pressure, with the pad of your index finger, on the point. Hold 60 seconds at each point. Follow the order of the sequence of points given on the previous page. When the blocked meridian is found, make the associated organ point with that meridian a starting point to perform the energy balancing. For example, if the energy is blocked in the liver meridian, make the liver organ point (point 3) the first point to begin the finger pressure. If the heart is blocked, use the heart point (point 5) as the first point in the sequence of energy balancing.

STEP 3. Hold 60 seconds at each point and go through all 12 points and come back to the starting point. Then, hold 60 seconds at the starting point and stop the treatment. Always end at the starting point to complete the energy cycle. Some patients can experience physical or emotional pain during these treatment sessions. If the patient has an emotional blockage, it needs to be isolated and treated. Some patients can get pain in the blocked area of the meridians during the treatment. In such instances, please go through another cycle of treatment or until the pain stops, repeat the treatment every ten minutes. Often this will correct the problem.

Some commonly used acupuncture points, and their uses to help in emergency situations, are given below. Massage these points gently with the finger pads for one minute each. Please refer to the appropriate meridians in Chapter 7 or refer to the textbooks on acupuncture in the bibliography if you would like to learn more about these points.

RESUSCITATION POINTS

1. Fainting: GV 26, GB 12, LI 1, PC 9, KID 1
2. Nausea: CV 12, PC 6
3. Backache: GV 26, UB 40
4. Fatigue: CV 5, LI 1, CV 17
5. Fever: LI 11, LU 10, GV 16

For more information on revival techniques, refer to Chapter 3, pages 570 to 573, in "Acupuncture: A Comprehensive Text," by Shanghai College of Traditional Medicine, Eastland Press, 1981 or refer to "Living Pain Free with Acupressure" by the author. It is available at various bookstores and at our **website (naet.com).**

Allergy treatments require repeated office visits in the beginning. Once all the known allergens are eliminated, the patient is trained to find his/her own allergens. The patient then has to see the doctor only if he/she encounters an item that bothers him/her and cannot be eliminated using the above methods, or for annual follow-ups. All allergens cannot be eliminated in one or two office visits. In some severe cases, it may take more than a visit per item to clear completely.

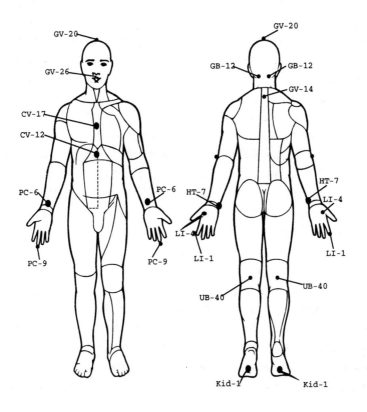

Figure 8-2

Resuscitation Points

There have been a few patients with mild cases of allergies who have completed the treatments in one or two visits or in two or three months. These patients were either not seen again, or only on a few follow-up visits. On the average, most patients have taken anywhere from eight to twelve months to achieve satisfactory results. Some extreme cases have taken three-and-half to four years to solve their problems. Allergic patients should keep this time span in mind when they approach any NAET specialists. If treatment is discontinued before completion of all the necessary treatments, the results will be unsatisfactory and allergic symptoms are very likely to recur. This will tend to make the patient feel that the allergy itself is to blame or that the treatment is useless. For this reason, it is better not even to start treatment, than to start and discontinue too soon, or to start and then cooperate in a half-hearted manner. The allergist will discharge his patients with proper instructions, just as soon as he/she feels it is safe to do so.

How can patients cooperate and help the doctor achieve maximum results in minimum time? After each treatment, patients are advised to stay away from the treated item for 25 hours. There are 12 energy meridians. In order for an energy molecule to pass through one meridian it takes two hours. To circulate through 12 meridians, it takes 24 hours. This means that the patient should not even come close to the object, as its electromagnetic field can interfere with the patient's own field and negate the treatment. Patients are also advised to maintain a food diary. Thus, if the patient reacts to something violently during treatment, the offender can easily be traced and treated, preventing further pain. During treatment, patients are placed on a strict diet of non-allergic items after the completion of three treatments. This helps the body to maintain good health without having to face possible allergic items.

The following is a list of general directions which, it is hoped, will be of assistance to allergic patients, regardless of the particular symptoms they may suffer.

1. The best time to begin treatments for your symptoms is now. Do not wait until it gets severe. It is not likely that the symptoms will decrease with the passing of time without doing anything; more likely, the symptoms will become more severe.

2. Report regularly for treatment and as often as directed by your NAET specialist. If necessary, long breaks should only be taken after completion of the treatment for each item. Never take more than two days off without completing a treatment for each item. For example, when getting treated for a milk allergy if you were to take five consecutive visits to clear the allergy to milk, you should take a few days or a week off after passing the treatment only. After being cleared of the milk, and before starting treatment for another item like beef, you may take a break.

3. Certain people may have a negative reaction to a treatment. One cannot predict reactions ahead of time. For this reason, the patient has to remain in the doctor's office anywhere from 15 minutes to half-an-hour following the treatment. During that time, if there is an unusual reaction, the doctor will treat the patient again. If there is no reaction, the patient will be sent home with certain instructions to follow.

4. The patient should not come close to the energy field of the items after he/she leaves the doctor's office for a period of 25 hours. This is a crucial time because the brain works on a biological time clock of 24-hour cycles. You should leave one hour extra for the brain to adjust. During this time, the brain can reject or

accept the treatment. If the brain accepts the treatment, it will generally not reject it for the rest of the patient's life.

5. Soon after treatment, patients should avoid strenuous activity, exercises, heavy meals, etc., for at least three to four hours. It is possible that any of these activities can cause a sudden blockage in the energy pathway causing unpleasant reactions.

6. Patients, who are allergic to many items, will experience various symptoms if they use the allergenic items while they are undergoing treatment. In NAET treatment, the patient is asked to use or eat anything he wants except for the item for which he/she is getting treated. If he/she is eating some other allergen, he/she can still react to that particular allergen even though this does not interfere with the current treatment; however, the patient may not feel very good. For better and faster results, the patient should avoid all other allergens.

If the patient is under any other medical care for any other symptoms, he/she is advised to continue those other treatments as before, along with the NAET treatments. This will help the patient keep his/her other health problems under control while going through the allergy treatments. This way the body does not have to fight stress or diseases from different causes while undergoing the stress of the new treatment. Patients with autism should continue their medicines or other treatments, so that they can get through these allergy treatments more easily than patients who refuse to seek western medical supportive treatments and rely on the allergy treatments alone.

7. During treatment, patients are advised to avoid exposure to extreme weather, such as excessive heat and cold drafts.

8. Patients are advised to practice good nutrition. They should try to eat non-allergenic items, or items that have been treated, while going through this program. Patients are also advised not to overeat or over-exercise, to drink plenty of liquids, have pleasant thoughts while preparing and eating the foods, and get plenty of rest.

9. Remember that it usually takes several years to build up sensitivity to the point where severe reactions occur. Do not get discouraged if relief from symptoms is delayed for some time. Just because all the symptoms do not disappear at the end of a few days or weeks of treatment, there is no reason for discontinuing a diet or the treatments. When a few major allergies are cleared, minor allergies may be noticed more easily. Your awareness of allergies will be more pronounced after a few items have been cleared. Some patients ask, "After being cleared for some items, do I become more allergic to things I was not allergic to before?" The answer is a definite "No." The person's awareness increases, or the allergic reactions stick out more noticeably after some major items have been cleared.

10. Avoid emotional stress and undue worry. This will bring down the immune system by increasing the energy blockages and cause more allergic reactions. If you are under a lot of stress, or sadness, you should avoid heavy meals, excessively spicy or salty meals. Try to eat simple foods in liquid or pureed form to allow the food to go through the digestive tract faster without dispensing a lot of energy from the energy reservoir.

11. As you improve, your symptoms will grow less severe and less frequent, but do not stop the treatments. Try to complete

treatments for all your known allergies. Otherwise, untreated allergens may build up and cause problems later.

12. Severely allergic patients should always try to carry antihistamines and oral medications or adrenaline shots with them. Severely allergic patients can get into life-threatening situations at any time with any kind of allergy. If the patient can administer the adrenaline shot or antihistamines immediately, the after-effect will be less severe preventing unfortunate incidents.

Additionally, specific instructions will be necessary for each patient, and these instructions vary depending on his/her sensitivities and allergic manifestations.

CHAPTER 9

TIPS TO BALANCE
THE BRAIN

9

TIPS TO BALANCE
THE BRAIN

Most of the cases of autism spectrum disorders I have seen fall into the category of allergy related autism. Children with different stages of autistic behavior respond differently. I have treated patients ranging in age from 4 to 31 years old. The younger we begin the treatment, the faster the results.

Allergy causes brain imbalances, as we have seen in the previous chapters. Brain imbalances arising from allergies are probably due to an improper response of the immune system affecting the brain or certain parts of the brain by otherwise harmless substances. An allergic person can react to anything around him, creating various health problems, which involve every part and organ of the body or impair any function of the body. So the brain and its associated organs are not any different from other vital organs in the body. The more exposure the brain had with numerous allergens, the greater the damage to the brain tissue. When autistic children grow up with allergies, their brains get the cumulative effects of the allergens. Repeated allergic reactions of the brain will cause repeated obstruction in the energy flow to the brain. Diminished energy flow will cause disturbances in the blood circulation. Poor blood circulation will cause reduced supply of oxygen and other essential nutrients to the brain tissue. Normal functions of the brain and brain tissue will get impaired due to lack of proper nutrients. Appropriate nutrients are necessary for certain enzymatic functions in the brain. With or without the nutrients, the enzymatic functions will go on in the brain. Substitute nutritional elements will replace the ingredients in the enzymatic function in the absence of proper nutrients. Substitute ingredients will not always produce the proper enzymes. Defective or incomplete enzymes will be produced and the brain will respond with abnormal reactions and responses in turn.

Autistic people with numerous food allergies suffer from poor absorption and assimilation of the essential nutrients. This may be due to an allergy of the child towards the nutrient. This allergy causes an energy blockage in the affected meridians giving rise to symptoms associated with the affected meridians. Sometimes various other adverse energies or unpleasant incidents can cause energy blockages in energy meridians giving rise to similar results as allergies. Some of the adverse influences are bacterial toxins (as seen in chicken pox, strep-throat, etc.), chemical toxins (as seen after vaccinations, immunizations, exposure to chemical spills, etc.), extreme starvation (absence of proper nutrients), and/or radiation (effect of powerful energy rays from external sources), etc., which can create energy blockages and damage to the brain tissue creating poor absorption and assimilation of nutrients. In allergic people where the brain is the target organ, all allergies affect their meridians that travel back and forth from brain, causing poor supply of energy, blood, and nutrients to the brain tissue. Because of this poor supply of essential nutrients, incomplete enzymes are produced causing improper brain function. Different parts of the brain may be affected in different people depending on the parts of nutrient(s) they are missing or the part(s) of the tissue that has been affected by the allergic reactions. In such people certain functions will be highly developed even though they may be completely non-functional in other areas. Some of these people can excel in math, playing certain musical instrument, drawing, painting, etc.

Most autistic children seem to be allergic to important brain enzymes or neurotransmitters such as dopamine, serotonin, adrenaline, nor-adrenaline and acetyl-choline. When a person is allergic to any substance, his/her body doesn't process that substance properly causing a deficiency or an accumulation of the substance. If the neuro-transmitters do not function properly, communication between the brain and different parts of the body does not take place properly causing abnormal or poor brain function. After eliminating the allergy to the neuro-transmitters, it is beneficial to supplement them with neuro-transmitters or precursors to neuro-transmitters for a while.

Symptomatic treatments are given to autistic children. If they are hyperactive, drugs are given to calm them. If they are too passive, stimulants are given. These drugs may help children to adjust to situations. However, they may not have long term effects. In fact if the child is allergic to the drug, it can do more damage to the already affected brain.

During the past decade many controversies and concerns have been raised about the use of medication for autistic children because children with autism have such severe allergies that they exhibit varying symptoms in varying degrees. As a result they respond differently to medications. Most autistic children are unable to report allergic reactions to their parents or caretakers due to their inability to communicate. If the parents and/or caretakers are taught Nambudripad's Testing Techniques (NTT) and MRT, parents can screen the medication for possible allergies before they administer it to the children. There is no harm in using drugs to handle appropriate situations as long as the person who administers the drug knows its purpose and the condition of the patient.

There are many books written on medications for autism, and since the autistic child needs to be under close supervision by a physician while on medication, parents are requested to check with the physician for more information on how to medicate or select the right medication for your child.

We now know that most of the causes of autism are in fact, undiagnosed allergies, which when left untreated, can become serious health problems in the future. An allergy is an over-reaction of the immune system. In NAET, allergies are viewed from a holistic perspective based on oriental medical principles.

When the body, or a magnetic field of the body, makes contact with an allergen, it causes blockages in the energy pathways called meridians. Put in another way, we can say, it disrupts the normal flow of energy through the body's electrical circuits. The energy flows in the body through the nerves with the help of various neurotransmitters. This energy blockage causes interference in appropriate neurotransmitter production and proper utilization causing poor communication between the brain, different parts of the body and the nervous system. The obstructed energy flow is the first step in a chain of events, which can develop into an allergic response. An allergic reaction is the result of continuous energy imbalances in the body, leading to a diminished state of health in one or more organs.

The spleen and liver meridians are most commonly affected in autistic people, the other meridians and related organs receiving disturbed energy flow are lungs, stomach, heart, gall bladder, small intestine, kidneys, and large intestine. NAET uses NTT to test the allergens and to detect blockages in meridians - Refer to Chapter Three. In some cases, all of the above meridians are affected by allergens. In others, just one or two meridians are affected with most allergens. Yet in some other cases, every allergen affects random meridian(s) without any regular pattern. NAET can treat all of these types with ease.

A DIAGNOSTIC EVALUATION OF AUTISM BY NAET SHOULD INCLUDE

■ A thorough medical and family history, pre-natal history of the mother (if she suffered from any potentially related condition or emotional trauma during pregnancy, etc.), emotional, social and environmental history (parental divorce, child abuse, death of a loved one, environmental or residential disruption, a newcomer in the family or arrival of a new sibling).

■ Behavior ratings completed by parents and teacher.

■ A physical examination (vital signs, etc.).

■ List of commonly consumed foods and drinks, commonly used clothes, chemicals in the environment, exposure to pesticides, immunizations, vaccinations, medications, any special addictions to toys, blankets, and furniture, etc. (could be allergic to any one of them).

■ Muscle Response Testing for possible allergens in relation to associated blocked organs.

■ A computerized non-invasive testing for possible allergens.

■ Heart Rate Variability test

■ Blood serum study either by ELIZA or ALCAT test.

WESTERN APPROACHES

Western medical approaches for such conditions are:
In less severe cases:

■ Behavior modification

■ Educational modification

■ Psychological counseling

■ Pharmaceutical drugs

In extremely severe cases none of the above works except pharmaceutical drugs to calm them down.

Medication has proven temporarily effective but does not provide long-term cure for many children with autism. It has been found helpful in alleviating the symptoms in some children and adults who take the medication. Some autistic children suffer from seizure disorders. Such children may need medication to keep their seizures under control. If there are no side effects, it is permissible to use medication to help the child function. But it is very important to check for an allergy to the medication before administering it. If the child is allergic to the drug, it is not going to give the expected results. In some children an allergy to drugs could make their condition worse. They may become hyper, violent, irritable beyond control, and may display unpleasant side effects like itching, hives, eczema, indigestion, bowel and bladder incontinence, bleeding from various parts of the body, etc. In such cases, medication must be stopped immediately and should not be used again until the allergy is eliminated.

In my experience, autistic children are usually allergic to many foods and chemicals they use in their daily lives. Some children may outgrow these allergic symptoms or change their symptoms into something totally new depending on the course of obstructed meridians on that particular day.

Even though western medical practitioners are using thoroughly researched pharmaceutical drugs, they are chemical compounds, which can have related allergy and side effects in certain individuals. The allergic reactions and side effects have created constant fear in some people discouraging them from using drugs. More and more people are becoming negative about taking drugs and are using natural products. Long term use of drugs can destroy the body's garbage disposal – the Liver—sometimes such damages are irreversible or very slow to reverse.

ALTERNATIVE THERAPIES

Practitioners and consumers are looking for natural means to control this disorder. Out of necessity, many alternative therapies have been developed and are available for autistic children today that produce inner calm and serenity in the victims without the usage of drugs.

These alternative therapies include:

Behavior modification in conjunction with:

- Vitamin-mineral therapy.
- Amino-acid therapy.
- Fatty Acid therapy.
- Various detoxification programs to remove toxins and parasites.
- Herbal supplementation, biofeedback, and living in a chemical-free environment.
- Diet management (removing sugar, artificial sweeteners, corn, gluten, milk, dairy products, yeast, food additives, food colors, and carbonated water from the diet entirely).
- Providing regular chiropractic and acupuncture treatments.
- Regular therapeutic massages, saunas.

- Encouraging Yoga and meditation practices.
- Magnetic therapy.
- Engaging in regular sports and exercise programs.
- Nambudripad's Allergy Elimination Treatments to maintain a balance between liver and spleen meridians by eliminating all possible allergies from his/her immediate environment.

NAET has proven to be the most effective allergy elimination treatment available so far.

THE STEPS OF NAET TREATMENT

Step-1

Isolate the offending allergen using NTT (Nambudripad's Testing Techniques - see Chapter three), comparing the strength of a particular muscle in the body in the presence and absence of a suspected allergen. It is also called Muscle Response Testing, slightly different from MRT as in applied kinesiology. A computerized skin resistance test is used with allergens and the use of standardized laboratory tests RAST, ELIZA (enzyme-linked immunozorbant assay), evaluation by HRV, etc., is encouraged.

Step-2

Mild acupressure on specific pre-determined acupuncture points by the practitioner on the specific meridians.

Step-3

Complete avoidance of the treated allergen for 25 hours following the treatment or otherwise determined by the practitioner. After 25 hours, the practitioner needs to retest the treated allergen to determine the completeness of the treatment. In most cases, it takes one treatment per single group of allergen (one office visit) to eliminate the allergy, if the treatment is administered properly and the 25-hour avoidance period is properly followed. In some extreme cases, it may take more than one office visit per group of items.

Avoiding the allergens is not always easy. In fact, it can be very cumbersome. The most effective treatment option for allergies until now has been complete avoidance of the offending allergens, which can be difficult and in some cases, impossible.

Can you imagine being on a diet month after month and year after year, especially if that diet contains no egg, soy, fruits, vegetables, wheat, corn, rice, sugar, chocolate, fats, hamburgers, French fries, ice cream, milk, butter, oils, gluten, MSG, spices, whiten-all, food additives, and food colorings, etc.? That's where NAET comes in. NAET will accommodate our "21st century lifestyles." It doesn't mean that you should go out of your way to eat any junk food available after completing NAET treatments. You should eat normal, healthy, unprocessed food most of the time. Unhealthy but commonly eaten zesty foods like chocolate, pastry, cream pies, etc. should be eaten once in a while only.

NAET can remove the adverse effect of any allergic food in the body and create homeostasis in the presence of the offending allergen (without avoiding it for life). During the NAET treatment, your brain will create a new friendly memory for the allergen and will imprint and store this new memory in your memory bank. During this proce: he old memory of the allergen's adverse effect is erased or forgotten. After completion of the NAET treatment, the allergen becomes a non-allergen, and an irritant becomes a non-irritant to your energy field. The body will learn to relax naturally in the presence of the new friendly substance. When the brain is not frightened about the contact with the new harmless substance (previously an allergen), natural calmness comforts the brain.

SUPPORTIVE TREATMENTS

Feed Your Brain

Start the day with this special rejuvenating brain tonic. Make sure the autistic person is allergy-free to the following ingredients before you prepare the food. If you find an allergy to one or two items, please exclude them from the drink until you clear the allergy to them. Each of these nutrients enters the respective meridians and associated organs and helps to enhance the functions of the area by eliminating the energy blockages in those meridians.

1/4 teaspoon barley green powder (St, Sp, brain)

6 ounces of apple juice (Liver, GB, Colon)

1/4 teaspoon of flax seed powder (GB, blood vessels)

1 pinch of cinnamon (Lu, PC & TW)

1 tablespoonful of honey (brain & nervous system)

50 mgs B6 (brain & nervous system)
50 mgs B complex (brain & nervous system)
2 drops grape seed oil (brain)
2 drops olive leaf extract or 1 capsule (immune system)
1 drop oregano oil (blood purifier)
1 pinch of epsom salt (liver, colon, brain & nervous system)
1 ounce cranberry juice (kid & UB)
1 scoop Biopure (a well balanced multivitamin - mineral formula from Metagenics. The address of this company is in the Resources section, or you may substitute any well balanced multivitamin-mineral formula).
2 tablespoonsful of prune juice (SI & LI).

Blend all the ingredients and drink six ounces once a day preferably in the morning after breakfast.

Brain Release

The child lies on his/her back. The mother/helper sits next to his/her head, supporting the head in her left palm as in diagram 9-1. Find the point just above the eyebrows on the forehead and with the right palm lightly massage up to the top of the head while the child breathes in. When you get to the top of the head, gently release the hand and the child breathes out. Do this sweeping massage three times. Turn the head to one side. Support the head on the bottom side with one palm, cupping the ear with the supporting palm (for eg. the left ear and side of the head), massage gently up the side of the cheek in front of the opposite ear (the side facing up, here for eg. in front of the the right ear), while the child breathes in. Do both sides this way three times each. Then cradle the head in both hands and hold it there for 30 seconds then release it. Finally, massage or rub the vertex or the top of the head for 30 seconds as in Fig. 9-2. This massage helps to get rid of the toxins from the brain.

Figure 9-1

BRAIN RELEASE

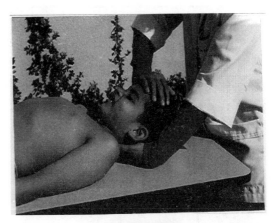

FIGURE 9-1
BRAIN RELEASE

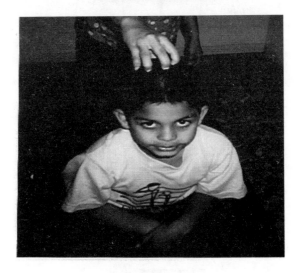

FIGURE 9-2

Vertex Massage

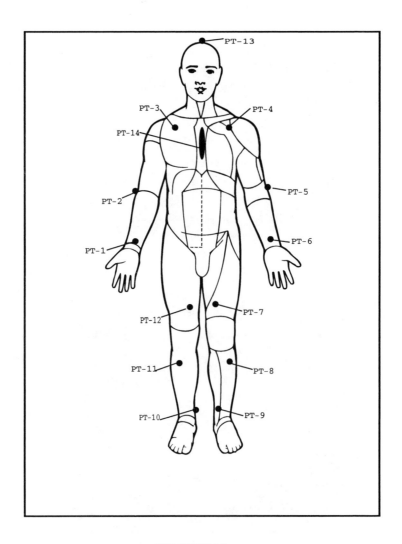

FIGURE 9-3

ACUPOINT MASSAGE

Acu-Point Massage

The right way to begin the day for an autistic child is with an acu-point massage using the acupoints as shown in the diagram 9-3. Simply apply gentle finger pressure on the points in the order given in the diagram. Fifteen seconds on each point twice a day, in the morning when waking up and before going to sleep. Begin from point 1 in the diagram and go in order to point 12 and finish up in the right hand at point1. This will encourage the energy to move in the right clockwise direction. When the energy circulates in the right direction, it will stabilize the body by bringing the body function into a homeostasis. The points are numbered in the right order of treatment for easy understanding. This is to balance the body only. It is not an NAET treatment. You don't have to make the autistic person hold the allergen while doing the technique.

Figure 9-4

Cross crawl

Cross-Crawl

Usually the balance between the left and right   ~s of
the brain is altered in an autistic child or adult. This is known
as switching. There are several reasons why one gets unbalanced or switched. Some of the common causes are anxiety,
fear, lack of liquids in the body and allergies. Hydrating the
patient alone helps to balance the two hemispheres most of
the time. The kinesiological exercise "cross-crawl" as given
in diagram 9-4 has been used for decades by kinesiologists to
balance the left and right brain very effectively.

Methodology

The child lies down in a supine position (on his back).
Make the child lift his/her right hand 90 degrees to the body
and the left leg 45-90 degrees to the body. Hold for 10 seconds, then relax. The child then lifts his/her left-hand 90 degrees to the body and right leg 45-90 degrees to the body.
Hold for 10 seconds, then relax. This completes one cycle.
Repeat this cycle five times in the morning and five times in
the evening.

Meridian Balancing

Have a set of meridian therapy cards, an energy chart
or look at the travel pathways of twelve acupuncture meridians in Chapter Seven of this book or Chapter 10 in "Say
Good-bye to Illness," by the author. Meridian therapy cards
and meridian charts are available from the NAET website
store: www.naet.com. Gently trace the meridians bilateral on
your child's body from the beginning of the first meridian of

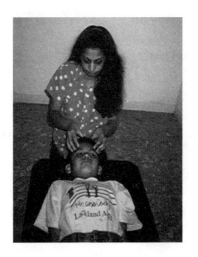

Figure 9-5

THE CEPHALIC RUB

the energy cycle (Lung meridian) to the last one (Liver meridian). Run your fingers over the meridians with a gentle caressing action toward their flow (marked with 'start' and 'end' in the beginning and end of the meridians and an arrow denoting the flow along the black long lines on the meridian therapy cards). Follow the order of the meridians as given in Chapter Seven. Do once a day, preferably at bedtime. This helps to calm all the nerves in the body by removing the energy blockages from the energy pathways by gentle massage towards the flow of meridians.

The Cephalic Rub

According to Chinese medical principles, all Yang meridians pass through the head traveling close to the superficial level reporting each and every energetic activity of every instant to the brain. All Yin meridians also pass through the head at a deeper level supporting and confirming the finding of their counterparts, Yang meridians, according to *Tang Dynasty physician Sun Si-Mo, "The three hundred connecting channels all rise to the head."* When you massage the whole head gently with a kneading movement, you are in fact invigorating all the energy meridians forcing the energy blockages to come out of the meridians and helping the energy to circulate freely through the energy pathways. When the energy circulates freely, blood circulation improves by allowing the oxygen and nutrients to reach every part of the brain evenly.

A-fifteen-minute massage, once every other day will help to nourish and stabilize the brain. After the head massage the person should lie down flat for an hour allowing the energy to concentrate in the brain tissues. The best time to do this head massage is before bedtime. The massage can be done using massage olive oil and coconut oil. Pioneer medical experts believed massaging with nourishing nutrients would help to nourish the brain faster. Massaging once a week with clarified butter, cooked mung bean paste or cooked brown rice with a few drops of grape seed oil and olive oil is beneficial in some cases. Method: Cook brown rice or mung bean with the skin still on. After bringing it to room temperature blend it with a few drops of grape seed oil and olive oil. Massage the whole head for 15 minutes with this nutrient paste once a week. Wait for 30 minutes to an hour, then wash the head thoroughly and dry it.

THYMUS STIMULATION

Thymus gland stimulation helps to improve the immune system reducing the allergic reactions. Since autistic children have poor immune systems and severe allergies, thymus stimulation has been very helpful in improving their immune system. A simple clockwise, gentle massage on the thymus gland for 1 minute daily preferably in the morning will be helpful. For location of the area refer to Figure 9-6.

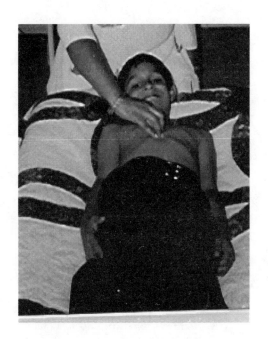

Figure 9-6

THYMUS STIM

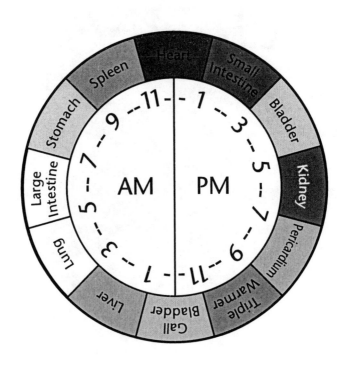

Figure 9-7
Meridian Clock

Meridian Clock

When the energy is blocked in a certain meridian, the affect of the blockage can be felt at its worst during the corresponding time of the meridian. When a person does not feel good, look at the meridian clock to find the corresponding meridian according to the time. Find the meridian pathway from Chapter 7 and apply gentle strokes using your finger pads along the flow of meridian from the beginning point towards the end point of the meridian to guide the blocked energy into the circulation. When the blockage is manually pushed forward, energy circulation will be re-established and you will feel better.

FOOD FOR A HEALTHY BRAIN
AND
NERVOUS SYSTEM

Autistic people have sluggish liver and spleen function, which leads to poor energy circulation in those areas. Foods with warming properties should be eaten more often to improve the energy flow to liver and spleen meridians and organs.

There are some suggestions for foods that can help your brain and nervous system. Please make sure your child is not allergic to these foods. If you find your child allergic to these foods, please take your child to an NAET practitioner to get him/her treated for the allergy to the item.

Grains: Brown rice, whole rolled oats, oat cereal, barley and millet. Wheat should be used with caution or after clearing the allergy since wheat and gluten are strong allergens to most people. Encourage more complex carbohydrates but if complex carbohydrates are hard to digest, semi-complex carbohydrates should be used initially. Semi-carbohydrates are easy to digest for people with allergies. Corn is a strong allergen to many. So caution should be applied when using cornstarch or products.

Dried Beans: Azuki beans, black beans, green mung beans, lentils, split peas and soy beans.

Vegetable proteins: Tofu, lentils, whey protein, tahini, butter, sesame, and sunflower butter.

Proteins: Lean meat, chicken, turkey, and fish.

Protein substitute: Good protein substitutes are available in the market. Any good product without allergy is ideal.

Vegetables: broccoli, cabbage, carrots, turnips, radish, cauliflower, spinach, onions, garlic, mushroom, shitake mushroom, green beans, beets, kholrabi, wintersquash, yams, sweet potato, cucumber, plantains, kale, dark leafy greens.

Fruits: dried raisins, prunes, figs, fresh apples, pears, peaches, prunes, dates, etc. one serving a day. Avoid eating too many raw fruits.

Juices and drinks: Vegetable juices and broths are preferred to fruit juices. Fruit juices should be taken in minimum quantity (four to six ounces daily). Eating many fruits, and sugar products, drinking a lot of fruit juices etc., can encourage candida growth. Autistic people are susceptible for candida-yeast overgrowth. After NAET, it is okay to have them in moderation. Herbal tea can be used as needed. Avoid carbonated drinks. Instead drink 5-6 glasses of purified or boiled cooled water daily.

Dairy: a couple of tablespoons of yogurt a day should be taken. Non fat or low fat milk is preferred. Clarified butter is preferred to real butter, and use sparingly.

Flesh foods: organically raised preferred. Beef once a week. Fowl, fish once or twice a week.

Cooking oils: Sesame oils, olive oils and clarified butter.

Dried or fresh herbs: Use as needed.

Spices and salt: As you need

Water: Purified water or boiled, cooled water 4-6 glasses daily

Herbal Remedy

1. **The Lindera formula** 1/2 gram x 2, 30 minutes after meals for children between the ages of 2- 10 years. For older children and adults adjust the dosage to 2 grams daily or follow the suggested dosage on the bottle.
(available at Lotus herbs. Address is given below).

2. **Agastache** 1 capsule x 2 daily after major meals.

3. **Sesame seed oil** or flax seed oil - 1/4 teaspoon daily for age 2-10 years; 1/2 teaspoon sesame seed oil daily for people older than 10 years.

4. **Cooked, pureed asparagus** one ounce daily for children between the ages of 2-10 years.
Cooked, pureed asparagus two-three ounces daily for children over ten years of age.

5. **Cooked mung beans** one to two ounces once daily. (tonifies and nourishes the brain, helps to balance the neurotransmitters).

6. **Minor Rhubarb formula** 1/2-1gram or as needed (adjust dosage according to the age and size of the person) once a week after supper to cleanse the digestive system. This will act like a laxative, but this will cleanse and detox the whole digestive system without causing depletion of vitamin-minerals or essential nutrients from the body.

Suggested dosage: 1/2 gram once a week 30 minutes after supper between the ages of 3- 10 years. For older children and adults adjust the dosage to 1-1/2 grams daily or follow the suggested dosage on the bottle.

All of the above should be checked for allergy and if found, should be eliminated with NAET prior to giving to the children. These herbal remedies are effective to reduce brain allergies and restore the function of the neurotransmitters. Find out the correct dosage and the length of supplementation for the individual child or adult using the method, "How to test and adjust the dosage of vitamins herbs, and medication" described in the NAET Guide Book. Always test for allergies before using it.

The NAET Guide Book is available at www.naet.com. bookstore.

The Chinese herbal formula is available at the following address. If you have questions about Chinese herbs you may request to talk to their herbal consultant. He/she will be happy to assist you with more information on herbs.

Lotus Herbs,
1124 N. Hacienda Blvd.
La Puente, CA 91626
(626) 916-1070

CHAPTER 10

NAET
AND
AUTISM

10

NAET AND AUTISM

C hildren and adults suffering from the symptoms of autism are usually allergic to the following food groups, which are listed according to their importance for the body. It is necessary to follow the restricted diet and your NAET specialist's instructions carefully during the 25 hours after the treatment in order to clear for the allergen being treated. You may also refer to the "NAET Guide Book" for more information on NAET treatments and specific instructions to follow during the 25 hour-avoidance period.

Most autistic children and adults can get their symptoms under control when they complete the NAET basic 30-45 groups of allergens successfully. Some autistic children and adults with mild to moderate symptoms may show marked improvements after they complete just five basic groups of allergens. But it is to their advantage to complete the 35-40 groups of allergens before they stop the treatments.

After treating each group of allergens, after 25 hours, each item should be tested individually to be certain that the treatment has been completed. Some children may need repeated treatments on egg white, egg yolk etc.

The 25 hour-food restriction should be observed on all treatments. Autistic children tend to fall out of treatments when the allergens are not avoided for 25 hours. In some children I have observed that it is necessary to avoid the treated food allergen for 30 hours. This may be due to the fact that autistic children have extremely fatigued and diminished brain function.

1. Egg Mix (egg white, egg yolk, chicken, and tetracycline.)
You may have brown or white rice, pasta without eggs, vegetables, fruits, milk products, oils, beef, pork, fish, coffee, juice, soft drinks, water, and tea.

To be checked individually: egg white, egg yolk, chicken, feather, tetracycline.

2. Calcium mix (breast milk, cow's milk, goat's milk, milk albumin, casein, coumarin, lactic acid and calcium)
You may have cooked rice, cooked fruits and vegetables (like potato, squash, green beans, yams, cauliflower, sweet potato), chicken, red meat, and drink coffee, tea without milk, and distilled or boiled, cooled water.

To be checked individually: Milk albumin, milk casein.

3. Vitamin C (fruits, vegetables, vinegar, citrus, and berry.)
You may have cooked white or brown rice, pasta without sauce, boiled or poached eggs, baked or broiled chicken, fish, red meat, brown toast, deep fried food, French fries, salt, oils, coffee without milk, and water.

4. B complex vitamins (17 B vitamins.)

You may have cooked white rice, cauliflower raw or cooked, well cooked or deep fried fish, salt, white sugar, black coffee, French fries, and purified, non allergic water. Rice should be washed well before cooking. It should be cooked in lots of water and drained well to remove the fortified vitamins.

To be checked individually: B1, B3, B6, choline, inositol.

5. Sugar Mix (cane sugar, corn sugar, maple sugar, grape sugar, rice sugar, brown sugar, beet sugar, fructose, molasses, honey, dextrose, glucose, and maltose.)

You may have white rice, pasta, vegetables, vegetable oils, meats, eggs, chicken, water, coffee, tea without milk.

To be individually checked for all sugars.

6. Iron Mix (animal and vegetable sources, beef, pork, lamb, raisin, date, and broccoli.)

You may have white rice without iron fortification, sour dough bread without iron, cauliflower, white potato, chicken, light green vegetables (white cabbage, iceberg lettuce, white squash), yellow squash, distilled water and orange juice.

7. Vitamin A (animal and vegetable source, beta carotene, fish and shellfish.)

You may have cooked rice, pasta, potato, cauliflower, red apples, chicken, water, and coffee without milk.

To be checked individually for: fish mix, shellfish mix, beta carotene.

8. Mineral Mix (magnesium, manganese, phosphorus, selenium, zinc, copper, cobalt, chromium, molybdenum, trace minerals, gold, mercury, lead, cadmium, aluminum, arsenic, copper, gold, silver, vanadium and fluoride.)

You may use only distilled water for washing, drinking, and showering. You may eat only cooked rice, vegetables, fruits, meats, eggs, milk, coffee, and tea. No root vegetables.

9. Magnesium

10. Salt Mix (sodium and sodium chloride.)
You may use distilled water for drinking and washing, cooked rice, fresh vegetables and fruits (except celery, carrots, beets, artichokes, romaine lettuce, and watermelon) meats, chicken, and sugars.

11. Corn Mix (blue corn, yellow corn, cornstarch, cornsilk, corn syrup.)

You may eat only steamed vegetables, steamed rice, broccoli, baked chicken, and meats. You may drink water, tea and/or coffee without cream or sugar.

12. Grain Mix (wheat, gluten, gliadin, coumarin, rye, oats, millet, barley, and rice.)

You may eat vegetables, fruits, meats, milk, and drink water. Avoid all products with gluten.

To be checked for: wheat, gluten, gliadin, coumarin, corn, oats, millet, barley, rye, and rice.

13. Artificial Sweeteners (Sweet and Low, Equal, saccharine, Twin, and aspartame.)

You may eat anything without artificial sweeteners. Use freshly prepared items only.

14. Yeast Mix (brewer's yeast, and bakers yeast, tortula yeast, acidophilus, yogurt, and whey.)

To be individually checked for: brewer's yeast, baker's yeast, whey, yogurt, and acidophilus.

You may have vegetables, egg, meat, chicken, and fish. No fruits, no sugar products. Drink distilled water.

15. Stomach acid (Hydrochloric acid.)

You may eat raw and steamed vegetables, cooked dried beans, eggs, oils, clarified butter, and milk.

16. Base (digestive juice from the intestinal tract contains various digestive enzymes: amylase, protease, lipase, maltase, peptidase, bromelain, cellulase, sucrase, papain, lactase, gluco-amylase, and alpha galactosidase.)

You may eat sugars, starches, breads, and meats.

17. Neurotransmitters: adrenaline, nor-adrenaline, serotonin, and acetylcholine.

18. Immunizations and Vaccinations: either you received or your parent received before you were born. Test them individually and if found treat them individually.

(MMR (measles, mumps, rubella), DPT (diphtheria, pertussis, tetanus), Polio vaccine, Small pox, Chickenpox, Influenza, hepatitis-B, hepatitis C.)

Each one of them should be checked and treated individually if it was found to be an allergen. Nothing to avoid while treating for these except infected persons or recently inoculated persons if there are any near you. MMR and DPT should be treated for the individual components since allergic reactions to these vaccines are causing imbalances in the brain in many children.

19. Pesticides (malathion, termite control chemicals, or regular pesticides.)
Avoid meats, uncooked vegetables and fruits, grasses, trees and flowers in the public areas where pesticides have been sprayed, ant sprays, insecticides, and other pesticides.

20. Alcohol (candy, ice cream, liquid medication in alcohol, and alcohol.)
Whether or not you drink alcohol, your body needs it. Alcohol is made from refined starches and other form of sugars. Many people are allergic to sugar and thus alcohol.

You may eat vegetables, meats, fish eggs, and chicken. Avoid hairspray, after shave, homeopathic remedies with alcohol.

Collect different food groups from every meal and treat for the mixture of breakfast, lunch and dinner. Collect this combined food sample at least four times a month and treat using NAET.

21. Coffee Mix (coffee, chocolate, caffeine, tannic acid, cocoa, cocoa butter, and carob.)

You may eat anything that has no coffee, caffeine, chocolate and/or carob.

22. Nut Mix 1 (peanuts, black walnuts, or English walnuts.)
You may eat any foods that do not contain the nuts listed above including their oils and butter.

23. Nut Mix 2 (cashew, almonds, pecan, Brazil nut, hazelnut, macadamia nut, and sunflower seeds.)

You may eat any foods that do not contain the nuts listed above including their oils and butters.

24. Spice Mix 1 (ginger, cardamon, cinnamon cloves, nutmeg, garlic, cumin, fennel, coriander, turmeric, saffron, and mint.)

You may use all foods and products without these items.

25. Spice Mix 2 (peppers, red pepper, black pepper, green pepper, jalapeno, banana peppers, anise seed, basil, bay leaf, caraway seed, chervil, cream of tartar, dill, fenugreek, horseradish, mace, MSG, mustard, onion, oregano.)

You may eat or use all foods and food products without the above listed spices.

26. Animal Fats (butter, lard, chicken fat, beef fat, lamb fat, and fish oil.)

You may use anything other than the above including vegetable oils.

27. Vegetable Fats (corn oil, canola oil, peanut oil, linseed oil, sunflower oil, palm oil, flax seed oil, and coconut oil.)

You may use steamed vegetables, steamed brown or white rice, pasta, meats, eggs, chicken, butter, and animal fats.

28. Vitamin F (Linseed oil, flax seed oil, sesame seed oil, grape seed oil, evening primrose oil, borage oil, wheat germ oil.)

You may eat anything that does not contain vegetable oils, wheat germ oil, linseed oil, sunflower oil, soybean oil, safflower oil, peanuts and peanut oil.

29. Dried Bean Mix (vegetable proteins, soybean, and lecithin.)

You may eat rice, pasta, vegetables, meats, eggs, and anything other than beans and bean products.

30. Amino Acids-1 (essential amino acids: lysine, methionine, leucine, threonine, valine, tryptophane, isoleucine, and phenylalanine.)

You may eat cooked white rice, lettuce, and boiled chicken.

31. Amino Acids 2 (non essential amino acids: alanine, arginine, aspartic acid, carnitine citrulline, cysteine, glutamic acid, glycine, histidine, ornithine, proline, serine, taurine, and tyrosine.)

You may eat cooked white rice, boiled beef (corned beef), and iceberg lettuce.

32. Dimethyl Glycine
You may eat white rice, white flower pasta, lettuce, oils and clarified butter.

33. Food additives (sulfates, nitrates, BHT. whiten-all)
You cannot eat hotdogs or any pre-packaged food. Eat anything made at home from scratch.

34. Food colors (different food colors in many sources like: ice cream, candy, cookie, gums, drinks, spices, other foods, and/or lipsticks, etc.)

You may eat foods that are freshly prepared. Avoid carrots, natural spices, beets, berries, frozen green leafy vegetables like spinach.

The items listed below are treated as needed and on a priority based protocol, which your NAET practitioner will explain to you.

35. Night-shade vegetables (bell pepper, onion, eggplant, potato, tomato (fruits, sauces, and drinks.)

Avoid eating these vegetables.

36. Starch Complex (Grains, root vegetables.)

You may have all vegetables except root vegetables, grains, yogurt, meats, chicken, and fish.

Refined starches are used as a thickening agent in sauces and drinks. Many people are allergic to starches. Refined starches should be avoided.

37. Drugs: Any drugs given in infancy, during childhood or taken by the mother during pregnancy.
antibiotics (Individual antibiotics), sedatives, laxatives recreational drugs.

38. Hormones (estrogen, progesterone, testosterone)
You may eat vegetables, fruits, grains, chicken, and fish.

39. Baking powder/ Baking soda (in baked goods, toothpaste, and/or detergents, yogurt, cosmetics.)

Avoid the items with baking powder and soda. You may eat or use anything that does not contain baking powder or baking soda including fresh fruits, vegetables, fats, meat, and chicken.

40. School work materials (crayons, coloring paper and books, inks, pencils, crayons, glue, play dough, other arts, and craft materials.)

Avoid using them or contacting them. Wear a pair of gloves if you have to go near them.

41. Fabrics (daily wear, sleep attire, towels, bed linens, blankets, formaldehyde.)

Treat each kind of fabric separately and avoid the particular cloth or kind of cloth for 25 hours.

42. Water (drinking water, tap water, filtered water, city water, lake water, rain water, ocean water, and river water.)
People can react to any water. Treat them as needed and avoid the item treated. Drink boiled cooled water during 25 hours following the treatment.

43. Chemicals (chlorine, swimming pool water, detergents, fabric softeners, soaps, cleaning products, shampoos, lipsticks, and cosmetics you or other family members use.)

Avoid the above items.

44. Plastics (toys, play or work materials, utensils, toiletries, computer key boards, and/or phone.)

Avoid contact with products made from plastics. Wear a pair of cotton gloves.

45. Hypothalamus
Nothing to avoid.

46. Brain Tissue
Nothing to avoid.
47. Parts of the brain: Cranial nerves, different lobes, gyrus, sympathetic and parasympathetic nerves, thalamus, hippocampus, corpus callosum, striatum, substantia nigra.)

48. Other brain enzymes: Secretin, cytokinine, dopamine, histamine, endorphin, enkephalin.

49. Perfume mix (room deodorizers, soaps, flowers, perfumes, or after-shave, etc.).

Avoid perfume and any fragrance from flowers or products containing perfume.

50. Gelatin
You may use anything that does not contain gelatin.

51. Gum Mix (Acacia, Karaya gum, Xanthiane gum, black gum, sweet gum, and chewing gum).

You may eat rice, pasta, vegeatables, fruits without skins, meats, eggs, and chicken, drink juice and water.

52. Paper Products (newspaper, newspaper ink, reading books, coloring books, books with colored illustrations).

Avoid the above items.

53. Fluoride
You may use or eat fruits, poultry, meat, potato, cauliflower, white rice, and yellow vegeatables. You may use distilled water, drink fresh fruit juices.

54. Vitamin E
You may eat fresh fish, carrots, potato, poultry, and meat.

55. Vitamin D
You may eat fruits, vegetables, poultry, and meats.

56. Vitamin K
You may eat fish, rice, potato, poultry, and meat.

57. Insect bites in infancy or childhood (bee stings, spider bites, or cockroach, etc.)

Treat for the individual insect and avoid it while treating.

58. Latex (shoe, sole of the shoe, elastic, rubber bands, and/or rubber bathtub toys.)

Avoid latex products.

59. Radiation (computer, television, microwave, X-ray, and the sun).

Avoid radiation of any kind.

60. Inhalants
Pollens, weeds, grasses, flowers, wood mix, room air, outside air, smog, cold (ice cube), heat (hot water in a glass bottle), dryness (heat up a piece of cotton towel on stove-top or in a microwave oven for a few seconds and put it in a glass jar with a lid to make the sample of dry heat), dampness (use a piece of wet cloth or paper towel along with a piece of ice cube in a glass jar to make this sample), and polluted air from nearby factories (place a piece of wet cloth in a flat open plate or container in the open air for 6-8 hours where the polluted

circulates and put it in a glass jar with lid immediately after removing from the plate), to make this sample.

61. Tissues and secretions (DNA, RNA, thyroid hormone, pituitary hormone, pineal gland, liver, urine, blood, and saliva)

Treat these items individually if needed. Avoid touching your own body. Wear a pair of gloves for 25 hours.

62. Allergies to people, animals and pets (mother, father, care takers, cats, and dogs)

Avoid the ones you were treated for 25 hours.

63. Emotional allergies (fear, fright, frustration, anger, low self-esteem, and/or rejection, etc.)

There is nothing to avoid for emotional treatment.

64. Other substances:

Cerebrospinal fluid, blood, parasites, other foods, environmental agents, detergent, handwashing soap, bed linen, night clothes, plastic toys on the crib, remote control for T.V., alarm clock on the bedside table, etc need to be checked for allergies.

After clearing the allergy to nutrients, appropriate supplementation with vitamins, minerals, herbs, enzymes etc., is necessary to make up the deficiency and promote healing. Please check with your NAET practi-

tioner or read the guidebook for information on how to take supplenents correctly.

Your NAET doctor will also do a few energy boosting and balancing techniques with vitamin B complex, calcium, vitamin F, neurotransmitters, sugar, trace minerals, and magnesium, etc. This should be done under proper supervision and you need to discuss this with your practitioner.

CHAPTER 11

AUTISM
CASE STUDIES

11

AUTISM: CASE STUDIES

The year was 1987. It was 11: 45 p.m on a winter night. I was still awake when the phone rang. It was Ray from Chicago. Ray is a good friend of our family. I was alarmed by his call, but I knew that he must have had a good reason to phone at such a late hour.

My first question was "Is everything okay with Anne?" (A year and a half ago, Ray's daughter, 9-year-old Anne had a severe anaphylactic reaction to peanuts and was in a coma for three months. Later with the help of NAET, she came out of coma and was able to lead an almost a normal life.)

"Yes," said Ray. "Anne is perfectly okay. Thanks to you and NAET, but I would like to discuss my dear friend Bob's son, Steve with you. He paused for a moment. "I didn't realize it was so late," he said apologetically. "If you like I can call tomorrow with my questions."

"It's perfectly okay," I said calmly trying to hide my curiosity. "I am not sleepy yet. Tell me about Bob and Steve and how I might be of help?"

"Bob and I went to school together," he continued, "after high school, we went different ways. He became a lawyer and I chose to become a scientist. After many years, I met Bob. He appeared very sad. During our conversation he told me about his tragic story. His only son Steve, who is ten-years old, had been diagnosed as severely autistic six years ago. I told him about Anne, you, your timely discovery of NAET and how it saved my daughter, etc." He paused again, then asked, "Do you think NAET could help with autism?"

"I haven't treated any autistic children, but there is always a first time. If it is allergy-related, it could help. No one knows the exact cause of autism, anyway," I said.

"Bob practices in New York. Do you think he should bring Steve to Los Angeles to see you for a few weeks?"

"NAET can't harm him." I said. "If it helped with peanut-anaphylaxis and brought Anne out of a coma, I am sure NAET is powerful enough to treat autism or anything else. If his autism is allergy-related, I am sure he will be helped. After I observe and test him I will be able to say more positively whether NAET would work in his situation. Yes, bring the child here and we will see what we can do."

The next week, Bob, Steve and Mary arrived with 10-year-old Steve, who looked well nourished and strongly built. I introduced myself and I held out my hand. The boy stood there staring at the wall. He was not aware of my presence. He was not aware of anything around him. He was in another world.

According to his father, Steve was normal until he was 18-months-old. He was speaking not only words clearly, but also short sentences. Every day, he used to wait along with his mother at the gate for his dad to return from work in the evening. He was the key-keeper. He would take the car key from his father and place it on a key-stand on the desk. In the morning when he was ready to leave, Steve would bring the key and put it in the key hole for dad. He was very intelligent. Then suddenly one day he had an attack of the flu, which lasted for a week; when he recovered he had lost his speech and mental capabilities.

Bob became emotional and couldn't speak for a few seconds. He wiped his tears and said, "He couldn't even say 'Mom' or 'Dad' after that."

I looked at the mother and then the father; both were controlling their tears. I was fighting tears myself. They were anxiously looking at me waiting for a verdict.

I felt uneasy because I had never treated anyone with autism before. I was going to experiment on him, but I couldn't tell them that. I didn't have words to console them. Could I give them hope or not? What if NAET didn't work on autism? Then my seven-year-old son barged into the room and asked, "Mommy, why can't this boy play with me? He won't talk to me. Can't you tell him to play with me?"

I saw the shadows of sadness flooding on Bob's and Mary's faces. I fumbled for words. "Well, son," I said. "He is not feeling very well today. He has allergies. When his allergies go away, he will become like you, Then he will play with you," and I said to the parents, "Why don't I test a few allergens and see if he has any allergies."

When I looked at my calm and concerned seven-year-old son (he was very attention-deficit and hyperactive and restless from the age of 18 months till he was six) and then the severely autistic ten-year-old Steve, a wave of deep pain pierced through my heart. I felt very emotional for a few minutes. My son might have been like Steve if I hadn't discovered NAET. God was certainly a lot kinder towards me and my family than he was towards Bob and his family.

I learned to test for allergies using MRT when my son was 16 months old. He was an allergic baby from birth. He was allergic to many foods, fabrics and chemicals. He used to have hives and runny nose frequently those days. But he was intelligent, calm, very matured for his age and probably beyond his age in understanding. He began walking when he was 7-months-old. He started talking in words and short sentences when he was 13-months-old. I started my medical education (chiropractic and acupuncture) when he 10-months-old. Attending two schools simultaneously didn't leave me much free time to play with him. But without any complaints, he sat near me quietly reading his own baby books while I studied mine. He never disrupted me while I studied, or destroyed any papers or his books. As he grew older he helped me to fold clothes, dry dishes, and bake cookies and cakes, etc. We went to the park every evening where he enjoyed feeding the ducks in the lake. He carried popcorn and bread to the lake. By the time he was fifteen months he knew his alphabet fluently and he could count to one hundred clearly. But when he was eighteen months old, he received the booster shot of DPT. He had mild fever (100 degrees F) for two days and his arm hurt when it was touched. After two days, his temperature was okay but his energy was still low. Two weeks after his DPT booster shot, he began flu-like symptoms and fever of 103-104 degrees everyday for 1 month. Thank God I knew how to test for allergies by MRT by then! I found him allergic to antibiotics and did not give him the antibiotics that the doctor prescribed for him. Instead, I found some Chinese herbal antibiotics that he was not allergic to. I also gave him Tylenol every four-six hours (he was not allergic to Tylenol), to keep his fever under control.

Roy was not the same ever since. He became very hyper, his vocabulary went down instead of getting better. He did not have the attention span as before. He began getting distructive by tearing books, newspaper, etc. He threw his toys all over and it was difficult to make him put them back in place. He was acting very wild and some of his friends began calling him "wild kid," etc. He forgot his alphabet and numbers. He became very hyperactive and unfocused. I began him on NAET treaments from the age of four. He was continuously treated until six and he became almost normal.

I had to teach him his alphabet and numbers all over again after he turned four. I remember the early years of his life between two and four, he had fever every day in spite of all the herbs and medications; he had a constant runny nose, hives, pain in the knees, severe cramps in the calf muscles, and pain in other joints, severe insomnia, temper tantrums, and he vomitted almost every meal he ate until I restricted his meals to cream of wheat, nonfat milk powder and water. They were the only things he was not allergic to at that time. On this restricted diet, he felt better.

Even after eliminating the allergy to DPT, he still continued to have mild residual symptoms: frequent respiratory problems like coughing, bronchitis and chronic insomnia. Another unusual symptom he noticed, four to five times a year, was a loss of memory for a moment while he watched T.V., for an hour or so continuously, or worked in front of the computer. I suspected a connection between the DPT booster shot and his strange behaviors all along. So I isolated the components of DPT (Diphtheria, Tetanus and Pertussis) and tested him again. Through NTT, I found pertussis was still causing his continuous health problems. He was treated for pertussis alone and in combination with brain, hypothalamus, nerves, lung tissue, and serotonin. He hasn't had any of the above residual symptoms for over a year now.

After many years, now when I think back and evaluate my son's condition, I have better understanding of the occurrences. Probably, when he got the booster dose of DPT, diphtheria reacted on him mildly causing pain, swelling and mild fever for a couple days and the symptoms subsided. The incubation period for diphtheria is only 2-6 days. But the incubation period for pertussis is 7-16 days. It took more than two weeks for pertussis to begin its action in his body. That was why his flu-like symptoms and fever started after two weeks.

The toxin produced by Pertussis affected his stomach, spleen, liver meridians and brain. The energy blockages in these meridians and associated organs caused his health disorders for the next two-three years until the allergy to the pertussis vaccine was eliminated.

Even though, the major symptoms were eliminated by treating by NAET on DPT, the minor residual symptoms continued until the pertussis was isolated and treated in combinations with the directly involved specific tissues as I stated earlier.

Many of the autistic children I have seen, had the history of the beginning of autism between the ages of 15 months to eighteen months. Most of the parents recalled their symptoms started after a "flu". This "flu" they are recalling may have been the reaction after the vaccination of DPT or MMR. Then according to the parents, all of them were treated with various antibiotics. These children may have been allergic to antibiotics. So when they took the antibiotics to fight off the mistaken "flu," the allergic reaction from the vaccination combined with the allergic reaction from the antibiotics together attacked the brain - the target organ; and the result was autism! Since I did not give my son the antibiotics he did not become autistic.

I learned muscle response testing to detect food allergies in acupuncture college. That changed my life..our lives. I wish everyone in the world could learn MRT and learn to test their allergies! If people learn how to test allergies using MRT, they could easily avoid the allergens until they find NAET to eliminate them. All the sicknesses arising from allergies would be reduced if you could just avoid them, even if you do not get treated. The "Touch for Health Organization," led by Dr. John F. Thie conducts lectures for the mass media through their continuous educational seminars. If people could over-come their skepticism and just pay attention to the holistic healing inventions, their suffering would be less severe.

Steve was allergic to almost everything. Amazingly, he sat through the computer testing without any trouble. Then we began NAET on him.

The first treatment was egg mix. The animal protein (egg mix) was causing energy blockages in his lung, small and large intestine meridians. Within two-three minutes of the first treatment, the egg mix, he began itching and developed hives all over the body. His face and ears turned red; cheeks be-came flushed. His body temperature rose to 101 degrees Fahr-enheit. After a few repeated spinal NAET (every 10 minutes for seven times), his face and ears returned almost to normal color, hives and rashes disappeared, temperature dropped to 98 degrees Fahrenheit and he fell asleep. His parents took him to the hotel.

The next day when I tested him, he had passed the egg mix, so I tested him for calcium mix. According to his mother, he craved milk and drank four to five glasses a day. The cal-cium mix (main component of this group is milk; other components are casein, albumin, globulin, cow's milk, goat's milk, and breast milk), caused energy blockages in liver and gall bladder meridians. I treated him for the calcium mix. Within a few minutes of this treatment, he began having spasms of his facial muscles, almost mimicking mild seizures. I was very nervous and shaky inside, but I couldn't show my nervousness. With a queasy stomach, I treated him eight more times every ten minutes. By the end of eight repeated NAET spinal stimulations, he began to yawn and his facial muscles relaxed and seizure-like movements stopped. He was sent home.

On the following day, he tested strong for calcium. The third treatment was for vitamin C mix. This caused energy blockages in the stomach, small intestine, urinary bladder and liver meridians. Everything went well until he was ready to leave. All of a sudden, he began acting violently, screaming and yelling, kicking his mother with his legs while she was trying to hold him. He had failed the treatment. He received the NAET treatments repeatedly five more times every ten minutes. Towards the end of the treatments, he became quiet. When I rechecked him, he was strong for the substance and he was sent home.

The next day, he tested strong for vitamin C mix. His mother reported that he slept through the night but wet his bed twice. The fourth treatment was for B vitamins. 15 B vitamins are in the sample. B complex caused energy blockages in his heart, stomach, spleen, liver, kidney and large intestine meridians. He became very restless and agitated during the treatment. I had to keep him in one room and repeat the spinal NAET every ten minutes for 11 more times until he began to relax. Then he fell asleep. After the 20 minutes waiting period, his parents had to carry him to the hotel.

Chapter 11: Autism Case Studies

The following morning, while I was treating a patient in the treatment room, I heard a child singing nursery rhymes in his loudest voice in the waiting room. I came out looking for the source. As far as I knew I didn't have a young child other than Steve in my waiting room. But to my amazement, it was Steve. I didn't expect such a miracle after just four treatments. He sat on his father's lap rocking himself gently and enjoyed singing the nursery rhymes without being aware of the surroundings. His father had a big smile on his face.

He began to talk nonstop from then on. He repeated everything one after the other that was taught or heard in his special school, from nursery rhyme stories, to the teacher's instructions. He remembered every line clearly. Until then nobody knew that he could even hear anything This clearly demonstrated that autistic children can hear everything that is said to them or around them even though they seem deaf or unresponsive. This taught us that they store everything in their memory to be recalled later. A branch of nerves that supplies the speech center gets blocked in autistic children. It would be beneficial if researchers could locate the nerve branch that is blocked in these cases. Since NAET is capable of removing nerve energy blockages, if someone could discover the nerves that are blocked in autistic children, the practitioners of NAET could unblock those specific nerves or specific nerve bundles to speed up the results.

But for some reason, Steve was able to remember and repeat things that were taught or heard in the school setting when he was with other children. I thought it was strange that he did not remember anything that his parents said to him, like their lullabies or bedtime stories. This could be due to two reasons: The parents might not have realized that he could hear, so they did not sing lullabies, or tell bedtime stories to him. So he didn't hear anything to remember or recall, or the autistic child could only remember what was taught in a group.

He did not hear us when we talked to him. He did not respond to any questions from his parents or from me. He continued to talk even in sleep. His father finally asked me, "Is there some way we can turn his voice box off? He talks constantly and loudly, causing all the neighbors in the hotel to be alarmed." He probably wanted to say that he was tired of listening to his constant talk, but he didn't say that.

I was confused and concerned. What turned his speech off initially? Now what turned it on? How am I going to turn it off again? Will I be ever able to do that? Which meridian is passing through the speech center? Which meridian is capable of unblocking and regulating the memory and speech? This is not taught specifically in any school.

I retested him for B complex; he had failed B vitamins. I tested him for all fifteen B vitamins individually to see if I could find any associations with his strange behavior. He had failed to pass B6 and choline. He had passed the rest of them completely. B6 caused energy blockages in spleen and kidney meridians and choline caused energy blockage in only the kidney meridian. I repeated NAET six more times every ten minutes for B6 and choline. He continued to talk incessantly. Towards the end of the treatments he became quiet and fell asleep as usual; his father's face also relaxed.

After 25 hours, when he passed the B vitamins, his voice box began to slow down. He continued to talk but not so loudly anymore. He was whispering or muttering things in a low voice. His father didn't mind that.

He was treated for sugar next, since sugar is essential for the assimilation and utilization of B vitamins. This caused energy blockages in his heart, stomach, spleen, kidney, liver, gall bladder and large intestine meridians. During treatment, he still continued to talk incessantly.

Suddenly, within the first ten minutes after the sugar treatment he became quiet. After 20 minutes, he fell asleep. By the next day, when he came to the office, his voice box was turned off naturally. He sat quietly and listened to people talking. He seemed to be hearing once again. He sat and listened to the conversations going on around him and stared at peoples faces as if he was seeing them for the first time.

When he was brought in to the examination room, I greeted him, "Good Morning!" He returned my greeting in a pleasant voice, "Good Morning!" He had a smile on his face. He looked at my face periodically. He was also circling in the room aimlessly.

I was surprised. I didn't expect such a quick transformation in him. "How do you feel today, Steve?" I asked him again. "How do you feel today, Steve?" He repeated after me. "What did you have for breakfast, today?" I asked again. "What did you have for breakfast, today?" He repeated after me. Things couldn't be that simple, I knew that all along. His brain needed more repair obviously.

But his father was overjoyed. He said he was very happy with his son's progress. He wanted to give him a treat for being such a good boy. I suggested that he get some ice cream. He took him to a nearby Baskin-Robbins and treated him to a strawberry-vanilla swirl. He didn't react. In fact, he was calmer than before.

When he returned from his treat, he was tested for iron mix and was found to be very allergic to it. This caused energy blockages in the spleen and heart meridians. He was treated for iron mix. Within five minutes of the treatment he fell asleep. On the following visit he had passed the iron mix with flying colors. He murmured words repeatedly in a low voice. No one could understand him or recognize the words. They didn't make any sense whatsoever. He also continued to respond to others by repeating their questions whenever the questions were asked to him directly.

Vitamin A mix (included fish, shell fish, beta carotene) was treated on the following visit. This caused energy blockages in the lung and large intestine meridians. He had dry and slightly scaly skin on his arms and legs. Soon after he was treated for vitamin A mix, he began coughing. His MRT tested strong after 20 minutes. He was still coughing occasionally when he left the office.

He appeared very sick the next day. He had severe nasal congestion, a repeated dry cough, throat irritation, mild fever and hives on the front and back of the body. According to his mother, he had lost his appetite for food or drinks and was also very constipated. He was tested for vitamin A mix and found to be passing the sample. But he was evaluated further due to his symptoms and needed a combination treatment with vitamin A mix and Base. He was treated for the base combination immediately. He continued to cough through the treatment. It took two treatments 15 minutes apart for MRT to become strong. Soon after the second treatment, he coughed continuously for almost a minute then he vomitted about an ounce of yellow liquid. Then he stopped coughing and began sleeping.

On the following day, his parents reported that he slept for twelve hours straight. He did not cough after the last treatment and his appetite had returned. He had passed the treatment for vitamin A mix completely. He continued to respond inappropriately by repeating whatever was asked of him or told to him.

The next treatment was for mineral mix which contained 63 essential trace minerals. No one knows the actual functions of these precious trace minerals in the human body. Mineral mix caused energy blockages in his lungs, heart, stomach, liver, gall bladder, small intestine, large intestine, bladder and spleen meridians. He only needed one treatment for mineral mix. 20 minutes after the initial treatment, he fell asleep. By now we had come to recognize his sign of passing a treatment as falling sound asleep. His parents took him home. According to his parents, he remained very quiet the rest of the day after the mineral treatment. But they had no clue that they were in for a big surprise when he came to my office that morning.

He appeared tired and quiet. He rested his head on his father's shoulder while he was in the waiting room. When his name was called he jumped out of his father's lap and walked into my room. When I greeted him "Good Morning" he just smiled. " Steve, Did you eat your breakfast today?" I asked. To our amazement, he nodded his head in "yes" mode. So I asked again, "Do you want to drink some water?" He nodded his head sideways indicating a "no." He had stopped the stereotype (parrot-like) talk. What a relief!

I still have no idea what blockage in which meridian, branch of the nerve, gyrus (fissures) or parts of the brain that stopped his speech and understanding initially and unblocking of which area helped him to recover his ability to understand and talk, recall and respond. I hope, some of the talented, superintelligent, anatomists and physiologists could solve the puzzle for me.

He didn't talk much anymore. He seemed very happy and peaceful. He looked tired or he seemed to enjoy resting his head on his father's shoulder. He responded appropriately by shaking his head or by saying "yes" or "no." In other words, his vocabulary was limited to just to two-three words.

He was found to be allergic to artificial sweeteners, and corn mix. After treating for each one of these, he seemed to have uncomfortable feeling in his head. After the treatment he began hitting his head with his two hand on the sides above the ears. Then he began banging his head on the wall near his seat. That was a clue to treat him again repeatedly until he stopped banging. When the allergen gets through with its journey through the meridians without any more obstruction, he would fall asleep. Then he was treated for grain mix. He did not have major physiological reactions to this item. He reacted to yeast and candida treatments severely. He began banging his head on the wall, and on the furniture. He couldn't communicate with us in words about his discomfort. Head banging was the sign of his discomfort of the candida treatment. We treated him every few minutes for candida until he relaxed and began to sleep. Yeast and candida took three days to clear.

Then he was treated for stomach acid (hydrochloric acid), intestinal enzymes (called "Base" in the NAET test kit: this contains amylase, protease, lipase, maltase, peptidase, cellulase, sucrase, lactase, alpha galactosidase, and bromelain), serotonin, neurotransmitters, childhood immunization DPT. He had a very difficult time while treating for DPT. It took about seven days to complete the DPT and combinations. With each treatment he became better and better with his behaviors. Then he was treated for MMR, and influenza. With these treatments he did not experience unusual reactions. But we noticed significant changes in him. He became calmer, developed good eye contact, increased his vocabulary, showed interest in playing and interacting with other children, began dressing himself, began asking for food and drinks whenever he was hungry, etc.

He continued with our program for the 52 NAET groups: this included caffeine mix (coffee mix, chocolate mix), nuts, spices, fats, amino acids, alcohol, vitamin E, fatty acids, food colors, food additives, starches, night shade vegetables (pepper, tomato, onion, eggplant, potato), modified starches, MSG and then received treatments for pesticides, petrochemical sensitivity, virus and bacteria mix. He received treatments for all the antibiotics and other medicines taken in the past, parts of the brain (cranial nerves, sympathetic nerve, para-sympathetic nerve, thalamus, corpus striatum, hypothalamus, hippocampus, pineal gland, frontal lobe, occipital lobe, parietal lobe, pre motor cortex, prefrontal cortex, cingulate gyrus, temporal gyrus, corpus callosum); brain chemicals (dopamine, adrenaline, norepinephrine, cytokinin), cerebrospinal fluid, blood, parasites, other foods, environmental agents, chemicals, schoolwork materials, animal dander and fabrics, etc. His brain responded slowly but surely to NAET. 52 treatments later, he was able to respond to questions appropriately. Later he graduated from his special education school and his autism was said to be under remission. He continued his education in a regular school and is functioning normally now.

MY SON'S ROAD TO RECOVERY

I think back three years to the day my youngest son was diagnosed with autism three weeks before his third birthday. I was numb from shock. You always think these kind of things can only happen to other people. Eric seemed to develop normally from birth but started to regress in his second year. We knew something was wrong but thought he might have a hearing problem of some sort because he had no speech, would not respond when we called him, and had many temper tantrums. I was scared but as I began to research and educate myself as to what autism is and the prognosis, scared turned into petrified. Petrified as to what the future would hold for Eric. It looked pathetically grim. Things were worse than I originally thought, but I decided we were going to beat this disorder, disease, or syndrome. I didn't even know what to call it.

Not knowing how difficult it was going to be, we started our journey. After hundreds of hours of research my husband and I would make decisions as to what therapies might be able to help Eric. For two years we went all over the country seeing doctors we thought might have some answers. We dedicated ourselves to months of exhausting detoxification programs, doing chelation therapy and allergy shots, I'm not saying these therapies are not good, but they can be expensive, difficult to do, and Eric did not show the slightest bit of improvement from them. Next we tried a gluten free diet, a sugar free diet, and avoidance of all known allergens. He did show a little improvement with these, but they are tough on both parents and children to adhere to, plus autistic children are allergic to so much, foods and environmentally, it is impossible to keep them away from everything. These diets made me realize that allergies are a huge problem when it comes to children with autism and other learning disabilities.

Frustrated with diets and allergy shots a friend informed me that she had heard of another treatment called NAET that sounded a lot easier than what we are doing. She explained that kinesiology is used to find out what the allergies are, the child is then exposed to the item and after treatment does not reject it as with an allergen. To tell you the truth it sounded to good to be true. After going to NAET web site and making a few telephone calls I began to feel that maybe this could help Eric.

We began NAET treatments right away. After clearing the first five items, Eric picked up some blocks with numbers on them; he had never shown any interest in these blocks in the past. As my husband and I sat in the living room observing him, Eric lined the numbers up in the correct order on a window ledge and said each number out loud. We had never heard him talking in his little voice before. What a joy this brought us. We continued NAET treatments regularly with improvement. After Eric cleared for wheat and gluten he could eat wheat without any problems. Candida was a big problem for Eric and once he was cleared of sugar and yeast he no longer had to be on an anti-candida diet and there have been no signs of candida. NAET has made life a lot easier and enjoyable for Eric. Today Eric is able to ask for things he wants. He is starting to put words together to form phrases.

He can say his ABC's and count to thirty. I can point out any letter or number to him and he can tell me what it is. He is much calmer and able to sit for an hour and a half straight, which makes it easier for him to learn. His eye contact is much improved along with his eating habits. Instead of looking at my son with sorrow as I did in the past, I can look at him with hope for the future. He is happier than I have ever seen. He is really starting to excel.

I want to thank Dr. Devi for sharing her discovery with the world and also those who have made Eric's treatments possible. NAET has given Eric the opportunity to live life. He still has areas needing improvement but his progress is ongoing as we clear his many allergies.

Our journey to get Eric better has taken us on many roads but Dr. Devi's allergy elimination technique has put Eric on the road to good health and it appears the sign up ahead just might say RECOVERY.

Sharon Racette
Quincy, MA

Simon's Progression through NAET

Simon age 9, was diagnosed as having autism spectrum disorder with occasional seizures since the age of four. He was categorized as high functional. He had all the classical behaviors of autism. According to his parents his autistic traits increased ten fold whenever he ate certain foods. His mother observed that his occasional seizures were connected with high consumption of refined sugar. His mother made a list of these foods: milk, eggs, wheat, bread, corn, sugar, chocolate, candy, fruits, oats, fish, beans, jelly beans, his prescription medication, hot dogs, barbecued beef, pork, chicken, brown rice, raisins, nuts, ice-cream, ice cubes, potato, tomato, oranges, grapes, banana, avocado, cheese, and salsa. Certain foods made him violent and aggressive for a number of hours. He consumed enormous amounts of food which made him grow fast. He weighed 110 pounds at the age of nine. He was on a rotation diet with a limited number of foods. It was not easy to plan his meals avoiding all of the above listed food items.

When Simon was evaluated in our office, we found the following symptoms: he avoided eye contact, played alone, showed no awareness of people, resisted physical touch by anyone including his mother, lacked appropriate social or emotional responses, lacked communication skills, was unable to talk, made unusual sounds, had extreme need for sameness, was attached to a cream colored old baby blanket, was preoccupied with twirling and pulling his hair or chewing the sleeve of his long sleeve shirt, refused to try new foods, refused to chew foods, insisted on eating fried foods and swallowed them in big chunks, was startled by any external noises, had severe insomnia, flapped his hand over his left side of the face repeatedly, showed distress and cried every now and then without any reason, wet his pants periodically, and was uncooperative in learning or doing school work. He also suffered from repeated dry skin, patches of scattered dermatitis and/or eczema, itching of his body, drooling, runny nose, canker sores, bad breath, abdominal bloating and constipation.

He sat through the computer testing for allergies. He was tested for 156 food items. The interpretation of the computer reading is on a scale of 0-100, (50 is normal, 100 is the maximum allergy at an inflammatory level, and zero is a possible hidden allergy or an artifact).

His computer test results showed:

148 items	100/100
6 items	96
2 items	92

MRT was done through his mother using her as the surrogate. He had weakness on 20 groups of basic allergens when tested with MRT. He was also found to be allergic to cotton, polyester and acrylic fabrics.

His vital signs were within normal limits. He had some scratch marks and a few scattered hives on his body. He also suffered from mild upper respiratory problems including mild dry cough (suffered for six months), itching of his nostrils, red cheeks and malar flush.

He was treated for egg mix on the first visit. On the following visit, his mother reported that he stopped coughing within hours after the first treatment (egg mix). One week after the first treatment, he still remained free of his coughing.

He was then treated for calcium mix. This included milk and milk products, calcium and vitamin D. On the following visit, his mother reported that his canker sores were healed completely. His abdominal bloating was slightly better.

Next he was treated for vitamin C mix. This included vitamin C, ascorbic acid, oxalic acid, citrus mix, vegetable mix and fruit mix. On the following visit, he appeared restless and refused to sit in the chair to wait his turn. Instead, he rushed into my office. My quick impulse was, "How are you Simon?"

"How are you Simon?" He repeated my question.

"Ah! Simon, you are speaking!" I exclaimed.

He snorted back "Ah! Simon, You are speaking!" Then his mother walked in and stood behind him with a beaming smile. I looked at his mother and said, "Wow! Did you hear him speak?" Simon immediately responded, "Wow! Did you hear him speak?"

He repeated every word his mother said for the next few minutes He had a smile on his face all along. His mother said he was chirping away nonstop after the treatment for vitamin C. His talk didn't make any sense. He repeated everyone's conversation throughout the week. She was so relieved to hear him speak even though his speech didn't make any sense. All these years, she never knew that he could say even one word. Now he was speaking fluently without any accent or hesitation, the words just flowed. "He did not even appear that he was listening," she said, "How could he have learned all these words and sentences without anyone teaching him I wonder!" She was still amazed at his sudden progress.

He was next treated for B complex, again through his mother using her as a surrogate. After the treatment, he was asked to sit outside along with his mother with the sample placed inside his sock. In a few minutes he got up from his seat, rushed into my office and fell on the treatment table. Another patient was sitting at the same table discussing her treatment plan with me. I looked at his face. His cheeks and ears were turning red. He was burning with fever. I immediately took the sample of B vitamins out of his sock, called his mother in and repeated NAET until his temperature became normal. It took about an hour to get his temperature down to normal. He became very quiet and appeared tired. After he became stable, his mother took him home.

On the following visit, Simon sat quietly in his seat. He did not jump around or move from his seat this time. His mother said he was extremely quiet after the B complex treatment. He did not talk but nodded his head for all the questions appropriately by "yes" or "no." She said he looked as if he had no energy to say a word. He passed the treatment for B complex with flying colors.

He was treated for sugar mix next. In less than a few minutes, he broke out in hives all over his body. NAET was repeated immediately on him through a surrogate (his mother). We repeated NAET every five minutes for six times until he passed the sugar mix. His hives faded away in just a few minutes and he fell asleep. His mother had to carry him to the car since he refused to wake up. He seemed to be having a very restful sleep.

On the following visit, he looked cheerful, quiet, calm, and appeared shy. He wouldn't look at other patients and he used his mother's body as a shield to hide behind her. He covered his face with his hands and peeked through his finger-gaps. But he kept smiling all along. His mother said, she had not noticed this kind of behavior before.

He was treated for iron mix that day. Soon after the iron treatment, we noticed a sudden change in his calm disposition. In a few minutes, he became very aggressive. He began kicking his mother, tried to push her out of the chair, and his smiling face was replaced by an angry and unhappy one. Then he began to bang his head on the wall and scream.

He wouldn't cooperate to walk to the treatment room. He crawled his way to the corner then went under the treatment table in the acupuncture room and hid there like a frightened kitten. He refused to come out. We had to move the table physically to get him out of there. We had to carry him to the NAET treatment room. NAET was repeated through the surrogate every five minutes for four more times. By then, he calmed down. His calmness projected as deep sleep. He curled up into a fetal position. By then we were familiar with his response. After the 20 minute waiting period from the last NAET treatment, his mother carried him to the car.

On the next visit, his mother said, he slept for 18 hours without eating, drinking, or moving from his fetal position. When he woke up he looked tired. He was too tired to eat anything. His mother fed him. He ate slowly and calmly. Then he went to sleep again. He slept for three days intermittently for hours. He was not interested in any activities. So his mother let him sleep. After three days when he woke up, he was his usual self again. But he was less aggressive and behaved somewhat normal. He pointed to certain foods like ice creams, cookies, etc., indicating that he wanted to eat them, which he had never done before. His mother let him have the cookies and ice cream since he was treated and cleared for sugar and milk.

On the following visit, he came and sat down on the chair in the waiting room. He had a serious look on his face.

Kevin, another seven-year-old, was demanding that his mother to take him to Burger King. Simon watched him for a while and stood up from his chair pointing his index finger towards Kevin and told him in a firm voice, "You are naughty!" Everyone in the waiting room laughed and complemented him saying, "Very good, Simon!" He smiled. He began to develop appropriate responses.

He was treated for vitamin A mix next. This included fish, shellfish, beta carotene and fish oils. In a few minutes after the treatment, he began itching all over his body. He was treated two more times for vitamin A, every five minutes and his itching stopped. Compared to all other previous treatments, the vitamin A treatment seemed easy. He fell asleep again demonstrating that his brain and body were happy to have another culprit out of his body.

On the next visit, his mother was beaming with joy. She said Simon's skin felt very soft and all the eczema and dermatitis cleared up. He stopped scratching his body. His dry scalp also cleared up. He was treated for mineral mix. Once again, he became very aggressive in the office. I had to treat him five times every five minutes to make his brain accept the mineral mix. After the treatment, he fell asleep again and his mother had to carry him to the car.

On the following visit, he seemed to be full of energy. When the car stopped in the parking lot, he ran ahead of his mother into the office, ran to Mala who was standing in the front office and hugged her and kissed her hand. Then without a word, he ran into my office, and hugged me, looked into my eyes and said: "I love you, Dr. Devi." His mother stood at treat the rest of the items in the basic allergen kit. After completing all the basic allergens, he was treated for serotonin, dopamine, neurotransmitters, secretin, dimethyl glycine, tap water, amino acids, starch complex, alcohol, caffeine, chocolate, food colors, food additives, stomach acids, digestive enzymes, parasite mix, childhood immunization (MMR, DPT, Polio), his past and present medications, pesticides, fabrics, plastics, latex, and chemicals. He was also treated for his father, mother, grandmother and all the animals and toys in his house. Soon after the treatment for vaccinations, his seizures stopped. He is now attending regular school. He is a healthy teenager now.

Spenser's Journey through NAET.

Treating NAET Practitioner:
Jaque Smiley, Riverside, CA

July 20, 1999

Spencer was 4-years-old at the time of his first visit. His mother said that he was developing normally until his 18-month booster shot. Following the shot he ran a fever for three days, slept for 18 hours, and would spend his time staring at the TV. In public he would scream.

He came into the office with a bag of potato chips. His mother said that was all he would eat and insisted on always taking them with him. He was treated for the potato chips first, and Spencer immediately lost his craving for them. Within two treatments he was able to give them up and begin to eat better food.

He was treated for: frontal and temporal lobes, B complex, potato chips and B complex, sugars, TB, small pox, measles, chicken pox and mumps vaccines. At this point his teacher said he was interacting more, and speaking with three words. He was involved with other children for the first time.

Spencer was then treated for minerals, Vit. A, French-fries, fats-repeated one time, DPT—repeated one time and Pertussis—repeated one time. After these treatments Spencer was asking questions like, "What's in there?"

At this point, Oct. 31, 1996 Spencer took a 5-month break from his sessions. During this time he stopped making the expected progress in his therapy classes. It was apparent that the sessions not only helped him with allergens but also balanced his energy so he could be more receptive to learning. His mother stated, "Every time Spencer stops his NAET treatments, he stops progressing in other areas of his life."

Resuming in April Spencer was treated for:

Amino acids
Salts and Chlorides
Artificial Sweeteners
Potatoes
Hong Kong Flu
Food colors and Additives
Flax oil
Tetracycline
Doughnuts—repeated
 Wheat+ Yeast+ Sugar
 Wheat+ Milk mix+ Sugar
 Udo's oil

Vit. E
Vit. F
(Vit. K & D were good)

By this time, Spencer was making such developmental progress that he was signed up for public schooling for the fall semester.

Next we treated him for:
Herpes virus
Food Color and Serotonin
Chemicals
Vit. T
Red Candy
Candida & Mercury
Eggs & Chicken
Opioids
Virus & Brain
Calcium

His mother summarized Spencer's NAET experience by saying, "It was so beneficial and natural. He can talk, focus and learn. To be able to do this naturally, without drugs or dietary changes is tremendous. He eliminated his allergies to the environment and food with NAET. He never needed a casein or gluten free diet."

NAET DAYS OF DYLAN O.

Dylan O. was five-years-old when he began NAET. He suffered from ADD and PDD/ mild autism. Along with this he exhibited angry behavior. He had been expelled from 4 preschools. His diet was almost totally sugar based, and he craved sugar and doughnuts.

His sessions followed the standard order. After the basics we treated him for doughnuts. It took five treatments for him to clear them. After thirteen treatments his behavior has greatly improved. He now gets good reports from his teachers and he has attended the same preschool for over one year now. He is craving less sugar and is off the Ritalin.

FOOD-INDUCED AUTISM

Clayton, age 9, has a food-induced autism. He tests very well and has no autistic traits whatsoever unless he eats certain foods. If his mother gives him a hot dog before testing he tests severely autistic. In addition to autism, he exhibits violent/psychotic behavior. He had been placed on anti-psychotic medication to curb the violence, which had helped for a time, however, he was beginning to break through the medication. For example he chased his younger sister around the house with a knife. His parents knew if they couldn't calm him down, he would have to be placed in another home in order to protect their daughter.

While Clayton's mother was pregnant with him their neighborhood was sprayed with malathion. While eight months pregnant she had intrauterine seizures. At birth his blood sugar level dropped. At one-month-old he had pneumonia and was placed on antibiotics. The mother noticed quite a difference in him after this. He was lethargic, would cry a lot, scream and stiffen his body.

We followed the Basics beginning with eggs/chicken. After the Basics we did diphtheria, tetanus, pneumonia, and fruit mix. Clayton's violence abated and he was able to go off the anti-psychotic medication. His mother was so relieved that he could remain at home. At this point she got a job and was unable to bring him in. In only 10 treatments he has made significant progress. Further treatments would greatly enhance his well being. We have yet to treat him for hot dogs, for example.

IT WAS DRUG INDUCED

Christian Rogers, age 2 ¾ was born addicted to Methadone and, most likely, other drugs as well. He was in drug withdrawal for the first three months of life. A foster family had raised him his entire life as his mother is still in jail. In addition to ADD he was very violent. He was unable to play with other children because he would harm them. His physician had placed him on Riserdol for his aggression but it wasn't helpful. As a matter of fact, most drugs were useless for him. The week before his first NAET treatment his neurologist told his foster mother, "Sometimes with these drug addicted children it just doesn't work out and they need to be institutionalized."

On the first visit to my office he punched and kicked his foster mother and foster sisters. He screamed the entire time as well. He did all of this while on 12 mg. of Ritalin. In just one treatment of egg/chicken he was able to go off the Ritalin.

Here is an account of the progress he has made thus far according to his foster mother:

Egg mix/chicken: no Ritalin for 25 hours.

Calcium mix/Milk mix: he was normal, quiet but still failed the treatment.

Calcium mix/Milk mix: He is a kid instead of a frustrating kid. He sat in a grocery cart one whole hour for the first time.

Infant formula—At nearly three-years-old, he would live on formula and didn't like food. He tested very allergic to the formula. We had to treat him emotionally for the formula as well.

Vitamin C mix (Bioflavonoid/Citrus).

B Complex/Wheat, Gluten: slept two nights, very unusual. His behavior has been awful since then. He was tested for Dimetapp. This was causing his hyperactive behavior. He had to be treated for Dimetapp and combinations:

Dimetapp/Tryptophane, Dimetapp/Brain.

Vitamin A mix /Fish, shellfish mix: No screaming, but constant movement.

Mineral Mix: Nothing unusual.

Salt mix, Chlorides: Treatment not needed.

Grain mix: No treatment.

Stomach Acids: Nothing unusual.

Macaroni.

Stomach
Stomach/Enzymes/Secretin/Sugar enzymes.
Candida
Candida/Brain.
Candida/Heavy Metals/Mercury.
Virus mix
Food color
Food additives
Food color and food additives/adrenals.
Food color and additives/sugar
Cocaine-made symptoms worse.
Marijuana—was real calm for a day, then awful.
Marijuana—the second treatment calmed him down
    again
Methadone
Methadone/Hormones
LSD
Bacteria mix
Bacteria/Eustatian tubes/Ear mix/Cochlea
String cheese
String cheese/Thymus/Lymph.
Pollen mix: failed the first time.
Pollen mix.
Pollen/mountain pollen/ local pollen.
Otter Pops
Weeds/Pigweed/Local weeds
Spice mix 1
Spice mix 2

At this point, Christian is on no medication, doesn't scream or hit. He is much calmer than before. His body temperature is still too low, 94.5 degrees. He needs to clear MSG, soy and many other items. He is such a different child that his other treating doctors (pediatrician, child specialist, neurologist) are amazed. His mother is committed to giving him the full NAET treatments. Her commitment has greatly helped him. He is still unable to maintain emotional balance on his own. During a month long break, he began to revert back. It will take more time for him to maintain balance on his own. However, he used to require two treatments weekly for emotional balance and now he can go up to two weeks before he loses his emotional balance.

Jacqueline Smillie
NAET Specialist
Redlands, CA
(909) 335-1980

Date: Wed, 8 Sept. 1999

Dr. Devi,

Thank you for taking the time to speak to me today. I will give you as much detail as possible regarding my boys, hopefully it will be of some benefit to other parents with autistic children. My life was not an easy one until I found NAET. I do not wish any parent to go through the nightmares I went through not finding the proper guidance to help my children. NAET is so easy and simple but very effective beyond belief! I wish I discovered NAET sooner!

I am a chiropractor in New Jersey and a mother of two beautiful boys ages 7 and 5.

As an infant my oldest child was diagnosed with asthma and eczema. The asthma was so severe the child had to throw up the mucus that blocked his throat. His eczema was so bad he had open wounds in the anticubital areas, behind his ears and knees. The diaper rash was almost as bad and he also had acne all over his face. All medications including immunizations were not tolerated, therefore my second child was kept away from these. My youngest suffered from severe colic and appeared to have a problem with growth. His pelvis was not getting larger, I rarely needed to advance to larger diapers.

Although he was on the charts as far as the pediatricians were concerned, his abdomen appeared to be large and his buttocks were too small. In addition, he not only looked malnutritioned, he had loose stools (like his brother) and had hypotonic musculature which bothered me. Both children had the allergy look. They had dark rings under their eyes, pale skin, red ears, cheeks and ring around the anus as well as loose, light brown stools, stomach aches and headaches too often.

After learning about food allergies from Doris Rapp's book, I put my oldest on an elimination diet and determined he had multiple food allergies. While away from these foods his asthma and eczema cleared up. Unfortunately, I let family and friends talk me into seeing a pediatric allergist in Philadelphia.

She determined he had only a few allergies such as to dogs and goat's milk. After resuming a normal diet, his asthma and eczema did clear up.

At age 3, he was classified as PDD/mild Autism. After the shock wore off I decided to stop fighting the pediatricians and listening to family and friends and go the alternative route. With the help of a nutritionist we proceeded to do all the necessary testing including blood, urine and stool.

ELIZA food allergy tests confirmed multiple food allergies including all gluten products, milk products, soy and most nut products, as well as some spices and herbs. After staying on a strict diet, yeast and parasite elimination, herbs, homeopathy, vitamins, acidophilus, minerals, amino acids, enzymes, auditory training, play therapy and chiropractic care since birth, we were able to make profound changes. He is now seven and has had the autistic classification removed. His is being mainstreamed and is academically age appropriate.

The experience with my oldest lead me to believe my youngest may have a problem, which he did, notably after testing he had all the same sensitivities.

For almost 4 years my children have been on a very strict diet. All baked goods were made at home and with rice and stevia (sugar also was a very big offender). Whenever an allergen was ingested a reaction of multiple symptomatology lasted approximately 2 weeks. These symptoms would keep them out of daycare/school and would land them in bed with lots of cleaning up after vomiting and diarrhea.

My children could attend parties and school, but could not partake in the goodies, which until you go through, the ramifications are hard to explain and understand. Halloween was a nightmare. Traveling was almost impossible without a room with a kitchen. Going out to eat was always scary wondering what might happen that night or the next. Life was very difficult and almost ruined my marriage.

When I learned about NAET I cried, I was so happy.

Needless to say, I did what I had to do to get trained and began to treat my children.

I have treated my children for multiple allergens and the results have been remarkable. They are eating everything they want and more. My life is so much easier and relaxed. An occasional reaction occurs, but nothing like before and now I have the knowledge and tools I need to prevent any further reactions.

This is the answer to so many parents prayers.

YOUR CHILD DOES NOT HAVE TO LIVE A CASEIN AND GLUTEN FREE LIFE!!!!!!!

Thank you so much Devi. I hope you understand that you have made such an impact on the world of allergies.

Dr. Maribeth Mydlowski,
New Jersey

STEPHEN S. AGE 9, AUTISM AND PDD

NAET Practitioner: Glenn Nozek, D.C., Tom River, NJ.

Stephen S. was diagnosed as autistic when he was four-years-old. His family heard about NAET in March 1998 when he was nine years of age. NAET treatments were started on March 19, 1998, when he was treated for egg mix.

March 23: Calcium mix. For 15 minutes after the NAET treatment for calcium, his left ear turned red and hot.

March 26: Calcium mix was repeated.
For 15 minutes after treatment, his left ear turned red and hot. After this treatment, his teacher wrote a note and stated, "Stephen's behavior is exceptional. I don't know if you are doing anything different, we are not. He seems to really enjoy learning now and he is understanding direction which lessens his frustrations." I also note an increase in receptive language. He will now answer most questions by nodding his head yes or no. He also is more aware of everything.

On March 28th, he played outside appropriately all day (Stephen usually chooses to stay indoors watching T.V.). He was running and kicking and throwing a ball. He had appropriate interactions with a neighbor boy and his sister.

March 30: He was tested for vitamin C (found negative). Then I tested him and treated for B complex. For 15 minutes his ears were red and hot. He developed hives on his face and a few on his torso. A note came from his speech therapist the next day stating that "his receptive language/vocabulary has grown incredibly high. He understands everything!"

April 2: Vitamin B complex repeated with RNA and DNA.
During the 15 minutes after treatment, his ears were red and hot. Hives appeared around his eyes and his eye lids reddened. A few hives were seen on the torso, which subsided after 10 minutes.

Stephen's other basic NAET treatments passed without any significant reactions. He is a normal child now.

Glen Nozek, D.C.,
Toms River, New Jersey.

ALLERGY TO B COMPLEX AND SUGAR

Dear Dr. Devi,

We were at your clinic for two weeks, two treatments a day, and I had no choice but to become an advocate of NAET. Alex is so thrilled to be able to eat cheese, catsup, and drink milk without her stomach blowing up like a balloon, and be able to eliminate two to three times a day instead of once a week, painfully. But, more than that, once you treated her for the chemicals that her parents were using before her gestation period, we saw a transformation before our very eyes. The trip home in the motor home was a whole new experience, so quiet and peaceful. No fights with her sister or temper tantrums. She looked at books, watched *her* favorite movies and even took a nap! It seemed too good to be true.

She has had several days in school now and they think that they have a new Alex in school. They are highly curious about what type of treatment could possibly make this kind of transformation in a child.

Alex has never known any other way to express herself except in anger and fits of crying and tantrums. It is so wonderful to watch her try some of the same habits when she wants things her own way, and see the smile she has on her face when she realizes it doesn't feel right anymore. I can tease her out of her old habits now. I have never seen her positive side in such full bloom. We have also had to train ourselves to be more positive and to display our pleasure with her in her new found excitement.

"Grandma, I didn't cause any trouble at school today."

Dr. Devi, I feel as if there is hope for Alexandria in the school systems, in interpersonal relationships, and in life. I'm sure you will see us again as soon as possible to follow up on the additional treatments that time didn't allow. But, for now I thank you from the bottom of my heart! This is the most amazing, exciting experience I have had in my lifetime. We all benefited from your treatments, but Alexandria being the most crucial and in the most crisis benefited the most!

Sincerely yours,
Daisy L. Costa,
CALIFORNIA

AUTISM

NAET Practitioner:
Glenn Nozek, D.C.,
Tom River, NJ

My son Daniel was diagnosed as autistic when he was three. We didn't find out about NAET until October of 1998. He is seven now. We immediately began NAET.

It is now February of 1999. So far he has had over 20 treatments. Daniel is autistic and has many communications problems as well as many allergies., which I believe to be connected in many ways. As a result of the NAET treatments that Daniel has received, there has been marked improvements in both the communicative and allergic areas for Daniel.

When I started bringing him to Lifeline, I thought, well, I know it can't hurt him as the treatments are non-invasive... but what I did not expect was how well he has done with the treatments. When we started the treatments Daniel had a constant skin rash on his face and significantly less than it was previously. I am convinced that with perseverance we will find the culprits and eliminate all of the allergic reactions that Daniel has.

In particular, I am so appreciative for Dr. Nozek, especially with respect to his true concern and caring for Daniel and myself. I feel that he has a deep caring for his patients and is always willing to listen to concerns. Although Daniel's situation is difficult at times, I am enjoying my journey down the NAET path and the freedom I have started to feel with my son. We have a long way to go, but working with the Lifeline staff makes the journey much more pleasurable. I am so very thankful that I found this method of treatment... more than words can say.

Rosemary Dubrowsky
NJ

FROM A UNIVERSAL REACTOR
TO FUN AT DISNEY WORLD!

My four-year-old son was becoming a universal reactor right before our very eyes. My husband and I were desperate. In only a few months his allergy symptoms had gone from problematic to debilitating, and he seemed to be becoming allergic to truly everything! The eczema he had since infancy raged out of control, and he began to suffer horrible attacks, which included wild crying spells, bizarre behavior and near fainting. He seemed to be allergic to almost all foods, and it was becoming impossible to find something safe to feed him. He was becoming sensitive to chemicals, inhalants as well (not to mention mold, dust, pollen and all those common al-lergens).

Ian began NAET treatments immediately and we saw results right away: and I mean dramatic results! Within a matter of days I had several "safe" foods that Ian could eat without getting sick. In about a month the " frightening attacks" stopped forever (they decreased rapidly in that month, too), and gradually most of his symptoms have been disappearing.

After half a dozen treatments my son has made a lot of progress. Yes, he still has a lot of symptoms and a restricted diet, but we are happy to have a variety of foods to eat again. Ian is so happy to be able to eat fruit and cheese and butter! He is eating these things for the first time in months without turning red and itchy. For the first time in a long time he can drink something other than bottled water.

He has been receiving treatments for about three months at this point and he can now eat almost everything--even things like peanuts, to which he has been extremely allergic to his entire life! Ian still has some (relatively) minor symptoms and we are still getting treatments. I have every reason to believe that soon he will actually be symptom free.

NAET has saved my son and there aren't words to express my gratitude to you for helping us find it. I would not hesitate to recommend it to anyone with allergies, mild or severe. It is amazing that the treatments are non-invasive, not the least bit uncomfortable and are much less restrictive than EPD. These are important considerations for any patient, but especially for children! Even more amazing, it would appear that Ian allergies are not being "managed" or kept under control: I think they are really gone!

I just came back from vacation and felt like telling you how Ian is doing. We took the kids to Disney World for a few days-- which ordinarily might not be the best choice for vacation for Ian but it worked out great. I was amazed to note how wonderful Ian is now. He was wearing shorts and running around eating ice cream just like other normal kids. Somehow away from home I was able to see that and appreciate it. Also, since the fall, we have been having a lot of work done in our house and Ian has had no problems with any of the construction material. Do you know what a miracle that is? !

Kathryn Moore, NJ

NAET Treatment Observation

From birth James has had many food sensitivities. His symptoms as a baby included explosive diarrhea, gas, abdominal cramping, red ears and cheeks as well as skin rashes. He reacted to most foods except rice and Nutramigen baby formula. As he developed his symptoms grew to include hyperactivity, irritability, language regression and social withdrawal. He was diagnosed as autistic when he was 2 years of age.

Having allergies myself for 35 years, I was aware that traditional allergy medicine had little to offer for treating food allergies except for avoidance. As James appeared allergic to almost everything --- I was desperate! I researched alternative allergy treatments and in 1996 found information on E.P.D. (Enzyme Potentiated Desensitization) on the internet. This treatment, brought from England, looked promising both for food and environmental allergies.

James and I followed this treatment regime very carefully for 2 1/2 years, which at times was very difficult. For weeks at a time we were not allowed to eat certain foods, use certain common products or take any over the counter medication including aspirin for fear we would negate the treatment. We each received a treatment every other month, at a cost of $275 per person. He was gradually able to reintroduce some foods into his diet, such as bananas and apples, however he still was not able to tolerate any eggs, soy, dairy products and grains. If he accidently got a food that contained "whey" for instance - he would immediately turn into an extremely irritable, noncooperative, screaming, hyperactive mess! This behavior would usually last anywhere for 2 to 3 days! Even minutes after certain foods could literally turn James from Dr. Jekyl to Mr. Hyde within minutes. He was going to be starting kindergarten soon and I was terrified to think that he may ingest one of these foods at school and they were not going to realize what was happening to him - let alone understand that these reactions were beyond his control! Needless to say E.P.D. had not delivered what it had promised - it was time to search again.

In July of 1999, we had our first NAET appointment with Judith Abrams of Ithaca, NY. We had heard some incredible things from a friend who had taken her autistic son for several treatments and was now able to eat foods that previously turned him into a Mr. Hyde! During the first visit, Judith tested James for the 10 basics - James was allergic to 7! James was still a very allergic child - even after 2 1/2 years of E.P.D.! We began the NAET treatments and saw impressive results almost immediately.

He was first treated for eggs, chicken, and feathers. During the 20 minute waiting period following the acupressure treatment James displayed allergic reactions similar to what we normally saw if he actually ate these foods. His ears turned bright red and he became very irritable and hyperactive. Within 10-15 minutes these symptoms disappeared. Each time we treated a new substance we again saw different reactions during the 20 minute waiting period and each time they would disappear before we left the office. Within days he was eating eggs and after several weeks of treatments he was able to eat a whole wheat bagel with cream cheese! All without one single reaction. No stomach pains, diarrhea, hyperactivity, irritability, screaming - no Mr. Hyde!!! It was simply incredible!

We have now completed treatment #17 and he is eating meals with us - running to the table when it's time to eat! Before NAET James was never excited about eating - in fact he rarely expressed hunger or a desire to eat. No wonder, eating had never been a pleasurable experience for James! Now, thanks to NAET eating is fun for James!!

Since beginning the NAET we have not seen a single reaction to the foods he has been treated for. We have "discovered" other foods to be a problem that we previously thought were safe or he never had before of his limited diet. We are systematically treating each one of these. We are very excited about the results we have so far with NAET.

Although we know it is far from finished in terms of NAET and my optimism is high. He was allergic to almost every vitamin and every single fat. I am sure once we start supplementing these he will continue to improve. He already is much calmer and seem more "together" than ever before. We can't thank Dr. Devi Nambudripad enough for sharing her discovery with the world - especially for those of us who have not been offered any support by the traditional medical community. I highly recommend it.

Teri Hirsh, NY

CHAPTER 12

NUTRITION CORNER

12

NUTRITION CORNER

Many people take vitamin and mineral supplements nowadays. The quality of the food is far inferior than a few years ago. The food products we buy in the market has less food value. So it has become a necessity to supplement our food if we need to prevent malnutrition.

Vitamins and trace minerals are essential to life. They contribute to good health by regulating the metabolism and assisting the biochemical processes that release energy from the foods and drinks we consume. Vitamins and trace minerals are micronutrients, and the body needs them in small amounts. The lack of these essential elements even though they are needed in minute amounts can create various impairments and tissue damage in the body. Water, carbohydrates, fats, proteins and bulk minerals like calcium, magnesium, sodium, potassium and phosphorus are considered to be macronutrients, taken into the body via regular food. They are needed in larger amounts. Both macro- and micronutrients are not only necessary to produce energy for our daily body functions, but also for growth and development of the body and mind.

Using macronutrients (food & drinks) and micronutrients (vitamins and trace minerals), the body creates some essential chemicals called enzymes and hormones. These are the foundations of human bodily functions. Enzymes are the catalysts or simple activators in the chemical reactions that are continually taking place in the body. Without the appropriate vitamins and trace minerals, the production and functions of the enzymes will be incomplete. Prolonged deficiency of these vitamins and minerals can produce immature or incomplete enzyme production, protein synthesis, cell mutation, immature RNA, DNA synthesis, etc., which can mimic various organic diseases in the body.

Deficiency of vitamins and other essentials in the body can be due to poor intake and absorption. Nutritional imbalances can mainly be attributed to allergies.

Many autistic children and adults have nutritional deficiencies due to poor eating habits and will benefit from nutritional supplements and megavitamin therapy. Others may have nutritional deficiencies due to food allergies and will not show any improvements on vitamin therapy.

All autistic people should be tested for possible allergies. If they are found to be allergic, they should be treated for the allergies before they are supplemented with vitamin and minerals.

Apart from allergies, one needs to know a few things about taking vitamins and minerals. Of the major vitamins, vitamin C and B complex vitamins are water-soluble (in autism cases especially B6, B12 and PABA are depleted very fast or these are found very low). A, D, E, and K are fat-soluble. It is believed that water-soluble vitamins must be taken into the body daily, as they cannot be stored and are excreted within one to four days, (although our clinical experience has proven otherwise).

When a patient is allergic to vitamin B complex, in many cases he/she cannot digest grains, resulting in B complex deficiencies. When one gets treated for allergies via NAET, he/she can eat grains, without any ill effect and will begin to assimilate B complex vitamins. In some cases through NTT, I have found B complex deficiency amounting to fifteen to twenty times the normal daily-recommended allowances. After supplementing with large amounts of B complex for a few weeks (10 – 20 times of RDA amount per day for a week or so), the deficiency was eliminated. Over and over in hundreds of patients, after supplementing for weeks, we have been able to remove their vitamin B complex deficiency symptoms completely. This proves that even though water soluble, vitamin B complex is stored in the body. We have received similar results with vitamin C. But more research is needed on a larger number of patients to verify these findings.

Fat-soluble vitamins are stored for longer periods of time in the body's fatty tissues and the liver. When you are allergic to fat soluble vitamins, you begin to store them in unwanted places of the body. Some of the abnormal fat-soluble vitamin storage can be seen as lipomas, warts, skin tags, benign tumors inside or outside the body, etc.

Taking vitamins and minerals in their proper balance is important for the correct functioning of all vitamins. Excess consumption of an isolated vitamin or mineral can produce unpleasant symptoms of that particular nutrient. High doses of one element can also cause depletion of other nutrients in the body, leading to other problems. Most of these vitamins work synergistically, complementing and/or strengthening each other's function.

Vitamins and minerals should be taken with meals unless specified otherwise. Oil-soluble vitamins should be taken before meals, and water-soluble vitamins should be taken between or after meals. But when you are taking megadoses of any of these, they should always be taken with or after meals. Vitamins and minerals, as nutritional supplements taken with meals, will supply the missing nutrients in our daily diets.

Synthetic vitamins are produced in a laboratory from isolated chemicals with quality similar to natural vitamins. Although there are no major chemical differences between a vitamin found in food and one created in a laboratory, natural supplements do not contain other unnatural ingredients. Supplements that are not labeled natural may include coal tars, artificial coloring, preservatives, sugars, and starches, as well as other binding agents and additives. Vitamins labeled natural may not contain vitamins that have not been extracted from a natural food source.

There are various books available on nutrition today that are helpful in understanding vitamins and their assimilative processes. If you are interested in learning more about nutrition, if you did not get enough understanding about vitamins and other nutritional supplements from this concise chapter you are advised to read the appropriate book titles listed in the bibliography section, at the end of this book.

VITAMIN A

Clinical studies have proven vitamin A and beta-carotene to be very powerful immune-stimulants and protective agents.

Vitamin A is necessary for proper vision and in preventing night blindness, skin disorders, and acne. It protects the body against colds, influenza and other infections. It enhances immunity, helps heal ulcers and wounds and maintains the epithelial cell tissue. It is necessary for the growth of bones and teeth.

Vitamin A works best with B complex, vitamin D, vitamin E, calcium, phosphorus and zinc. Zinc is needed to get vitamin A out of the liver, where it is usually stored. Large doses of vitamin A should be taken only under proper supervision, because it can accumulate in the body and become toxic.

Many teenagers with an allergy to vitamin A have acne, blemishes and other skin problems. People with allergy to vitamin A develop skin tags, and warts, and pimples around the neck, arms, etc. It causes premenstrual syndrome in sensitive people causing to retain water in the tissue. When they get treated and properly supplemented with vitamin A, the skin clears up and PMS problems become less severe.

VITAMIN D

Vitamin D is often called the sunshine vitamin. It is a fat-soluble vitamin, acquired through sunlight or food sources. Vitamin D is absorbed from foods, through the intestinal wall, after they are ingested. Smog reduces the vitamin D producing rays of the sun. Dark-skinned people and sun-tanned people do not absorb vitamin D from the sun. Vitamin D helps the utilization of calcium and phosphorus in the human body. When there is an allergy to vitamin D, the vitamin is not absorbed into the body through foods, or from the sun. People with an allergy to vitamin D can exhibit deficiency syndromes: rickets, severe tooth decay, softening of teeth and bones, osteomalacia, osteoporosis, sores on the skin, blisters on the skin while walking in the sun, severe sunburns when exposed to the sun, etc. Sometimes allergic persons can show toxic symptoms if they take vitamin D without clearing its allergy. These symptoms include mental confusion, unusual thirst, sore eyes, itching skin, vomiting, diarrhea, urinary urgency, calcium deposits in the blood vessels and bones, restlessness in the sun, inability to bear heat, sun radiation, electrical radiation, emotional imbalance like depression, suicidal thoughts in the winter when the sunlight is diminished. Some people in Alaska and other cold countries suffer emotional instabilities during winter where they have a few hours of daylight in winter. When they get treated for vitamin D, and combinations, with NAET, they do not suffer from depression anymore. From this experience, it should be assumed that vitamin D is very necessary to maintain mental stability. Vitamin D works best with vitamin A, vitamin C, choline, calcium, and phosphorus.

When an allergy to vitamin D is treated by NAET, the deficiency or toxic symptoms can be eliminated and gradually with the proper supplementation, normal health can be restored.

VITAMIN E

Vitamin E is an antioxidant. The body needs zinc in order to maintain the proper levels of vitamin E in the blood. Vitamin E is a fat-soluble vitamin and is stored in the liver, fatty tissues, heart, muscles, testes, uterus, blood, adrenal glands and pituitary glands. Vitamin E is excreted in the feces if too much is taken.

VITAMIN K

Vitamin K is needed for blood clotting and bone formation. Vitamin K is necessary to convert glucose into glycogen for storage in the liver. Vitamin K is a fat-soluble vitamin, very essential to the formation of prothrombin, a blood-clotting material. It helps in the blood-clotting mechanism, prevents hemorrhages (nosebleeds and intestinal bleeding) and helps reduce excessive menstrual flow.

An allergy to vitamin K can produce deficiency syndromes such as prolonged bleeding time, intestinal diseases like sprue, etc., and colitis.

VITAMIN B

Approximately 15 vitamins make up the B complex family. Each one of them has unique, very important functions in the body. If the body does not absorb and utilize any or all of the B-vitamins, various health problems can result. B complex vitamins are very essential for emotional, physical and physiological well being of the human body. It is a nerve food, so it is necessary for the proper growth and maintenance of the nervous system and brain function. It also keeps the nerves well fed so that nerves are kept calm and the autistic person can maintain a good mental attitude.

B-vitamins are seen in almost all foods we eat. Cooking and heating destroy some of them, others are not destroyed by processing or preparation. People who are allergic to B-vitamins can get mild to severe reactions just by eating the foods alone. If they are supplemented with vitamin B complex, without being aware of the allergies, such people can get exaggerated reactions. One has to be very cautious when taking B complex, commonly called stress vitamins.

Dr. Carlton Frederic, in his book, "Psychonutrition," tried to point out that nutritional deficiencies are the causes of most of the mental irritations such as extreme anger, severe mood swings, bipolar diseases, schizophrenic disorders, frontal lobe disorders, anxiety disorders, attention deficit disorders, hyperactivity disorders, various neurological disorders, mental sicknesses including mild to moderate to severe psychiatric disorders. He tried to prove his theory by giving large doses of vitamin B complex, especially B-12, to some of the psychiatric patients. Fifty percent of the patients got better, were cured of their mental sickness and went back to live normal lives. But another 50 percent made no progress or got worse. He couldn't explain why the other 50% got worse. His theory was ridiculed and his treatment protocol with mega B complex vitamin therapy for mental disorders was thrown out for the want of proof. He did not think in the direction of allergies. When I discovered the allergic connection, I tried to contact him to let him know that his theory was absolutely right and I had proof to support his theory. Unfortunately, I was a year late to reach him...he had passed away a year before my discovery of NAET.

A few minerals are extremely essential for our daily functions. While some metals and trace minerals are mentioned here, for more information on other minerals, please refer to the appropriate references in the bibliography.

CALCIUM

Calcium is one of the essential minerals in the body. Calcium works with phosphorus, magnesium, iron, vitamins A, C and D. Calcium helps to maintain strong bones and healthy teeth. It regulates the heart functions and helps to relax the nerves and muscles. It induces relaxation and sleep.

Deficiencies in calcium result in rickets, osteomalacia, osteoporosis, hyperactivity, restlessness, inability to relax, generalized aches and pains, joint pains, formation of bone spurs, backaches, PMS, cramps in the legs and heavy menstrual flow.

Many autism children and adults respond well to calcium supplementation. Often autistic people suffer from abdominal pains, dysentery, insomnia, skin problems, nervousness, dyslexia, canker sores, post-nasal drip, hyperactivity, obesity, and joint disorders. They all respond well to calcium supplementation after allergy elimination. When people are on cortisone treatment, they need to take more calcium.

IRON

Poor diet is certainly one cause of iron deficiency but if you are allergic to iron, you do not absorb iron either. Iron is absorbed better in the acid medium (stomach) but in the intestine where the digestive juices are basic, iron does not absorb well. If you have a deficiency of iron, or if you have an allergy to iron and base in combination, all iron contained food can cause bloating and abdominal distention. Iron deficiency results in anemia. If you have an iron deficiency you can get various health problems. If you are allergic to iron, and if you supplement with iron or eat iron-containing foods, you may experience various allergic reactions like dry mouth, fatigue, dizziness, nausea, loss of appetite, restlessness, a short attention span, feeling extreme cold, cold limbs, internal cold and tremors, cold extremities, feels better in warm weather, poor circulation in the fingers and toes, varicose veins and fragile arteries, hair loss, insomnia (unable to fall asleep), swelling of the feet and ankles, etc. Iron deficiency also can give rise to above symptoms. Iron is also necessary to maintain the health of blood cells especially red blood cells. This improves the absorption of oxygen and elimination of carbon dioxide and other toxins from blood. Iron plays an important role in awareness and alertness. An imbalance in iron in the blood causes sluggish synaptic functions in the nerve endings causing the neuro-transmitters function poorly resulting in behavior and learning disability in young children. So good assimilation and utilization of iron is necessary for body's natural detoxification and maintenance function. Vitamin C can enhance the iron absorption. A high fiber diet, and the repeated daily use of laxatives can deplete iron from your body. Drinking tea can deplete iron in the body. Drinking tea (tannic acid) with meals can inhibit the iron absorption from food.

Food sources: chicken liver, beef liver, beef, crab, soybean, blackstrap molasses, spinach, beets, beet green, beef, potato, scallops, sunflower seeds, pistachio, broccoli, cashew nuts, lima beans, swiss chard, turkey dark-meat, lobster, tuna, almonds, sesame seeds, peanuts, peas, prunes, apricot, Brussels sprouts, cod, raisins, haddock, and endive.

CHROMIUM

Chromium is a natural insulin regulator. It is essential for insulin to work efficiently in our bodies. Insulin is required to remove glucose (sugar) from the blood. Chromium helps the insulin to do its job so that blood sugar can be kept at a normal range.

Food sources: sugar, whole grains, wheat germ, corn, corn oil, brewers yeast, mushrooms, red meat, liver, shellfish, clams and chicken.

COBALT

Cobalt is essential to form quality red blood cells, since it is part of vitamin B-12. Deficiency results in B-12 anemia. Multiple chemically sensitive people have low tolerance to any external smells like gasoline, smoke, chemical fumes, sprays, perfumes, etc. Maintaining a good level of cobalt along with selenium and molybdenum helps to reduce the smell-sensitivity in MCS people. If they are allergic to any of the trio, should be treated singly or in combination before supplementation.

Food sources: green leafy vegetables, milk, buckwheat, figs, red meat, liver, kidney, oyster, and clams.

COPPER

Copper is required to convert the body's iron into hemoglobin. Combined with the thyroxin, it helps to produce the pigment factor for hair and skin. It is essential for utilization of vitamin C. Deficiency results in anemia and edema. Toxicity symptoms and allergic symptoms are insomnia, hair loss, irregular menses, joint pains, arthritis and depression. Food sources: almonds, green beans, peas, green leafy vegetables, whole wheat, other whole grains, dried beans, prunes, raisins, beef liver, shellfish, and fish.

FLUORIDE

Sodium fluoride is added to drinking water. Calcium fluoride is seen in natural food sources. Fluorine decreases chances of dental carries, (too much can discolor teeth). It also strengthens the bones. Deficiency leads to tooth decay. Toxicity and allergy symptoms include dizziness, nausea, vomiting, fatigue, poor appetite, skin rashes, itching, yeast infections, mental confusion, muscle spasms, mental fogginess and arthritis. Treatment for fluoride will eliminate possible allergies.

Food sources: fluoridated water, gelatin, sunflower seeds, milk, cheese, carrots, almonds, green leafy vegetables and fish.

IODINE

Two thirds of the body's iodine is in the body's thyroid gland. Since the thyroid gland controls metabolism, and iodine influences the thyroid, an under supply of this mineral can result in weight gain, general fatigue and slow mental reaction. Iodine helps to keep the body thin, promotes growth, gives more energy, improves mental alertness, and promotes the growth of hair, nails and teeth. Autistic children are found to be allergic to iodine causing poor absorption of the substance. Some autistic children crave salt. They may not be receiving sufficient iodine in their diet or may have poor absorption of iodine due to an allergy. A deficiency in iodine can cause overweight, hypothyroidism, goiter and lack of energy.

Food sources: kelp, seafood, iodized salt, vegetables grown in iodine-rich soil and onion.

MAGNESIUM

This is one of the important minerals to help with irritability and hyperactivity. Magnesium is necessary for the metabolism of calcium, vitamin C, phosphorus, sodium, potassium and vitamin A. It is essential for the normal functioning of nerves and muscles. Autistic and hyperactive children need more magnesium in their diet to maintain the stability of the nervous system. It also helps convert blood sugar into energy. It works as a natural tranquilizer, laxative and diuretic. Diuretics deplete magnesium. Alcoholics and asthmatics are deficient in magnesium.

Food sources: Nuts, soybean, green leafy vegetables, almonds, brown rice, whole grains, sesame seeds and sunflower seeds.

MANGANESE

Manganese helps to activate digestive enzymes in the body. It is important in the formation of thyroxin, the principal hormone of the thyroid gland. It is necessary for the proper digestion and utilization of food. Manganese is important in reproduction and the normal functioning of the central nervous system. It helps to eliminate fatigue, improves memory, reduces nervous irritability and relaxes the mind. A deficiency may result in recurrent attacks of dizziness and poor memory.

Food sources: green leafy vegetables, beets, blueberries, oranges, grapefruit, apricot, the outer coating of nuts, and grains, peas, kelp, raw egg yolk, nuts and wheat germ.

MOLYBDENUM

Molybdenum helps in carbohydrate and fat metabolism. It is a vital part of the enzyme responsible for iron utilization.

It also helps reduce allergic reaction to smell in chemically sensitive people in combination with selenium and cobalt.

Food sources: whole grains, brown rice, brewers yeast, legumes, buckwheat, millet, and dark green leafy vegetables.

PHOSPHORUS

Phosphorus is involved in virtually all physiological chemical reactions in the body. It is necessary for normal bone and teeth formation. It is important for heart regularity, and is essential for normal kidney function. It provides energy and vigor by helping in the fat and carbohydrate metabolism. It promotes growth and repairs in the body. It is essential for healthy gums and teeth. Vitamin D and calcium are essential for its proper functioning.

Food sources: whole grains, seeds, nuts, legumes, egg yolk, fish, corn, dried fruits, milk, cheese, yogurt, chicken, turkey and red meat.

POTASSIUM

Potassium works with sodium to regulate the body's water balance and to regulate the heart rhythm. It helps in clear thinking by sending oxygen to the brain. A deficiency in potassium results in edema, hypoglycemia, nervous irritability, and muscle weakness.

Food sources: vegetables, orange, banana, cantaloupe, tomatoes, mint leaves, water cress, potatoes, whole grains, seeds, nuts and cream of tartar.

SELENIUM

Selenium is an antioxidant. It works with vitamin E, slowing down the aging process. It prevents hardening of tissues and helps to retain youthful appearance. Selenium is also known to alleviate hot flashes and menopausal distress. It prevents dandruff. Some researchers have found selenium to neutralize certain carcinogens and provide protection from some cancers. It has been also found to reduce the sensitivity to smells and odors from plastics, formaldehyde, perfume, molds, smoke, and gasoline etc. It works when combined with cobalt and molybdenum.

Food sources: brewers yeast, wheat germ, kelp, sea water, sea salt, garlic, mushrooms, sea food, milk, eggs, whole grains, beef, dried beans, bran, onions, tomato and broccoli.

SODIUM

Sodium is essential for normal growth and normal body functioning. It works with potassium to maintain the sodium-potassium pump in the body. Potassium is found inside the cells and sodium is found outside.

Food sources: kelp, celery, romaine lettuce, watermelon, sea food, processed foods with salt, fast foods, table salt, fish, shellfish, carrots, beets, artichoke, dried beef, cured meats, bacon, ham, brain, kidney, coffee, watercress, sea weed, oats, avocado, Swiss chard, tomatoes, cabbage, cucumber, asparagus, pineapple, tap water, canned or frozen foods.

SULFUR

Sulfur is essential for healthy hair, skin and nails. It helps maintain the oxygen balance necessary for proper brain function. It works with B-complex vitamins for basic body metabolism. It is a part of tissue building amino acid. It tones up the skin and makes the hair lustrous and helps fight bacterial infection.

Food sources: radish, turnip, onion, celery, string beans, watercress, soybean, fish, meat, dried beans, eggs and cabbage.

VANADIUM

Vanadium prevents heart attacks. It inhibits the formation of cholesterol in blood vessels.

Food sources: fish, sea weed, sea food.

ZINC

Zinc is essential to form certain enzymes and hormones in the body. It is very necessary for protein synthesis. It is important for blood stability and in maintaining the body's acid-alkaline balance. It is important in the development of reproductive organs and helps to normalize the prostate glands in males. It helps in treatment of mental disorders and speeds up healing of wounds and cuts on the body. Zinc helps with the growth of fingernails and eliminates cholesterol deposits in the blood vessels. It helps to improve the immune system.

Food sources: wheat bran, wheat germ, seeds, dried beans, peas, onions, mushrooms, brewers yeast, milk, eggs, oysters, herring, brown rice, fish, lamb, beef, pork, green leafy vegetables and mustard.

TRACE MINERALS

Even though trace minerals are needed in our body, they are seen in trace amounts only. The researchers do not know definite functions of the trace minerals but deficiencies can definitely contribute toward health problems.

AMINO ACIDS

All proteins are made up of amino acids. They are the building blocks of protein. There are 22 different types of amino acids. Some can be made in the body and are called non-essential amino acids. Eight are not produced in the body and are known as essential amino acids. These essential amino acids that have to be absorbed from food are lysine, methionine, leucine, threonine, valine, tryptophan, isoleucine and phenylalanine. Children also need histidine and arginine. Autistic children require a lot of glycine in their diet.

LECITHIN

Every living cell in the human body needs lecithin. Cell membranes, which regulate which nutrients may leave or enter the cell, are largely composed of lecithin. Cell membranes would harden without lecithin. Its structure protects the cells from damage by oxidation. The protective sheaths surrounding the brain are composed of lecithin, and the muscles and nerve cells also contain this essential fatty substance. Lecithin is composed of choline, inositol, and linoleic acids. It acts as an emulsifying agent. Lecithin is considered a "brain food." It is very essential in autistic child's (person's) diet. In an autistic brain, there are less active axons and dendrites (nerve energy transportation). So messages get lost or distorted. The emulsification action of lecithin can make the nerves smooth and open up the transportation channels to allow the messages to be transported.

It helps prevent arteriosclerosis, protects against cardiovascular disease, increases brain function, and promotes energy. It promotes better digestion of fats and helps disperse cholesterol in water and removes it from the body. The vital organs and arteries are protected from fatty build-up with the inclusion of lecithin in the diet.

Food sources: soybean, eggs, brewer's yeast, grains, legumes, fish, and wheat germ.

The body needs all of the essential vitamins and minerals in proper proportion for its normal function. If there is any deficiency of the vitamins, minerals, trace minerals, or amino acids, it can be seen as some functional disorder or other problem. If it can be found in time and treated or supplemented with appropriate amounts, many unnecessary discomforts can be avoided.

CHAPTER 13

DESTROYING AUTISM

13

DESTROYING AUTISM

Most children with autism share communication and social deficits, but their symptoms can present themselves in many ways and in combinations, ranging from mild to severe, making diagnosis, treatment, and everyday living difficult. There are no "set" or "typical" behaviors in children with autism. You will hear a variety of terms used to describe different children such as high or low functioning, more or less-abled, autistic-like or autistic tendencies depending upon where the children fall on the continuum. Terms change over the years, but the important thing to remember is that all children are different and their reactions, progress, and length of time necessary to learn proper behaviors, etc. will be different. But they can learn and be productive as well. It takes much time, patience, fortitude, and love.

Children can suffer from various degrees of autism. Their ability to interact with the world will be affected depending on the degree of the involvement. No one has definite answers to the cause of Autism. I believe strongly from my limited experience that most of the cases we see are due to some type of allergies. From the previous chapters, you may have seen how every day food, chemicals and environmental items inhibited the brain and nerve function in a few cases. They are actual case studies from my practice and from other NAET practitioners' cases. You have seen how these children, once diagnosed non-functional, got back on the right track after just a few allergy elimination treatments. If they all could get well and be productive after NAET, it is not a small matter anymore. It is true that I have not treated hundreds of cases of autism yet, so I do not have a large number of cases to prove my theory. But when we look at the results of a few patients we have treated, the future is promising. We need to pay more attention to NAET and the effectiveness of NAET. We need to treat a large number of autistic children with varying stages of autism to study the effect of NAET.

So far no other treatments have worked and produced such outstanding results in such a short a period of time as NAET. As I mentioned earlier, autism is on the rise at an alarming rate. We have to stop this now before it gets out of hand. We need to find a way to stop it before it becomes a problem; before many of our children become handicapped, before we lose our children, our productive future citizens of the country - to autism! We need to nip autism in the bud. When we look at the history of the autistic children, every one of them suffered from a number of allergic health disorders from birth. They were born allergic. Later when they were exposed to a strong allergen like an antibiotic, chemical spray, pesticide, vaccination, immunization or a bacterial or viral toxin, their brain was affected. The nervous system did not know how to shake it off. So they lost the power to communicate properly, to comprehend adequately, and to hear, feel and speak appropriately. Since they could not hear, understand, and communicate with others, they began to withdraw and hide within themselves. So they became "autistic" to others.

We can help them to come out of their cocoons. We can help them to hear things again; we can assist them to comprehend again; and we can stimulate them to communicate again like normal people. We need to understand them first. We need to find the root of their problems that brought them to the present state. This can be done easily by process of elimination. That is what we do in NAET. We find the allergens and eliminate them one by one. During this systematic process, the major allergen is detected. In some cases there may be more than one or a few major allergens causing the problem and the autism in a child. When all the allergens and the major offenders are removed, healing can take place almost immediately. Then they need to go through some behavior modification. After the allergies are eliminated, behavior modification becomes easier for the children and the therapist.

NAET is a simple procedure. We need to make the parents and medical practitioners aware of NAET. This can be done only through news media and support groups. Let us join forces with all other autism support groups, autism associations, hospitals and private clinics treating autistic children and adults. We need to encourage all medical professionals and parents to learn NAET, and eradicate this "incurable" brain disorder once and for all using allergy elimination with NAET as the tool to "defeat and destroy" autism.

We need to work on the following areas if we want to eradicate autism permanently.

1. Let's bring all the autistic communities and supporters together to "defeat and destroy" AUTISM and educate them about NAET.

2. Let's teach the incredible, simple muscle response testing to test allergies and other side effects of substances we expose our children to.

3. Let's make NAET available to all presently affected children and adults.

4. Alert all the parents (present and future) about the importance of testing their children for allergies using MRT for all drugs, immunizations, possible chemical and environmental toxins, and foods before they expose their children to these items.

5. If they are found to be allergic to any of these items, please get them treated with NAET before using them. There are thousands of NAET practitioners all over the world. (please look at the website for practitioner location: www.naet.com).

6. Vaccinations and immunizations are life-savers probably to some people. You don't want your child to miss the opportunity of the possible benefits from immunizations if it is as good as it sounds. But as a parent, as a doctor, as a healthcare provider, as a teacher, you should be aware of the possible allergic reactions and after-effects if the child is allergic to the immunizations. 90% of our autistic children recovered from autism when they successfully completed the NAET treatments for MMR and DPT immunizations. According to their parents, most of these children were fairly normal until they received the booster doses of immunizations. If the healthcare providers who injected the children with vaccines were aware of MRT and NAET, we could have prevented these children from becoming autistic.

If there is an allergy, it can harm the child in many ways, one of which may be autism. If you just spend five extra minutes to test your child with MRT before you inject the child, you could easily prevent this disaster---Autism!

Autism can be defeated and destroyed if we work together and follow the six steps listed above.

If parents take their autistic children to an NAET practitioner, after they receive a few basic treatments, most children will become manageable. If they complete the full course of treatments the results have been more than satisfactory in the cases with allergies, (that is giving the benefit of the doubt that there may be some cases without allergies). However, I haven't come across any case of autism without an allergy involved so far.

The earlier you begin NAET, the faster the results. Children treated under the age of ten have achieved faster results than adults treated for autism with NAET.

Even though autism is currently associated with biological or neurological differences in the brain, the lay public still views autistic children and adults as weird, abnormal and/or eccentric people. They may be mistreated by their siblings, relatives, classmates, playmates, and other neighborhood children by name calling and teasing, etc. Parents need to educate relatives, friends, and neighbors. Once people understand, especially other children, they would be less likely to make fun of the child or his/her weaknesses. It is everyone's responsibility, the teacher, counselor, principal, coach, as well as the parents to use appropriate medical terminology to explain the child's health problem to other children, so they will not tease or annoy the child and leave him/her alone. Not only that, if the need arises, other children should be willing and ready to help the child with any of his difficult chores.

If the child's root problem is not eliminated, an autistic child's future depends on how the family (parents), siblings, teachers, caretakers and friends present him/her to the world. There are many excellent autistic training centers like "The Option Institute," in this country, which take pride in their productive behavior modification programs and help many autistic children to become normal. Parents should enroll their children in those centers to give them an adequate education. After removing the known allergies, it will take less time in such institutes to retrain your child.

SELF ESTEEM

There are many ways that parents can begin training even the youngest child to be responsible for his/her actions and build self-confidence as well. Everyday life is not only stressful, but also quite a challenge with an autistic youngster. However, you should have certain expectations in mind for your child. They give you something to look forward to and build responsibility in your child. He/she should learn to contribute to and be part of the family. Mastering simple tasks will make the child feel good about himself/herself, and build a positve self image. You can do this by developing a daily structured routine: washing, brushing teeth and hair, dressing, etc. Allow your child to make simple decisions. Would you like to wear the red shirt or the blue one? Do you want the peanut butter or the turkey sandwich? As the child matures, add responsibilities. By learning to choose he/she learns to make decisions. These tasks may seem small at first but they represent stepping stones to accomplish difficult tasks later on. Your child may be reluctant to cooperate at first but do not give up, take it one step at a time. Remember the goal is to try to foster as much independence as possible.

BEHAVIOR MANAGEMENT

Tantrums, aggression, unpredictability, repetitive behaviors, and uncontrolled outbursts present some of the greatest challenges to parenting an autistic child. The autistic child's brain works very slowly; sometimes messages are crisscrossed in the brain; their comprehension is limited due to the inefficient nervous system. So you need to get to the child's level and explain things very slowly or talk to the child very softly, word by word if necessary, to make the child understand. If you take enough time and explain, they will understand better and you will get faster results.

By the end of the day you may be completely drained but through consistent, positive behavior modification, your child will begin to react appropriately to situations. The key word is consistent. Reward behaviors you want the child to repeat. Praise him/her, smile, encourage or reward. This form of behavior modification helps your child to learn the correct action or response to a situation. It offers an orderly plan of rewards and punishments (verbal reprimands) to strengthen acceptable responses and discourage unacceptable ones. Be careful not to use behavior modification for everything that happens during the day. Begin by picking one or two behaviors you would like to change. Select a reward for your child. It may be difficult to know what to choose, especially if your child is not responsive. It might be something the child likes to eat, or a hug or smile, a game to play, etc. Try to keep a record of the child's progress with a chart. You might place a sticker or a happy face by the behavior that he/she has done correctly.

Sometimes the behavior may require a " time-out." A "time-out" gives your child a chance to calm down. You simply remove your child from the situation and place him in a chair or another room for a specific period of time. You can set a timer and when the timer goes off the child can return to the family. Learning to live within parameters is not easy for a child who is autistic but it is the only way to a productive, responsible life.

EARLY INTERVENTION

The first few years of a child's life is most important to his/her development and so it is with an autistic child. There are special educational services available for children with handicaps or who are at risk of developing them from infancy until the age of five. Early intervention is conducted at home and/or at school. An individual learning plan is designed by an early intervention team, made up of school specialists. The program may include play therapy, teaching social skills, speech therapy etc. It also helps parents cope with every day problems. There is also time for group activities with normal children, which have proven to improve autistic children's skills. As parents you cannot do everything alone. You need support. Early intervention is a legal right and it has been proven to benefit autistic children by enchancing communication, cognitive, social and self-help skills. The staff can work with you to plan goals based on your child's individual needs.

AS A TEACHER OF AN AUTISTIC CHILD

Teachers need special training in handling difficult cases like autism. Parents should visit the school and observe teachers with special educational backgrounds. Usually teachers in preschools and other small classes are well trained to observe any imbalances in small children. If the teacher notices any symptoms of autism he/she should give special attention to the child to determine if whatever he/she is observing is true. He/she should meet with the child alone to evaluate the mental status and behavioral pattern of the child. He/she should document the child's behavior and inform the parents, school authorities, and the school psychologist about the findings. He/she should work individually with the child and help him/her to improve in his identified areas one at a time. The teacher should pay special attention to introduce the child to the rest of the class and to include him/her in all class activities.

A teacher should know his/her students and make learning fun, making the presentation more interesting by using appropriate visual and auditory aids. Autistic children on the road to recovery, can do many things like other normal children. If a child cannot focus, understand, or pay enough attention to things being said or demonstrated by the teacher, the child should be placed among children who understand slightly better than he/she does. The child will watch the other children and try to imitate them and learn from others. High functioning autistic children cannot focus or concentrate on any task for more than a few minutes at a time. Do not force them. They become frustrated and irritable. By alternating and rotating the visual and auditory stimuli every few minutes, the teacher will encourage the child to be attentive and focus so he/she can learn. Try to bring out the best in the children. Avoid focusing on the child's weakness and avoid speaking negatively about the child to others. Children hear everything and keep it in their memory even though the child appears to be deaf, dumb and unresponsive to the surrounding stimuli. The teacher should be patient with the child. Care should be taken not to lose your temper or tease him/her in front of other children. The teacher should not impose excessive punishments for minor things, or forget to reward the child when he/she does accomplish small tasks.

We tend to think that the child cannot understand if he cannot talk, or interact. We have numerous examples to share with you that these deaf, dumb and inactive children can hear every word that is said around them.

Michael was nine-years-old when his parents brought him to our office for treatment. Michael had never spoken a word until then. He was very restless, never looked you in the eyes while talking to him, appeared as if he did not understand anything that happened around him. Nothing significant happened during the first three treatments. The fourth treatment was for B complex vitamins. He reacted to the B complex treatment differently. Soon after the treatment, he went into a crying spell. He began screaming in his loudest voice and started banging his head on the wall. He couldn't explain how he felt. His symptoms were of some discomfort in his body. I took him into the treatment room and repeated NAET on him every five minutes for three more times. By this time he calmed down. Suddenly, he began yawning. Then he was moved into another room and helped to lie down and the mother was asked to sit with him. In less than five minutes, he was fast asleep. After 20 minutes I rechecked him and then his parents carried the sleeping child home.

During his next visit, he walked into the office along with his parents singing nursery rhymes. He sat in the waiting room of the clinic and repeated all the nursery rhymes taught in school loud and clear, without a mistake or a pause. His parents were surprised to hear him say the words so clearly, for they had taken it for granted that their son was born dumb. This clearly demonstrates that these children hear and store everything in their memory ready to retrieve it if the situation permits. In his case, an allergy to B vitamins caused him to be dumb and unresponsive to everything in his surroundings. When the energy blockage was removed, his restrictions released. The nerves supplying energy to the vocal cords were no longer blocked and the words flowed out of his memory bank. He took many more treatments (about 50 treatments) to eliminate all his known allergies. He is a normal teenager now.

NAET TREATMENTS

An autistic child should be tested and treated for all basic allergies as soon as possible. If possible he/she or the parents should be taught how to self-test for his/her allergies. Make a point to test everything before using them. Any item tested as allergic, should be avoided until he/she gets treated with NAET.

After the NAET allergy treatments, the offending allergen should not cause problems. But even after the successful NAET treatment, always remember to test for allergy to every item, including the kind you have been treated for in the past, before you use them. You may have been treated for an apple six months ago, but the new apple may have something else in it, like a new pesticide, chemical spray, grown in a new soil, etc., and anything new in it can trigger a reaction in a child with autism.

NUTRITION

After treating for the NAET basics, proper care should be taken to maintain a well balanced diet from the non-allergic food groups. The day can be started with the brain nectar tonic. Autistic children and adults deplete B complex vitamins and trace minerals very quickly. These vitamins should be replaced appropriately in their daily diets. They should be encouraged to drink plenty of water (4-6 glasses daily).

EXERCISE

Various brain balancing exercises and activities are described in Chapter 9. The parents should make a regular habit of implementing some of those exercises every day to help them maintain a stable mind.

PARENT AND SELF AWARENESS

Parents should be educated and trained to pay attention to the presence of any commonly seen autistic-like behaviors in their children. Any new allergen is capable of reproducing the old physical symptoms or creating a new symptom in a sensitive person. If the parent or child is aware of this and exhibits any of these symptoms unexpectedly (when in contact with a new allergen in a new place), the parent or child will not panic and would be able to pay more attention and make a conscious effort to prevent them in front of strangers. Self-instruction, where a child is mentally trained to remind himself/herself is an effective form of mental exercise that can help the child to act and react appropriately in social situations, and can also develop organizational skills. It is okay to take an appropriate drug prescribed by your physician in uncontrollable situations. Have your physician prescribe a non-allergic medication for symptomatic relief. If the child is allergic to the medication, he/she should be treated for the allergy to the medicine with NAET. The child doesn't have to take the medication regularly after sufficient NAET treatments have been received. But always make it a point to have the prescription medication available for any emergency that occurs without warning.

AS A PARENT OF AN AUTISTIC CHILD

As a parent, care of the autistic child should begin before anyone else detects your child's abnormality. There are many books written on normal growth and development of children. All parents should begin reading these books when you plan to have a child, and read through these educational materials during pregnancy. Watch the child closely when he/she is growing up. Pay attention to his /her emotional and physical needs wisely. It is advisable to take your infant to a NAET practitioner and get his/her allergies tested and treated if needed before they become a problem. NAET can be used as a good preventive measure.

Parents should make enough time to spend with the child from infancy, by touching, cuddling, caressing, talking to them and visiting places and meeting people with them. Parents should tell the child repeatedly how much they love him/her and how important he/she is in their lives. The child should be made to feel worthy from infancy by the action of the parents. If the infant seems to be restless, hyper, suffers from insomnia, repeated crying spells, temper tantrums, test all his foods, drinks, clothes, chemicals, detergents, toys, etc., by MRT. If you find an allergy by MRT, please find an NAET practitioner near you and get him/her treated immediately. You may also use all the mind calming techniques in Chapter 9 from the very beginning. Whenever such uncomfortable symptoms are exhibited, it is due to some irritation in the body. So hold the child and massage the vertex of the head (top of the head) for a few minutes. This reduces the irritability temporarily. If parents learn to pay enough attention to the child's every day changes, the problem can be caught at an early age and the treatment can be provided immediately, sparing them from unnecessary anxious moments in the future.

If the parents did not discover the abnormalities in infancy, they do not have to feel guilty or less efficient. Whenever the problem is discovered in your child, begin working with these methods immediately and results will happen before you know it.

A diagnosis of autism in a child affects the entire family. Usually most parents go into a denial stage initially. But it shouldn't last too long. An autistic child brings tremendous inconvenience and re-adjustments in the parents' and other siblings' lives. But they all should learn to cooperate and help the child to grow up into a normal adult. Family members should be very patient with the child. It doesn't mean that parents shouldn't discipline the child. Take extra time to calmly explain all the rules of the family and what is expected if the child can understand and follow through. If you lay out the rules and never ask the child to follow them, or never check to see if he has followed them, children, even an autistic child, will lose respect for the parent. Children watch you closely and if they think they can get away with something they will try every possible avenue. So it is for the parents to teach the child the right course of action from the beginning: putting toys away after play, washing hands after play, teaching him/her to appreciate things, to respect other's toys, books; teaching him/her to say 'thank you' and 'please', etc. Spend time with the child at bedtime telling him/her a bedtime story; giving him/her a gentle vertex massage. If there are more children in the family, consider reading bedtime stories as a group. If the child is not capable of understanding your demands and rules, you still need to take time and explain to them. As I have described to you earlier, the child understands and stores all messages inside the brain. For some reason the child is not able to respond to you appropriately. When the time comes, he will utilize the knowledge. If you never told him/her he/she will never know it.

If there are siblings, make them take part in his/her daily activities, like washing him/her, dressing, feeding, etc. Siblings will feel very important and give them a sense of responsibility in rearing him/her and this will reduce your burden and solve the sibling rivalry. As the child grows up, parents should include him/her in everyday house chores, like cleaning house, mowing the lawn, making breakfast, lunch and dinner, setting the dining table, etc. This gives them enough training and confidence, making them feel important in the family and that improves self-image. Improving family life with an autistic child takes understanding, patience, effort and love. Love conquers all obstacles in life. All the children (siblings) should be taught to share and care, love, and support each other from the beginning. With everyone's support and effort, an autistic child should grow up as normal as any other child in a loving, caring atmosphere.

SEEKING PROFESSIONAL HELP

When behavior management enforced by parents and teachers turns ineffective, professional help from counselors and psychotherapists may be necessary to guide him/her properly. There are psychologists and therapists with special training and experience in specific areas of behavioral problems of children with different disorders. Their services often prove invaluable in controlling your child. Parents also could benefit from some counseling to cope with the situation.

MEDICATION

Stimulants, antidepressants, beta-blockers, lithium, Naltrexone, and megavitamin therapy have all been used as interventions with autism. However, no single drug or pill has been found to treat the disorder. More research is needed in this area. There are various reasons for someone to depend on medication. Some parents feel they have to keep their children medicated. In some severe cases, it may be necessary to keep them medicated to help them go through school, and other activities of life. In some cases, when both parents are working to find enough income to make ends meet, it may be very straining for parents to find the extra time to spend with the child. So keeping the child on medication reduces the stress and gets the work done. Some special schools make it mandatory for the child to be on medication. Otherwise, it is hard for them to manage the kids. Whatever the reason may be to give medication to your child, at least make sure that he/she is not allergic to it. Medication may be okay for a short term. Long term medication should be avoided. If the child gets his/her allergies eliminated through NAET, he/she may not require long term medication.

AUTISTIC ADULTS

Society today recognizes that everyone no matter how disabled or handicapped can contribute to the community as a productive citizen. Locating employment to fit your child's needs and abilities may take time and planning, but it is worth it. There are many supportive businesses today that are flexible and open to helping adults with special needs find employment. There are many federal and state agencies that help locate appropriate jobs as well as universities and vocational schools. Some lucky adults get a break and discover NAET. Others will never hear about NAET or will refuse to seek help.

EVALUATING AUTISTIC ADULTS

The procedure for evaluating and establishing the diagnosis for autistic adults is the same as evaluating a child with autism. The classical signs of poor communication skills, lack of social interaction, and sensory impairment are seen in autistic adults just the way they are seen in children with this disorder. The impact of autism on an adult might be the same as it is for children. But it is reflected on an adult differently due to the fact that an adult's life is totally different with different demands and expectations. A child is under the care or supervision of a parent, guardian, teacher or care taker. An adult is expected to work, meet other demands of life, live in a community doing some community work, and meet social obligations within the community, family or friends. The impact of life can be overwhelming to an autistic adult

Autistic adults always find difficulty sitting still for a long time anywhere. So they would tend to be very restless most of the time. If they could be placed in jobs of their interest, they could work long hours without getting tired. This should be kept in mind when job placement is arranged.

Autistic adults have difficulty with conversations. They tend to use a limited range of words in their conversations. Sometimes they reverse pronouns using "you" instead of "I." They include irrelevant details, shift topics or persevere on certain topics. They often can recall dates, ages, telephone numbers and addresses as well as factual information like events and measurements. They interrupt people during conversations, get into arguments without respecting others' ideas, and can talk inappropriately or make foolish remarks. Laughing might occur when they are anxious or crying for no apparent reason. They are unable to understand that other people have beliefs and feelings that might be different from their own. Their interpersonal difficulties create problems in making and keeping friends.

Rote memory is strong in autistic adults (memorizing facts, dates, addresses, etc.), but other types of memory are impaired. Their language difficulties compound their memory deficits.

Organizing materials at work, or home is also a problem for an autistic person. They will fall in the group of procrastinators, always late getting up, late getting to work, have difficulty keeping on a time schedule, get an anxiety attack, crying spells, etc.

Some of the above symptoms may be familiar to some of the chemically sensitive people. You don't have to be autistic to experience these symptoms because, these are the common symptoms suffered by chemically sensitive individuals. That knowledge gives us hope that most autistic children have allergies like multiple chemical sensitivity persons. These symptoms are the reactions of certain irritations in the body, which could be caused by allergies. When we look around, we see variations of these symptoms displayed in many people among us. We do not consider all these people to be autistic adults. Some display a few of these symptoms at one time whereas others display one or two of the symptoms ocassionally. But people with autism display most of these symptoms most of the time. This knowledge also comforts us that if autism is allergy-related, we can eliminate their allergies with NAET and they may be able to lead a normal life.

The symptoms of autism vary from person to person and range from mild, to moderate, or to severe. People with mild symptoms can function and lead a life as close to normal as possible. All others may face difficulties in varying degrees throughout their lives.

NAET is not just for autistic children, it can help an autistic person regardless of age or intensity of the disease. So a parent of an autistic adult should find an NAET practitioner near him/her and begin NAET treatments as soon as possible so they too can "SAY GOOD-BYE to Allergy-related Autism," and lead productive lives.

GLOSSARY

Acetaldehyde: An aldehyde found in cigarette smoke, vehicle exhaust, and smog. It is a metabolic product of Candida albicans and is synthesized from alcohol in the Liver.

Acetylcholine: A neurotransmitter manufactured in the brain, used for memory and control of sensory input and muscular output signals.

Acid: Any compound capable of releasing a hydrogen ion; it will have a pH of less than 7.

Acute: Extremely sharp or severe, as in pain can also refer to an illness or reaction that is sudden and intense.

Adaptation: Ability of an organism to integrate new elements into its environment.

Addiction: A dependent state characterized by cravings for a particular substance if that substance is withdrawn.

Additive: A substance added in small amounts to foods to alter the food in some way.

Adrenaline: Trademark for preparations of epinephrine, which is a hormone secreted by the adrenal gland. It is used sublingually and by injection to stop allergic reactions.

Aldehyde: A class of organic compounds obtained by oxidation of alcohol. Formaldehyde and acetaldehyde are members of this class of compounds.

Alkaline: Basic, or any substance that accepts a hydrogen ion; its pH will be greater than 7.

Allergenic: Causing or producing an allergic reaction.

Allergen: Any organic or inorganic substance from one's surroundings or from within the body itself that causes an allergic response in an individual is called an allergen. An allergen can cause an IgE antibody mediated or non-IgE mediated response in a person. Some of the commonly known allergens are: pollens, molds, animal dander, food and drinks, chemicals of different kind like the ones found in the food, water, air, fabrics, cleaning agents, environmental materials, detergent, make-up products etc., body secretions, bacteria, virus, synthetic materials, fumes, and air pollution. Emotional unpleasant thoughts like anger, frustration, etc can also become allergens and cause allergic reactions in people.

Allergic reaction: Adverse, varied symptoms, unique to each person, resulting from the body's response to exposure to allergens.

Allergy: Attacks by the immune system on harmless or even useful things entering the body. Abnormal responses to substances usually well tolerated by most people.

Amino acid: An organic acid that contains an amino (ammonia-like NH3) chemical group; the building blocks that make up all proteins.

Anaphylactic shock: Also known as anaphylaxis. Usually it happens suddenly when exposed to a highly allergic item. But sometimes, it can also happen as a cumulative reaction. (first two doses of penicillin may not trigger a severe reaction, but third or fourth one could produce an anaphylaxis in some people). An anaphylaxis (this life threatening allergic reaction) is characterized by: an immediate allergic reaction that can cause difficulty in breathing, light headedness, fainting, sensation of chills, internal cold, severe heart palpitation or irregular heart beats, pallor, eyes rolling, poor mental clarity, tremors, internal shaking, extreme fear, angio neurotic edema, throat swelling, drop in blood pressure, nausea, vomiting, diarrhea, swelling anywhere in the body, redness and hives, fever, delirium, unresponsiveness, or sometimes even death.

Antibody: A protein molecule produced in the body by lymphocytes in response to a perceived harmful foreign or abnormal substance (another protein) as a defense mechanism to protect the body.

Antigen: Any substance recognized by the immune system that causes the body to produce antibodies; also refers to a concentrated solution of an allergen.

Antihistamine: A chemical that blocks the reaction of histamine that is released by the mast cells and basophils during an allergic reaction. Any substance that slows oxidation, prevents damage from free radicals and results in oxygen sparing.

Assimilate: To incorporate into a system of the body; to transform nutrients into living tissue.

Autoimmune: A condition resulting when the body makes antibodies against its own tissues or fluid. The immune system attacks the body it inhabits, which causes damage or alteration of cell function.

Binder: A substance added to tablets to help hold them together.

Blood brain barrier: A cellular barrier that prevents certain chemicals from passing from the blood to the brain.

Buffer: A substance that minimizes changes in pH (Acidity or alkanity).

Candida albicans: A genus of yeast like fungi normally found in the body. It can multiply and cause infections, allergic reactions or toxicity.

Candidiasis: An overgrowth of Candida organisms, which are part of the normal flora of the mouth, skin, intestines and vagina.

Carbohydrate, complex: A large molecule consisting of simple sugars linked together, found in whole grains, vegetables, and fruits. This metabolizes very slowly into glucose than refined carbohydrate.

Carbohydrate, refined: A molecule of sugar that metabolizes quickly to glucose. Refined white sugar, white rice, white flour are some of the examples.

Catalyst: A chemical that speeds up a chemical reaction without being consumed or permanently affected in the process.

Cerebral allergy: Mental dysfunction caused by sensitivity to foods, chemicals, environmental substances, or other substances like work materials etc.

Chronic: Of long duration.

Chronic fatigue syndrome: A syndrome of multiple symptoms most commonly associated with fatigue and reduced energy or no energy.

Crohn's disease: An intestinal disorder associated with irritable bowel syndrome, inflammation of the bowels and colitis.

Cumulative reaction: A type of reaction caused by an accumulation of allergens in the body.

Cytokine Immune system's second line of defense. Examples of cytokines are interleukin 2 and gamma interferon.

Desensitization: The process of building up body tolerance to allergens by the use of extracts of the allergenic substance.

Detoxification: A variety of methods used to reduce toxic materials accumulated in body tissues.

Digestive tract: Includes the salivary glands, mouth, esophagus, stomach, small intestine, portions of the liver, pancreas, and large intestine.

Disorder: A disturbance of regular or normal functions.

Dust: Dust particles from various sources irritate sensitive individual causing different respiratory problems like asthma, bronchitis, hay-fever like symptoms, sinusitis, and cough.

Dust mites: Microscopic insects that live in dusty areas, pillows, blankets, bedding, carpets, upholstered furniture, drapes, corners of the houses where people neglect to clean regularly.

Eczema: An inflammatory process of the skin resulting from skin allergies causing dry, itchy, crusty, scaly, weepy, blisters or eruptions on the skin. skin rash frequently caused by allergy.

Edema: Excess fluid accumulation in tissue spaces. It could be localized or generalized.

Electromagnetic: Refers to emissions and interactions of both electric and magnetic components. Magnetism arising from electric charge in motion. This has a definite amount of energy.

Elimination diet: A diet in which common allergenic foods and those suspected of causing allergic symptoms have been temporarily eliminated.

Endocrine: refers to ductless glands that manufacture and secrete hormones into the blood stream or extracellular fluids.

Endocrine system: Thyroid, parathyroid, pituitary, hypothalamus, adrenal glands, pineal gland, gonads, the intestinal tract, kidneys, liver, and placenta.

Endogenous: Originating from or due to internal causes.

Environment: A total of circumstances and/or surroundings in which an organism exists. May be a combination of internal or external influences that can affect an individual.

Environmental illness: A complex set of symptoms caused by adverse reactions of the body to external and internal environments.

Enzyme: A substance, usually protein in nature and formed in living cells, which starts or stops biochemical reactions.

Eosinophil: A type of white blood cell. Eosinophil levels may be high in some cases of allergy or parasitic infestation.

Exogenous: Originating from or due to external causes.

Extract: Treatment dilution of an antigen used in immunotherapy, such as food, chemical, or pollen extract.

Fibromyalgia: An immune complex disorder causing general body aches, muscle aches, and general fatigue.

"Fight" or "flight": The activation of the sympathetic branch of the autonomic nervous system, preparing the body to meet a threat or challenge.

Food addiction: A person becomes dependent on a particular allergenic food and must keep eating it regularly in order to prevent withdrawal symptoms.

Food grouping: A grouping of foods according to their botanical or biological characteristics.

Free radical: A substance with unpaired electrone, which is attracted to cell membranes and enzymes where it binds and causes damage.

Gastrointestinal: Relating both to stomach and intestines.

Heparin: A substance released during allergic reaction. Heparin has antiinflammatory action in the body.

Histamine: A body substance released by mast cells and basophils during allergic reactions, which precipitates allergic symptoms.

Holistic: Refers to the idea that health and wellness depend on a balance between physical (structural) aspects, physiological (chemical, nutritional, functional) aspects, emotional and spiritual aspects of a person.

Homeopathic: Refers to giving minute amounts of remedies that in massive doses would produce effects similar to the condition being treated.

Homeostasis: A state of perfect balance in the organism also called as "Yin-yang" balance. The balance of functions and chemical composition within an organism that results from the actions of regulatory systems.

Hormone: A chemical substance that is produced in the body, secreted into body fluids, and is transported to other organs, where it produces a specific effect on metabolism.

Hydrocarbon: A chemical compound that contains only hydrogen and carbon.

Hypersensitivity: An acquired reactivity to an antigen that can result in bodily damage upon subsequent exposure to that particular antigen.

Hyperthyroidism: A condition resulting from over-function of the thyroid gland.

Hypoallergenic: Refers to products formulated to contain the minimum possible allergens and some people with few allergies can tolerate them well. Severely allergic people can still react to these items.

Hypothyroidism: A condition resulting from under-function of the thyroid gland.

IgA: Immunoglobulin A, an antibody found in secretions associated with mucous membranes.

IgD: Immunoglobulin D, an antibody found on the surface of B-cells.

IgE: Immunoglobulin E, an antibody responsible for immediate hypersensitivity and skin reactions.

IgG: Immunoglobulin G, also known as gammaglobulin, the major antibody in the blood that protects against bacteria and viruses.

IgM: Immunoglobulin M, the first antibody to appear during an immune response.

Immune system: The body's defense system, composed of specialized cells, organs, and body fluids. It has the ability to locate, neutralize, metabolize and eliminate unwanted or foreign substances.

Immunocompromised: A person whose immune system has been damaged or stressed and is not functioning properly.

Immunity: Inherited, acquired, or induced state of being, able to resist a particular antigen by producing antibodies to counteract it. A unique mechanism of the organism to protect and maintain its body against adversity of its surroundings.

Inflammation: The reaction of tissues to injury from trauma, infection, or irritating substances. Affected tissue can be hot, reddened, swollen, and tender.

Inhalant: Any airborne substance small enough to be inhaled into the lungs; eg., pollen, dust, mold, animal danders, perfume, smoke, and smell from chemical compounds.

Intolerance: Inability of an organism to utilize a substance.

Intracellular: Situated within a cell or cells.

Intradermal: method of testing in which a measured amount of antigen is injected between the top layers of the skin.

Ion: An atom that has lost or gained an electron and thus carries an electric charge.

Kinesiology: Science of movement of the muscle.

Latent: Concealed or inactive.

Leukocytes: White blood cells.

Lipids: Fats and oils that are insoluble in water. Oils are liquids in room temperature and fats are solid.

Lymph: A clear, watery, alkaline body fluid found in the lymph vessels and tissue spaces. Contains mostly white blood cells.

Lymphocyte: A type of white blood cell, usually classified as T-or B-cells.

Macrophage: A white blood cell that kills and ingests microorganisms and other body cells.

Masking: Suppression of symptoms due to frequent exposure to a substance to which a person is sensitive.

Mast cells: Large cells containing histamine, found in mucous membranes and skin cells. The histamine in these cells are released during certain allergic reactions.

Mediated: Serving as the vehicle to bring about a phenomenon, eg., an IgE-mediated reaction is one in which IgE changes cause the symptoms and the reaction to proceed.

Membrane: A thin sheet or layer of pliable tissue that lines a cavity, connects two structures, selective barrier.

Metabolism: Complex chemical and electrical processes in living cells by which energy is produced and life is maintained. New material is assimilated for growth, repair, and replacement of tissues. Waste products are excreted.

Migraine: A condition marked by recurrent severe headaches often on one side of the head, often accompanied by nausea, vomiting, and light aura. These headaches are frequently attributed to food allergy.

Mineral: An inorganic substance. The major minerals in the body are calcium, phosphorus, potassium, sulfur, sodium, chloride, and magnesium.

Mucous membranes: Moist tissues forming the lining of body cavities that have an external opening, such as the respiratory, digestive, and urinary tracts.

Muscle Response Testing: A testing technique based on kinesiology to test allergies by comparing the strength of a muscle or a group of muscles in the presence and absence of the allergen.

NAET: (Nambudripad's Allergy Elimination Techniques): A technique to eliminate allergies permanently from the body towards the treated allergen. Developed by Dr. Devi S. Nambudripad and practiced by over 3,500 medical practitioners worldwide. This technique is completely natural, non-invasive, and drug-free. It has been effectively used in treating all types of allergies and problems arising from allergies. It is taught by Dr. Nambudripad in Buena Park, CA. to currently licensed medical practitioners. If you are interested in learning more about NAET, or NAET seminars, please visit the website: www.naet.com.

Nervous system: A network made up of nerve cells, the brain, and the spinal cord, which regulates and coordinates body activities.

Neurotransmitter: A molecule that transmits electrical and/or chemical messages from nerve cell (neuron) to nerve cell or from nerve cell to muscle, secretory, or organ cells.

Nutrients: Vitamins, minerals, amino acids, fatty acids, and sugar (glucose), which are the raw materials needed by the body to provide energy, effect repairs, and maintain functions.

Organic foods: Foods grown in soil free of chemical fertilizers, and without pesticides, fungicides and herbicides.

Outgasing: The releasing of volatile chemicals that evaporate slowly and constantly from seemingly stable materials such as plastics, synthetic fibers, or building materials.

Overload: The overpowering of the immune system due to massive concurrent exposure or to low level continuous exposure caused by many stresses, including allergens.

Parasite: An organism that depends on another organism (host) for food and shelter, contributing nothing to the survival of the host.

Pathogenic: Capable of causing disease.

Pathology: The scientific study of disease; its cause, processes, structural or functional changes, developments and consequences.

Pathway: The metabolic route used by body systems to facilitate biochemical functions.

Peakflow meter: An inexpensive, valuable tool used in measuring the speed of the air forced out of the lungs and helps to monitor breathing disorders like asthma.

Petrochemical: A chemical derived from petroleum or natural gas.

pH: A scale from 1 to 14 used to measure acidity and alkanity of solutions. A pH of 1-6 is acidic; a pH of 7 is neutral; a pH of 8-14 is alkaline or basic.

Postnasal drip: The leakage of nasal fluids and mucus down into the back of the throat.

Precursor: Anything that precedes another thing or event, such as physiologically inactive substance that is converted into an active substance that is converted into an active enzyme, vitamin, or hormone.

Prostaglandin: A group of unsaturated, modified fatty acids with regulatory functions.

Radiation: The process of emission, transmission, and absorption of any type of waves or particles of energy, such as light, radio, ultraviolet or X-rays.

Receptor: Special protein structures on cells where hormones, neurotransmitters, and enzymes attach to the cell surface.

Respiratory system: The system that begins with the nostrils and extends through the nose to the back of the throat and into the larynx and lungs.

Rotation diet: A diet in which a particular food and other foods in the same "family" are eaten only once every four to seven days.

Sensitivity: An adaptive state in which a person develops a group of adverse symptoms to the environment, either internal or external. Generally refers to non-IgE reactions.

Serotonin: A constituent of blood platelets and other organs that is released during allergic reactions. It also functions as a neurotransmitter in the body.

Sublingual: Under the tongue, method of testing or treatment in which a measured amount of an antigen or extract is administered under the tongue, behind the teeth. Absorption of the substance is rapid in this way.

Supplement: Nutrient material taken in addition to food in order to satisfy extra demands, effect repair, and prevent degeneration of body systems.

Susceptibility: An alternative term used to describe sensitivity.

Symptoms: A recognizable change in a person's physical or mental state, that is different from normal function, sensation, or appearance and may indicate a disorder or disease.

Syndrome: A group of symptoms or signs that, occurring together, produce a pattern typical of a particular disorder.

Synthetic: Made in a laboratory; not normally produced in nature, or may be a copy of a substance made in nature.

Systemic: Affecting the entire body.

Target organ: The particular organ or system in an individual that will be affected most often by allergic reactions to varying substances.

Toxicity: A poisonous, irritating, or injurious effect resulting when a person ingests or produces a substance in excess of his or her tolerance threshold.

RESOURCES

RESOURCES

American Association of University
Affiliated Programs for Persons with Developmental Disabilities
8630 Fenton Street, Ste. 410
Silver Spring, MD 20910
(301) 588-8252

Autism Outreach Project
123 Franklin Corner Road, Ste. 215
Lawrenceville, NJ 98648
(609) 895-0190

Autism Research Institute
4182 Adams Avenue
San Diego, CA 92116
(619) 281-7165

Autism Society of America
7910 Woodmont Avenue, Ste. 650
Betthesda, MD 200814
(800) 3-AUTISM

Autism Support Center
64 Holten Street
Danvers, MA 001923
(508) 777-9135

Center for the Study of Autism
2207 B Portland Road
Newberg, OR 97132
(503) 538-9045

**National Information Center for
 Children and Youth with Disabilities**
P.O. Box 1492
Washington D.C. 20013

(800) 695-0285Metagenics
100 Avenida La Pata
San Clemente, CA 92673
(949) 366-0818/ 800-692-9400
Nutritional supplements.

Lotus Herbs
1124 N. Hacienda Blvd.
La Puente, CA 91626
(626) 916-1070

Say Good-bye to Allergy-related Autism

BIBLIOGRAPHY

BIBLIOGRAPHY

American Psychiatric Association. (1994). *Diagnostic and Statistical Manual of Mental Disorders*. (4th ed.). Washington, D.C: American Psychiatric Association, 1994

Asperger, H. (1979). Problems of Infantile Autism. *Communication.* 13, 45-52

Baron, Judy and Sean Barron. *There's a Boy in Here.* New York: Simon and Shuster, 1993

Baron-Cohen, Simon, and Patrick Bolton. *Autism: The Facts.* Oxford: Oxford University Press, 1993

Bettelheim, B. *The Empty Fortress: Infantile Autism and the Birth of Self.* New York: Free Press, 1967

Betts, Carolyn. *A Special Kind of Normal.* New York Scribner, 1983

Brandl, Cherlene. *Facilitated Communication: Case Studies-- See Us Smart!* Ann Arbor Maine: Robbie Dean Press, 1999

Braverman, Eric R., with Carl Pfeiffer. *The Healing Nutrients Within.* New Canaan, CT: Keats Publishing, 1987

Callahan, Mary. *Fighting for Tony.* New York: Simon and Schuster, 1997

Capps, L., Sigman, M., and P. Mundy. Attachment Security in Children with Autism. *Development and Psychopathology,* 6, 24999-261

Castleman, Michael. *Nature's Cures.* Emmaus, PA: Rodale Press, 1996

Chopra, Deepak. *Perfect Health---The Complete Mind/ Body Guide.* New York: Harmony Books, 1991

Cohen, D.J., Donnellan, A. and R. Paul (eds). *Handbook of Autism and Pervasive Development Disorders.* New York: Wiley, 1987

Dillon, Katleen M. *Living with Autism: The Parents' Stories.* Boone, NC: Parkway, 1995

Firth, U. *Autism and Asperger Syndrome.* Cambridge, England: University Press, 1991

Garrison, William. *Small Bargains: Children in Crisis and the Meaning of Parental Love.* New York: Simon and Schuster, 1993

Gerlach, Elizabeth K. *Autism Treatment Guide.* Four-Leaf Press, 1993

Kephart, Beth. *A Slant of the Sun: One Child's Courage.* W.W. Norton: 1998

Harrington, Kathie. *For Parents and Professionals: Autism.* Lingui Systems, 1998

Kaufman, Barry Neil. *Son-Rise.* New York: Harper and Row, 1976

Kaufman, Barry Neil and Samarhia Lyte Kaufman. *Son-Rise: The Miracle Continues.* Kramer, 1994

Landrigan, P., and J. Witte. *Neurologic Disorders Following Measles Virus Vaccinations.* JAMA233: 1459 (1973)

McBean, Eleanor. *Vaccinations Do Not Protect.* Manachaea, TX: Health Excellence Systems, 1991

McGilvery, Robert W., and Gerald W. Goldstein. *Biochemistry---A Functional Approcah.* Phillllladphia, PA: W.B. Saunders Company, 1983

Miller, Neil Z. Vaccines: Are They Really Safe and Effective? Santa Fe, New Mexico: New Atlantian Press, 1992

Oppenheim, Rosalind. *Effective Teaching Methods for Autistic Chil
dren.* Springfield, Illinois: Charles C. Thomas, 1974

Rutter, M. Autistic Children: Infancy to Adulthood. *Seminars in Psychiatry and Allied Disciplines,* 24, 513-531

Sanua, VD. Studies in Infantile Autism. *Child Psychiatry Hum. Dev.* 19(3):207-27, 1989

Smalley, S.L., Asarnow, R.F. and A. Spence. (1988) Autism and Genetics: A Decade of Research. *Archives of General Psychiatry,* 455, 953-961

Piaget, J. *The Construction of Reality in the Child.* New York: W.W. Norton, 1962

Rapp, Doris. *Is This Your Child?* New York: William Morrow and Company, 1991

Rea, William J. *Chemical Sensitivity.* Boca Raton, FL: Lewis Publishers, 1996

Rimland, Bernard. Controversies in the Treatment of Autistic Children: Vitamin and Drug Therapy, *J. Child*

Smith, M.D. *Autism and Life in the Community: Successful Interventions for Behavioral Challenges*. Paul Brooks, 1990

Stehl, Annabel. *The Sound of a Miracle, A Child's Triumph Over Autism*. Doubleday, 1991

Stehl, Annabel. *Dancing in the Rain: Stories of Exceptional Progress by Parents of Children with Special Needs* Georgiana, 1995

Strom, Charles M. *Heredity and Ability: How Genetics Affects Your Child and What You Can Do About It* New York: Plenum Press, 1990

Tager-Flusberg, H. Sentence Comprehension in Autistic Children. *Applied Psycholinguistics, 2, 5-24*

Volkmar, F.R. and D.J. Cohen. (1991). Debate and Argument: *The Ultility of the Term Pervasive Developmental Disorder. Journal of Child* scology and Pscyhiatry. 32, 1171-1172

Volkmar, F.R., Paul R., and D. Cohen. (1985). The Use of "Asperger's Syndrome." *Journal of Autism and Developmental Disorders*, 15, 437-439

Weil, Andrew. *Health and Healing---Understanding Conventional and Alternative Medicine*. Dorling Kindersley, 1995

Wild, Gaynor, and Edward c. Benzel *Essentials of Neurochemistry*. Boston, MA: Joues and Bartlett Publishers, 1994

Williams, Donna. *Nobody Nowhere* Random House, 1992

Wing, Lorna. *Early Childhood Autism.* Oxford: Pergamon Press, 1976

Wing, Lorna. *Autistic Children: A Guide for Parents and Professionals,* 2nd edition. New York: Brunner/ Mazel, 1985

INDEX

Index

Say Good-bye to Allergy -related Autism

NOTES ...

NOTES ...

NOTES ...

NOTES ...

NOTES ...

Books Order Form

Name of book	Price/book	No. of books	Price Total
Say Good-bye to Allergy-related Autism	$18.00	_____	_____
Say Good-bye to ADD & ADHD	$18.00	_____	_____
Say Good-bye to Illness	$24.00	_____	_____
Living Pain Free	$22.95	_____	_____
NAET Guide Book	$12.00	_____	_____

Shipping & Handling in U.S. per book $5.00 _____
Please allow two to three weeks for delivery.

Sales Tax (CA Residents, please add 7.75% Sales Tax) _____

Total _____

If you want to pay by credit card,
please fill in the information below.

Name of Cardholder: _____

Address: _____

Phone: _____

[ ] Visa [ ] MC   Exp. date: _____

Credit Card Number: _____

Signature of the Cardholder: _____

Today's date: _____

Books Order Form

Name of book	Price/book	No. of books	Price Total
Say Good-bye to Allergy-related Autism	$18.00	_____	_____
Say Good-bye to ADD & ADHD	$18.00	_____	_____
Say Good-bye to Illness	$24.00	_____	_____
Living Pain Free	$22.95	_____	_____
NAET Guide Book	$12.00	_____	_____

Shipping & Handling in U.S. per book $5.00 _____
Please allow two to three weeks for delivery.

Sales Tax (CA Residents, please add 7.75% Sales Tax) _____

Total _____

If you want to pay by credit card,
please fill in the information below.

Name of Cardholder: _____

Address: _____

Phone: _____

[ ] Visa [ ] MC   Exp. date: _____

Credit Card Number: _____

Signature of the Cardholder: _____

Today's date: _____